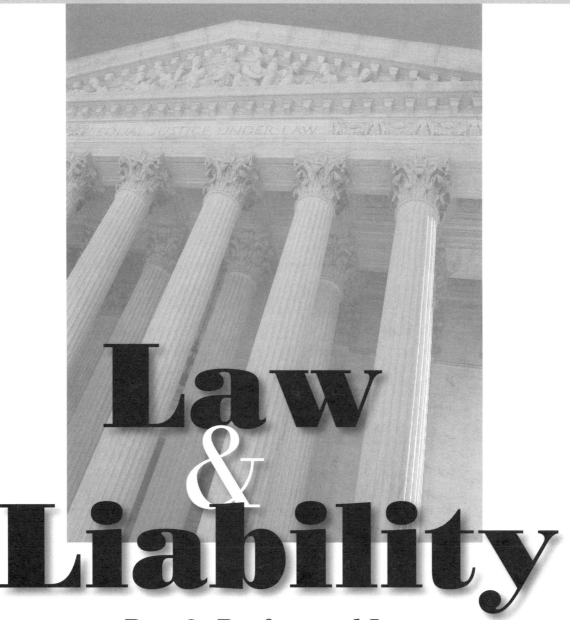

Law & Liability

Part 2: Professional Issues

AMERICAN PHYSICAL THERAPY ASSOCIATION

This monograph is a compilation of official documents of the American Physical Therapy Association and articles originally published in *Physical Therapy* and *PT—Magazine of Physical Therapy.*

ISBN 1-931369-24-0

For more information about this and other APTA publications, contact the American Physical Therapy Association, 1111 North Fairfax Street, Alexandria, VA 22314-1488, 800/999-2782, ext 3395, www.apta.org. [Order No. P-157-05]

Table of Contents

Acknowledgements iv

Introduction 1

Today's Health Care System 3

   Principles and Objectives for the United States Health Care System and the Delivery of Physical Therapy Services
      [HOD P06-04-17-16] 5

   Direct Access and Attainment of "Physician Status" as Applied Under the Medicare Program [HOD-P06-05-16-08] . . . 7

   Physical Therapy as a Mandated Service Under Medicaid [HOD-P06-03-21-17] 7

   No-Risk, All Gain Destinations/Kathy Lewis 8

Delegation and Supervision 11

   Direction and Supervision of the Physical Therapist Assistant [HOD P06-05-18-26] 13

   Provision of Physical Therapy Interventions and Related Tasks [HOD P06-00-17-28] 15

   Distinction Between the Physical Therapist and the Physical Therapist Assistant
      in Physical Therapy [HOD P06-01-18-19] 15

   Procedural Interventions Exclusively Performed by Physical Therapists [HOD P06-00-30-36] 15

   Student Physical Therapist Provision of Services [HOD P06-00-18-30] 16

   Supervision of Student Physical Therapist Assistants [HOD P06-00-19-31] 16

   Public Protection in the Delivery of Therapeutic Exercise [HOD P06-00-33-13] 16

   Cross-Trained Personnel [HOD P06-99-12-05] 16

   Credentialing of Physical Therapy Aides [HOD P06-99-12-14] 17

   Editor's Note: Support Personnel/Jules M Rothstein 18

   Stories From the Front—Supervision/Rita Arriaga 20

   Stories From the Front—PTAs and Safe Practice/Rita Arriaga 22

   Stories From the Front—Communication and the Use of Personnel/Rita Arriaga 24

   Stories From the Front—Supervision, Judgment, and the Physical Therapist Assistant/Rita Arriaga 27

   Stories From the Front—Part 1: Delegation/Rita Arriaga 30

   Liability Awareness: Stories from the Front—Part 2/Rita Arriaga 32

Pro Bono Services 35

   Guidelines: Pro Bono Physical Therapy Services [HOD G06-93-21-39] 37

   In Practice: "For the Public Good"/Ronald W Scott 38

   Liability Protection: What PTs Should Know/Lucie Lawrence 41

Disability Legislation 43

   Americans With Disabilities: Role of the American Physical Therapy Association in Advocacy, Promotion,
      and Accommodation [HOD P06-04-12-12] 45

   Non-Discrimination [HOD Y06-98-14-06] 45

   Affirmative Action [HOD P06-98-14-05] 45

   Responses Within Nonfederal Hospitals in Pennsylvania to the Americans With Disabilities Act of 1990/Dina L Jones,
      Valerie JM Watzlaf, Douglas Hobson, Jane Mazzoni 46

   ADA Q&A/John A Mirone 58

   A Practical Application of the ADA/Kim Osborne 60

   ADA Q&A/John A Mirone 64

   ADA Case Law: Cook v State of Rhode Island/John A Mirone 66

   ADA Case Law: Reasonable Accommodation in Disability Law/John A Mirone 67

   Capitol Watch: IDEA Legislation—A Positive for PT and Children With Disabilities/Pamela Phillips 69

ADA Case Law: Serving as an Expert/Miller 71

ADA Case Law: Preemployment Screening/Laurie Johnson 73

Capitol Watch: PTs Help Make IDEA a Reality/Steve Davolt 76

ADA Case Law: Technical Standards in Education Programs/Laurie A Walsh 78

Automony/Collaboration/Communication 85

Stories From the Front—Consultation/Rita Arriaga 87

Stories From the Front—Communication With Other Health Care Providers/Rita Arriaga 89

Stories From the Front—Complex Medical History and Communication/Rita Arriaga 91

The Screening Process/Lisa Culver 94

Screening: A Basic Obligation (in: Direct Access: Exploring New Opportunities)/Melanie Fosnaught 97

Autonomous Practice: Issues of Risk/Carol Schunk, Kathy Thut 98

Stories From the Front—Patient Management/Rita Arriaga 104

Producing Singular Results/CarolSchunk, Cathy Thut, Carol Davis 109

Employer/Business Issues 111

Non-Discrimination in the Provision of Physical Therapy Services [HOD P06-03-24-21] 113

Physical Therapy Practitioners With Communicable Diseases or Conditions [HOD P06-93-15-20] 113

Guidelines: Recruiting and Hiring Internationally Educated Physical Therapists [HOD G06-94-34-45] 113

Guidelines for Student and Employer Contracts [HOD G06-92-14-28] 114

Liability Awareness—A Risk Consideration for Contract Staffing/Kathy Thut 115

Stories From the Front—Modalities/Rita Arriaga 116

Stories From the Front—Recent PT Graduates/Rita Arriaga 118

Part 1: Physical Therapy Contracts/Kathy Lewis 120

Part 2: Physical Therapy Contracts/Kathy Lewis 124

Part 3: Physical Therapy Contracts/Kathy Lewis 129

Letters of Recommendation: To Write or Not to Write?/Ronald W Scott 134

OSHA Ergonomics Guidelines and the PT Consultant/Lauren Andrew Hebert 135

Managed Care, ERISA, and PT/John J Bennett 143

Tapping Technology: Legal and Liability Risks on the Internet/Kathy Lewis 148

Liability Awareness—Beyond the Borders of Hands-on Care/Joy Sterneck 152

Liability Awareness—Impacts and Implications of Employer Liability in a
Physical Therapy Practice/Scott Stephens 155

Referral/Advertising for Professional Services 159

Financial Considerations in Practice [HOD P06-99-13-17] 161

Opposition to Physician Ownership of Physical Therapy Services [HOD P06-03-27-25] 161

Referral Relationships [HOD P06-90-15-28] 161

Physician Ownership of Physical Therapy Services/ Michele Wojciechowski 163

A Plan of Care to Protect Physical Therapist Practices/Dave Mason 170

Advertising Professional PT Services: Legal Implications/Ronald W Scott 173

Federal Trade Commission Issues Landmark Ruling on a California Self-Referral Arrangement 174

Issues Related to Specific Settings 175

Physical Therapy for Individuals With Disabilities: Practice in Educational Settings [HOD P06-95-14-03] 177

In Practice—Home Health: Special Risks/Gloria J Young 178

Liability Considerations in Continuing Education/Ronald W Scott 180

In Practice—CIs and Liability/Ronald W Scott 185

Liability Concerns in Aquatic Physical Therapy/Annie Clement 187

Of Dignity and Mobility/Kimberly Wynn 192

Physical Restraint: Legal and Risk Management Issues/Johnathan M Cooperman, Ronald W Scott 198

Selected Readings 202

Acknowledgements

We gratefully acknowledge Ronald W Scott, JD, PT, OCS, who has contributed in so many ways to *PT Magazine*'s coverage of law and liability issues—from full-length articles, to companion pieces, to columns, to general review and consultation.

We also are grateful to the following individuals who reviewed the contents of the original edition as well as suggested additions for this second edition to ensure that the articles continue to be relevant, useful, and accurate. Thanks to Kathy Lewis, PT, MAPT, JD, Laura Lee (Dolly) Swisher, PT, PhD, Cathy Thut, PT, MBA, and Mary Ann Wharton, PT, MS.

And to the many authors of the articles that are included in this volume—thank you.

Introduction

> A physical therapist shall comply with laws and regulations governing physical therapy and shall strive
> to effect changes that benefit patients/clients. (APTA Code of Ethics, PRINCIPLE 3 [HOD 06-00-12-23])

APTA recognizes the unique challenges physical therapists (PTs) confront every day to understand and apply all the laws that relate to physical therapist practice. The APTA *Standards of Practice, Code of Ethics* and *Guide for Professional Conduct* direct PTs to comply with all applicable laws that govern the jurisdiction in which they practice. All physical therapists, from new practitioners to experienced clinicians, face legal considerations in all aspects of practice.

It is essential for PTs to understand and apply their knowledge of law and liability to their everyday practice, whether to employee relations or patient care.

However, law is not static—new legislation is passed, and current regulations are amended. In order to uphold their legal and ethical obligations, physical therapists must keep up with developments in laws to protect patients from harm, laws to uphold PTs' rights in dealing with payers, laws to protect the physical therapy profession from encroachment, and many more. The sheer amount of information can be overwhelming to the busy professional.

Recognizing this, APTA publications, including its professional issues magazine, *PT—Magazine of Physical Therapy*, frequently have covered both specific legislation affecting physical therapist practice and general trends in liability. Articles and columns have explained particular laws, examined risk management strategies, discussed repercussions of breach of confidentiality, and analyzed issues related to physical therapist practice beyond the scope of licensure. APTA's official peer-reviewed journal, *Physical Therapy*, has published manuscripts that have dealt with any number of legal considerations. In 1996, APTA's commitment to keeping readers up-to-date on these topics was supported by the launching of a *PT Magazine* column, "Liability Awareness," that continues today and from which many of the articles in this book were drawn.

This second edition of the two-volume *Law and Liability* is now part of APTA's Risk Management in Physical Therapy series, which also includes the two-volume *Ethics in Physical Therapy* and *Risk Management in Physical Therapy: A Quick Reference*. The second edition includes relevant articles published between 2000 and 2005, as well as the still-applicable articles from the first edition.

Both volumes in *Law & Liability—Part 1: Liability Issues*, and *Part 2: Professional Issues*—will be relevant to all PTs across all practice settings, including articles in Part 1 on licensure, documentation, liability insurance, malpractice, and patient relations, and articles in Part 2 on pro bono services, contracting, and principles of risk management.

In addition to articles with broad appeal, Part 2 also includes items on disability legislation, advertising, delegation and supervision, making referrals, and the hiring process. There is even a section in Part 2 specifically geared toward practitioners in specific settings, such as home health, continuing education, and aquatics.

Both volumes include several of APTA's core documents, policies, guidelines, standards, and procedural documents that represent the Association's stance on the basics of safe, ethical physical therapy practice that meets the appropriate standard of care. A list of suggested readings complements these, directing the reader to specific resources for in-depth information. Together with the articles, these guidelines and references provide physical therapists with a set of tools to help them understand their legal obligations, know their rights, minimize risk, and provide physical therapy services in accordance with the high standards of their profession.

*Readers should note that articles related to specific laws or citations of specific APTA documents provided current information at the time of original publication and may be outdated due to changes in the legal code or revisions in APTA official documents. None of the articles in this publication is intended to provide specific legal advice for any particular individual. Personal advice can be given only by personal legal counsel, based on current and applicable state and federal law.

APTA documents, positions, and policies are current as of September 2005. They may change based on annual APTA House of Delegates actions.

APTA documents are current as of September 2005. They may change based on annual APTA House of Delegates actions. Visit APTA's Web site, www.apta.org, for the most current versions of all documents.

Today's Health Care System

Principles and Objectives for the United States Health Care System and the Delivery of Physical Therapy Services
HOD P06-04-17-16

The American Physical Therapy Association (APTA) supports a health care system that provides all individuals within the United States with access to quality health care.

This system should provide comprehensive, cost-effective, and appropriate physical therapy services provided by a licensed physical therapist or by a qualified physical therapist assistant under the direction and supervision of a physical therapist. In primary care, physical therapists should be recognized as health care professionals who can and should play a major role in achieving clinically effective outcomes and cost efficiencies that are essential to comprehensive health care.

APTA endorses the following principles and objectives for a health care system in which physical therapy is acknowledged as an essential component of health care:

PRINCIPLE I: ACCESS TO CARE

The health care system should provide access for all individuals, and should:

- Enable patients/clients to select among providers, including physical therapists, who are qualified and authorized by state and other jurisdiction law to provide professional health care services.

- Permit patient/client direct access to physical therapists with no requirement of a referral from any other practitioner.

- Encourage employers to offer a choice of quality, affordable health care coverage to employees and their dependents.

- Enable patients/clients to select and participate in plans that allow the development of financial reserves to cover individual health care expenses, including those incurred for physical therapy and any catastrophic coverage.

- Include mechanisms to allow patients/clients to pay their provider of choice directly for health care services.

- Prohibit denials of coverage due to preexisting and/or congenital health conditions.

- Provide affordable fee-for-service options and other mechanisms to assure that patients/clients are able to choose their health care providers.

- Provide financial support for the education and training of sufficient numbers and types of health care professionals to assure appropriate access to care for all individuals.

- Include a requirement that all public and private health plans provide examination, evaluation, diagnostic, prognostic services provided by a physical therapist, and intervention services provided by a physical therapist or physical therapist assistant under the direction and supervision of a physical therapist in any setting.

- Provide coverage for programs and incentives that prevent injury, impairment, and illness, promote wellness and aid in maintenance of functional independence, and provide coverage for preventive and restorative care programs to reduce the incidence and long-term impact of disease, disability, and injury.

- Include a requirement that all public and private health plans provide adequate assistive technology, including but not limited to durable medical equipment.

PRINCIPLE II: QUALITY OF CARE

The plan of care for a patient/client should ensure that intervention is based on achieving appropriate outcomes specific to the patient's/client's needs. Although APTA endorses adherence to standards of practice and efficiency of care, the Association opposes any policy that places arbitrary limits on physical therapy services. To ensure quality of care and protection of the public's best interests:

- Professional practitioners should be involved in the development of practice parameters and guidelines specific to their scope of practice.

- Physical therapists should use clinical experience, literature-based evidence, and patient/client preferences and apply APTA's *Guide to Physical Therapist Practice* as the foundation of such parameters and guidelines.

- Decisions regarding the initiation, continuation, or discharge of a patient's/client's physical therapy should be determined by the physical therapist responsible for that patient's/client's management.

- Physical therapists should hold themselves accountable to the public and to third party payers through peer review, and should be recognized as the appropriate professionals to review the delivery and utilization of physical therapy services.

PRINCIPLE III: COST CONTAINMENT AND PAYMENT

Payment rates for health care services should be reasonable and equitable, and mechanisms to control costs in the health care system should not encourage providers to withhold, restrict, or deny essential patient/client services. Insurers should be required by law to disclose to patients/clients the services and types of care covered, including the extent of coverage of physical therapy services. To ensure appropriate payment and cost containment:

- Health care professionals should be involved in the development of standards, establishment of payment rates, and review of claims and utilization for their specific discipline.

- A referral from a physician or any other practitioner should not be required for payment for physical therapy services.

- No arbitrary criteria should be utilized to determine payment for physical therapy services.

- Practitioner self-referral arrangements, including physician ownership of physical therapy services, should be prohibited by law.

- The use of billing codes should be restricted to those professionals who are licensed to perform those services and payment for physical therapy services should be made only when the services have been provided by a physical therapist or by a physical therapist assistant under the direction and supervision of a physical therapist.

- Administration of health care benefits, coverage, and payment should be simplified, and patients/clients and providers should have access to a fair and expedited appeals process for denied claims.

- Payment for physical therapy services should occur only when adequate documentation exists, consistent with APTA guidelines, to support the need for physical therapy services.

- Payment for physical therapy services should be determined fairly in all settings, and guidelines should be consistent regardless of the setting in which the services are provided.

- Payment should cover all elements of the patient/client management model, including the education of the patient/client, family, and caregiver as a component of the physical therapist's plan of care.

- Health care professionals should seek optimal treatment effectiveness in consideration of cost efficiencies.

PRINCIPLE IV: STATE LICENSURE

The responsibility for licensure and regulation should remain exclusively within the purview of the state or other jurisdiction and should not be preempted by any federal or regional agency or process. There should be no credentialing of institutions that would override or eliminate the requirements of individual practitioner license laws.

Direct Access and Attainment of "Physician-Status" as Applied Under the Medicare Program
HOD P06-05-16-08 [HOD 06-73-30-37]

Whereas, Section 1861(r) of the Social Security Act currently recognizes certain health care professionals who do not have medical degrees, such as dentists, podiatrists, and optometrists, as having status equivalent to physicians under the Medicare program;

Whereas, Physical therapists have attained education and clinical preparation within their scope of practice at least equivalent to many of these professionals; and,

Whereas, Attainment of beneficiary's direct access to physical therapists and recognition by the Medicare program of physical therapists' advanced education, clinical preparation, and expertise are consistent with the achievement of American Physical Therapy Association Vision Statement for Physical Therapy 2020 and the goals and objectives of the American Physical Therapy Association;

Resolved, That the American Physical Therapy Association shall assign high priority in its federal government affairs activities to achieving the enactment of legislation and promulgation of regulations that shall result in beneficiary's direct access to physical therapists and the attainment of "physician status" as recognized under the Medicare program.

Physical Therapy as a Mandated Service Under Medicaid
HOD P06-03-21-17 [Initial HOD 06-97-21-30]

Physical therapy should be a mandated service as a basic component of health care under Title XIX of the Social Security Act (the Medicaid program) at both the federal and state levels. The American Physical Therapy Association supports state and federal government actions that retain or enhance physical therapy benefits and opposes state and federal government actions that reduce physical therapy benefits under Title XIX.

liability awareness

by Kathy Lewis, PT, MAPT, JD

No-Risk, All-Gain Destinations

Must-visit Web sites for help in anticipating, preventing, and insuring against risk.

As a physical therapist (PT) or physical therapist assistant (PTA), you are acutely aware that new professional liability issues, guidelines, edicts, and compliance strategies for health care practitioners are continuously coming to light.

You're familiar with media reports of patient injuries and deaths linked to medical errors, and you've seen the effects of such cases on the parameters and cost of professional liability insurance for physicians. You've read and heard much from APTA and other sources about the Health Insurance Portability and Accountability Act (HIPAA) and its patient privacy protections. (For a comprehensive summary of those provisions, revisit the Government Affairs column in the November 2002 issue of **PT**.[1]) With our profession advancing toward the goals of direct access for all consumers and "all the privileges of autonomous practice" for PTs (as highlighted in *APTA's Vision Statement for Physical Therapy 2020*[2]), you appreciate the importance of PTs and PTAs keeping up with all the latest developments in risk management.

You may be less aware, however, of the plethora of excellent risk management resources that are just a click of a mouse away. The following list of Internet sites can serve as your collective gateway to current information on a wide variety of risk management-related subjects and issues.

Risk Prevention

To ensure the provision of high-quality patient/client care and to avoid any activity that violates professional practice standards, and thus incurs risk, you must be knowledgeable about those standards. Your best source for this information is APTA's Web site (www.apta.org). Specifically, you'd do well to visit these links:

❖ **APTA core documents.** Here, you'll find links to the *Code of Ethics*, the *Guide for Professional Conduct*, the *Standards of Practice for Physical Therapy and the Criteria*, the *Standards of Ethical Conduct for the Physical Therapist Assistant*, and the *Guide for Conduct of the Physical Therapist Assistant*. From the APTA Web site's home page, click on "About APTA," then "APTA Core Documents."

❖ **House of Delegates and Board of Directors standards, policies, positions, and guidelines.** Each year the House of Delegates (HOD) and Board of Directors (BOD) revise and develop positions relative to current issues. The *2002 House of Delegates Standards, Policies, Positions, and Guidelines Manual* and Section I (Professional and Societal) of the *Board of Directors Policies, Positions, and Guidelines* are comprehensive, up-to-date, and downloadable compilations. From the APTA Web site's home page, click on "About APTA," "APTA Core Documents," then "House and Board Policies." To view the *2002 House of Delegates Standards, Policies, Positions, and Guidelines Manual*, click on "House of Delegates Policies." To view the *Board of Directors Policies, Positions, and Guidelines*, click on "Board of Directors Policies." Also, should you want to examine all HOD and BOD activity on a given subject—supervision, for example—you need only click on the binoculars icon on the PDF menu within the HOD or BOD document named above, then type in the word "supervision" to find activity on supervision-related issues in such diverse areas as continuing education, reimbursement, PTAs and ancil-

lary personnel, and students. The binoculars icon is a "find" feature that will direct you to the first appearance in the document of the word or phrase you've selected. For subsequent mentions of the word or phrase, click on the icon to the right of the binoculars icon; this is a "find again" feature.

❖ **Ethics and Judicial Committee (EJC) interpretations and opinions.** You'll find recent EJC opinions on such subjects as sexual relationships with patients/clients and former patients/clients; reporting obligations with respect to unethical, incompetent, or illegal acts; and conflict of interest in treating fellow employees. There also is a *Compendium of Interpretations and Opinions, 1980-1995*, in which the EJC addresses such specific ethical questions as truth in disclosure in advertising, division of fees and salaried arrangements, equipment endorsement, and much more. From the home page, go to "Practice," then "Ethics and Legal Issues in Physical Therapy," then "Ethics and Judicial Committee Opinions."

❖ **Reimbursement issues.** Here, you'll find information on compliance with HIPAA (which sets national standards for electronic health care transactions), advice on how to avoid and handle claims audits and retroactive denials, and risk awareness pointers for PTs who are starting independent private practices. From the home page, click on "Reimbursement."

❖ **"Stories From the Front."** An excellent tool for learning from others' mistakes, this collection of columns from the pages of **PT** is ideal for individual study and as a basis for departmental discussions. The author, Rita Arriaga, PT, MS (former chair of APTA's Committee on

Risk Management and Member Benefits), uses case studies based on real-life scenarios to illustrate actions (and inaction) that incur risk and can provoke lawsuits, and she offers strategies for avoiding such risks. From the home page, go to "Products and Services," then "APTA Affinity Benefits," then "Risk Management," then "Suggested Risk Management Readings," then "Stories from the Front."

The following non-APTA sites also are good sources of risk prevention information and guidance:

❖ *Malpractice cases posted by the Healthcare Providers Service Organization (HPSO).* HPSO, administrator of the APTA-endorsed professional liability insurance plan, each month posts the facts and outcomes of various malpractice cases—offering insights into risks and health care practitioners' failure to properly manage them. Go to www.hpso.com/case/caseindex.php3 and then scroll to the bottom of the page for links to previously posted cases and brief descriptions of the defendants. If your time is limited or you are interested only in physical therapy scenarios, you can search the archives for links to those specific cases.

❖ *Quality-of-care links from the National Committee for Quality Assurance.* You'll find links here to information about quality-of-care issues that is available at a number of government and nongovernment sites, including CNN, the Medicare Rights Center, the National Partnership for Women and Families, the Centers for Disease Control and Prevention, the Food and Drug Administration, and the National Institutes of Health. Go to www.ncqua.org and click on "Related Links."

❖ *Resources on "root cause analysis."* Root cause analysis is a process for looking at the potential risks revealed by "close calls" in health care and other fields—errors that might have resulted in an adverse event had they not been caught in time. An excellent article on root cause analysis is available on the Web site of Joint Commission Resources, Inc, a subsidiary of the Joint Commission on Accreditation of Healthcare Organizations (JCAHO). Type in www.jcrinc.com/publications .asp?durki+801. Additional links about root cause analysis are available from Duke University at http://faculty. fuqua.duke.edu/daweb/dalinks.htm.

Homing In

Some information on the Web sites of professional organizations may require membership in that organization. Also, some URLs may have changed by the time this column is published, or may subsequently change. If you experience difficulty with any of the links provided in this column, go to the home page of that site and conduct a search for the new URL. Home pages of the sites mentioned in this column are:

American Physical Therapy Association: www.apta.org
Harvard Medical Institutions Risk Management Foundation: www.rmf.harvard.edu
Healthcare Providers Service Organization: www.hpso.com
Joint Commission on Accreditation of Healthcare Organizations: www.jcaho.com
National Committee for Quality Assurance: www.ncqua.org

In addition to the links described in this column, you may be able to find further information on the particular subject in which you are interested by using such Internet search engines as Google (www.google.com) and Yahoo! (www.yahoo.com).

liability awareness

Also, JCAHO publishes "sentinel event alerts" on particular risk management issues that have undergone a comprehensive root cause analysis. Typically, these reports identify factors that may relate to the problem, risk factors that may cause the problem, and strategies by which to prevent the problem. Of particular interest to PTs is the sentinel event alert on preventing restraint deaths that is available at http://www.jcaho.com/about+us/news+letters/sentinel+event+alert/sea_8.htm.

Risk Protection and Claims Management

Adverse events may occur even when high-quality care was provided. You may well have considered professional liability insurance to protect your assets and for your own peace of mind, but you need reliable information on which to base your insurance and claims management choices. Here are some good places to start:

❖ *APTA resources.* A previous Liability Awareness column from **PT**, "Professional Liability for the Employed PT," provides detailed advice about why and when the employed practitioner should consider purchasing an individual professional liability policy. Another past Liability Awareness column, "Do the Write Thing: Document Everything!" is a detailed look at how documentation can be your best defense mechanism if you are the subject of a lawsuit. Also available on APTA's Web site is a page of links to online articles about filling out claims, adequate liability coverage in wellness and fitness niches, and the duty to report. For all of these resources, from the APTA Web site's home page, go to "Products and Services," then "APTA Affinity Benefits," then "Risk Management," then "Suggested Risk Management Readings." (For the links to online articles, click on "The Hot Topics.")

❖ *HPSO newsletter.* The *HPSO Risk Advisor,* a quarterly newsletter available at www.hpso.com/newsletters/newsindex.php3, has special editions devoted to physical therapy and offers a quick review of the hottest risk-related legal issues and trends in physical therapy and the health care industry. Several articles available at the site are particularly compelling from the standpoints of risk protection and claims management, including "The Liabilities of Working Under Contract" (www.hpso.com/newsletters/3-2002/w2002flash.php3), "The Right Way to Fill Out an Incident Report" (www.hpso.com/newsletters/3-2002/48850A.HTM), and "Gripped By a Lawsuit" (www.hpso.com/newsletters/archivesgripped.php3). (A note for first-time visitors: To move beyond the first page of a newsletter from winter 2001 to the present, use the navigation arrows in the upper left corner of the opening page.)

❖ *Harvard Medical Institutions Risk Management Foundation.* The foundation's Web pages (at www.rmf.harvard.edu) contain extremely valuable information on such subjects as what to do when a patient makes a liability claim; how to prepare for a deposition; how to best use clinical guidelines, advisories, and algorithms as evidence of standard of care; and how to improve communication skills with patients/clients.

In today's complex and rapidly changing health care environment, it behooves PTs who wish to avoid burdensome expenditures of time and money dealing with risk-related issues to expand their definition of "continuing education" to include making the most of resources that are readily available on the Internet. With so much information literally at our fingertips—on complying with the latest regulations, fashioning effective risk management strategies, acquiring professional liability insurance, and so much more—PTs and PTAs have nothing to risk and everything to gain by seeking out information and answers electronically. **PT**

Kathy Lewis, PT, MAPT, JD, is an Associate Professor in the Graduate Program in Physical Therapy at Wichita State University and chairs APTA's Committee on Risk Management and Member Benefits. She can be reached at 316/978-6156 or dknlewis@worldnet.att.net.

References

1. Ravitz K. The HIPAA privacy final modified rule. *PT—Magazine of Physical Therapy.* 2002; 10(11):21-25.
2. *APTA's Vision Statement for Physical Therapy 2020.* Available at www.apta.org/About/aptamissiongoals/visionstatement. Accessed September 18, 2002.

The information presented here is not to be interpreted as specific legal advice for any particular provider. Personal advice can be given only by personal legal counsel, based on applicable state and federal law.

Delegation and Supervision

Direction and Supervision of the Physical Therapist Assistant
HOD P06-05-18-26 [Initial HOD 06-84-16-72/HOD 06-78-22-61/HOD 06-77-19-37]

Physical therapists have a responsibility to deliver services in ways that protect the public safety and maximize the availability of their services. They do this through direct delivery of services in conjunction with responsible utilization of physical therapist assistants who assist with selected components of intervention. The physical therapist assistant is the only individual permitted to assist a physical therapist in selected interventions under the direction and supervision of a physical therapist.

Direction and supervision are essential in the provision of quality physical therapy services. The degree of direction and supervision necessary for assuring quality physical therapy services is dependent upon many factors, including the education, experiences, and responsibilities of the parties involved, as well as the organizational structure in which the physical therapy services are provided.

Regardless of the setting in which the service is provided, the following responsibilities must be borne solely by the physical therapist:

1. Interpretation of referrals when available.
2. Initial examination, evaluation, diagnosis, and prognosis.
3. Development or modification of a plan of care which is based on the initial examination or reexamination and which includes the physical therapy goals and outcomes.
4. Determination of when the expertise and decision-making capability of the physical therapist requires the physical therapist to personally render physical therapy interventions and when it may be appropriate to utilize the physical therapist assistant. A physical therapist shall determine the most appropriate utilization of the physical therapist assistant that provides for the delivery of service that is safe, effective, and efficient.
5. Reexamination of the patient/client in light of their goals, and revision of the plan of care when indicated.
6. Establishment of the discharge plan and documentation of discharge summary/status.
7. Oversight of all documentation for services rendered to each patient/client.

The physical therapist remains responsible for the physical therapy services provided when the physical therapist's plan of care involves the physical therapist assistant to assist with selected interventions. Regardless of the setting in which the service is provided, the determination to utilize physical therapist assistants for selected interventions requires the education, expertise, and professional judgment of a physical therapist as described by the *Standards of Practice, Guide to Professional Conduct,* and *Code of Ethics.*

In determining the appropriate extent of assistance from the physical therapist assistant (PTA), the physical therapist considers:

- The PTA's education, training, experience, and skill level.
- Patient/client criticality, acuity, stability, and complexity.
- The predictability of the consequences.
- The setting in which the care is being delivered.
- Federal and state statutes.
- Liability and risk management concerns.
- The mission of physical therapy services for the setting.
- The needed frequency of reexamination.

Physical Therapist Assistant

Definition

The physical therapist assistant is a technically educated health care provider who assists the physical therapist in the provision of physical therapy. The physical therapist assistant is a graduate of a physical therapist assistant associate degree program accredited by the Commission on Accreditation in Physical Therapy Education (CAPTE).

Utilization

The physical therapist is directly responsible for the actions of the physical therapist assistant related to patient/client management. The physical therapist assistant may perform selected physical therapy interventions under the direction and at least general supervision of the physical therapist. In general supervision, the physical therapist is not required to be on-site for direction and supervision, but must be available at least by telecommunications. The ability of the physical therapist assistant to perform the selected interventions as directed shall be assessed on an ongoing basis by the supervising physical therapist. The physical therapist assistant makes modifications to selected interventions either to progress the patient/client as directed by the physical therapist or to ensure patient/client safety and comfort.

The physical therapist assistant must work under the direction and at least general supervision of the physical therapist. In all practice settings, the performance of selected interventions by the physical therapist assistant must be consistent with safe and legal physical therapist practice, and shall be predicated on the following factors: complexity and acuity of the patient's/client's needs; proximity and accessibility to the physical therapist; supervision available in the event of emergencies or critical events; and type of setting in which the service is provided.

When supervising the physical therapist assistant in any off-site setting, the following requirements must be observed:

1. A physical therapist must be accessible by telecommunications to the physical therapist assistant at all times while the physical therapist assistant is treating patients/clients.

2. There must be regularly scheduled and documented conferences with the physical therapist assistant regarding patients/clients, the frequency of which is determined by the needs of the patient/client and the needs of the physical therapist assistant.

3. In those situations in which a physical therapist assistant is involved in the care of a patient/client, a supervisory visit by the physical therapist will be made:

    a. Upon the physical therapist assistant's request for a reexamination, when a change in the plan of care is needed, prior to any planned discharge, and in response to a change in the patient's/client's medical status.

    b. At least once a month, or at a higher frequency when established by the physical therapist, in accordance with the needs of the patient/client.

    c. A supervisory visit should include:

        i. An on-site reexamination of the patient/client.

        ii. On-site review of the plan of care with appropriate revision or termination.

        iii. Evaluation of need and recommendation for utilization of outside resources.

Provision of Physical Therapy Interventions and Related Tasks
HOD P06-00-17-28

Physical therapists are the only professionals who provide physical therapy interventions. Physical therapist assistants are the only individuals who provide selected physical therapy interventions under the direction and at least general supervision of the physical therapist.

Physical therapy aides are any support personnel who perform designated tasks related to the operation of the physical therapy service. Tasks are those activities that do not require the clinical decision making of the physical therapist or the clinical problem solving of the physical therapist assistant. Tasks related to patient/client management must be assigned to the physical therapy aide by the physical therapist, or where allowable by law, the physical therapist assistant, and may only be performed by the aide under direct personal supervision of the physical therapist, or where allowable by law, the physical therapist assistant. Direct personal supervision requires that the physical therapist, or where allowable by law, the physical therapist assistant, be physically present and immediately available to direct and supervise tasks that are related to patient/client management. The direction and supervision is continuous throughout the time these tasks are performed. The physical therapist or physical therapist assistant must have direct contact with the patient/client during each session. Telecommunications does not meet the requirement of direct personal supervision.

Distinction Between the Physical Therapist and the Physical Therapist Assistant in Physical Therapy
HOD P06-01-18-19 [Initial HOD 06-96-24-39]

The American Physical Therapy Association (APTA) is committed to promoting the physical therapist as the professional practitioner of physical therapy and promoting the physical therapist assistant as the only individual who assists the physical therapist in the provision of selected physical therapy interventions. APTA is further committed to incorporating this concept into all Association policies, positions, and program activities, wherever applicable.

Professional: The term "professional," when used in reference to physical therapy services, denotes the physical therapist.

Physical Therapist Assistant: The physical therapist assistant is an educated individual who works under the direction and supervision of a physical therapist. The physical therapist assistant is the only individual who assists the physical therapist in accordance with APTA's policies and positions in the delivery of selected physical therapy interventions. The physical therapist assistant is a graduate of a physical therapist assistant education program accredited by the Commission on Accreditation in Physical Therapy Education.

Practice: The practice of physical therapy is conducted by the physical therapist.

Procedural Interventions Exclusively Performed by Physical Therapists
HOD P06-00-30-36

The physical therapist's scope of practice as defined by the American Physical Therapy Association *Guide to Physical Therapist Practice* includes interventions performed by physical therapists. These interventions include procedures performed exclusively by physical therapists and selected interventions that can be performed by the physical therapist assistant under the direction and supervision of the physical therapist. Interventions that require immediate and continuous examination and evaluation throughout the intervention are performed exclusively by the physical therapist. Such procedural interventions within the scope of physical therapist practice that are performed exclusively by the physical therapist include, but are not limited to, spinal and peripheral joint mobilization/manipulation, which are components of manual therapy, and sharp selective debridement, which is a component of wound management.

Student Physical Therapist Provision of Services
HOD P06-00-18-30

Student physical therapists, when participating as part of a physical therapist professional education curriculum and when acting in accordance with the American Physical Therapy Association policy and applicable state laws and regulations, are qualified to provide services only under the direction and direct supervision of the physical therapist, who is responsible for patient/client management. Direct supervision means the physical therapist is physically present and immediately available for direction and supervision. The physical therapist will have direct contact with the patient/client during each visit that is defined in the *Guide to Physical Therapist Practice*, as all encounters with a patient/client in a 24-hour period. Telecommunications does not meet the requirement of direct supervision.

Supervision of Student Physical Therapist Assistants
HOD P06-00-19-31

Student physical therapist assistants, when participating as part of a physical therapist assistant education curriculum, and when acting in accordance with the American Physical Therapy Association policy and applicable state laws and regulations, are qualified to perform selected physical therapy interventions under the direction and direct supervision of either the physical therapist alone or the physical therapist and physical therapist assistant. The physical therapist is responsible for patient/client management. Direct supervision means the physical therapist is physically present and immediately available for direction and supervision. The physical therapist will have direct contact with the patient/client during each visit that is defined in the *Guide to Physical Therapist Practice*. Telecommunications does not meet the requirement of direct supervision.

Public Protection in the Delivery of Therapeutic Exercise
HOD P06-00-33-13

The American Physical Therapy Association (APTA), in an effort to safeguard the public, supports that persons with movement-related impairments, functional limitations, and disabilities will receive the highest quality of care when therapeutic exercise is delivered by qualified practitioners. APTA will monitor and respond to any proposed credentialing, accreditation, licensure, or other regulatory efforts of individuals or groups who seek to be recognized as qualified to perform therapeutic exercise on persons with movement related impairments, functional limitations, and disabilities.

Cross-Trained Personnel
HOD P06-99-12-05 [Initial HOD 06-95-27-17]

The American Physical Therapy Association (APTA) opposes the concept of the cross-trained professional practitioner, defined as "a health care practitioner who is cross-trained in area(s) of practice in which the individual is neither educated nor licensed." This position should not be interpreted as expressing opposition to coordination of care involving professional practitioners from different disciplines or dual credentialing through education and licensure.

APTA does not oppose the utilization of cross-trained support personnel who provide physical therapist-directed support services as aides. Cross-trained support personnel refers to individuals with "on-the-job training within applicable state laws and regulations to provide services outside or in addition to the scope of their educational preparation or training."

Credentialing of Physical Therapy Aides
HOD P06-99-12-14 [Initial HOD 06-86-10-23]

The American Physical Therapy Association continues to oppose certification or credentialing of physical therapy aides and, therefore, will not endorse or recognize such programs.

Support Personnel

Change the light cast upon an object and you can change how the object looks. Change the observer of an object and you can change how an object is described. These simple truths, exemplified in art by the work of the impressionists, are illustrated in the dialogue that follows Bashi and Domholdt's article this month, "Use of Support Personnel for Physical Therapy Treatment." Each commentator provides a unique impression of the research and its implications. When it comes to the use of personnel, we apparently have had very little data, and most of us have formed our opinions and behavioral patterns in the absence of dialogue and communication. Therefore it is not surprising that each commentator sees the work of Bashi and Domholdt very differently.

Physical therapists, like physicians, often see a dichotomy between those who deliver services (the practitioners) and those who administer the delivery system. Therapists who deliver hands-on care frequently consider administrative issues as irrelevant, non–patient-oriented topics. With our nation's newfound interest in recasting our health care system, this myopic view can no longer be tolerated. The business and administration of health care is of concern to all of us. Unless we as a profession are willing to examine how we provide services and how we might most effectively provide services, decisions about service delivery will be made by others.

Box, in her commentary on Bashi and Domholdt's article, alludes to a critical issue when she states, "We must remember that the profession of physical therapy belongs as much to the society it seeks to serve as it does to those who provide that service." The profession may not necessarily belong to society, but health care is a societal responsibility, and the management of that care cannot be the province of any group within society, or any subgroup within a profession.

When Bashi and Domholdt note, ". . . the use of nonprofessional support personnel in physical therapy has a long history . . .," they provide a poignant insight beyond their words. One may argue that the first physical therapists were seen by other professions as "nonprofessional support personnel." Too often the issue of personnel use revolves around words and pejorative connotations. Degrees and titles create pecking orders that seem inviolate, even though they are the products of evolution rather than logical development. Similarly, emotional and value-laden words are often used to defend roles and characterize health care workers. In concurring that in many settings physical therapist assistants play a vital role in our delivery of services, I need not engage in the dialogue about whether members of this group represent a "profession."

In determining who plays what role in health care, we are not valuing any group of health care workers as human beings. When we engage in discussions about the role of aides and assistants, we are not discussing the value of persons, but rather whether members of these groups should be assigned to tasks.

As can be seen from the commentaries in this issue, responsible and respectful
people can disagree on many aspects of this topic, but the real issue is who
can do what most effectively, efficiently, and safely. We have seen the divisive
effect of the strutting of credentials in the efforts of some physiatrists to exert
control over therapists. This resulted in diminished patient care and excessive
costs. We will do a great disservice to our profession and society if the data
Bashi and Domholdt provide become the grist for power plays by any group.

The leadership of our profession can continue to hold forums and to develop
practice guidelines relating to the use of support personnel. These are appropriate actions, but they will be insufficient without practitioner involvement.
Unless we have a general meeting of the minds, one developed through the
acquisition of more data and refined through discussions, our practice behaviors may not change. The overriding finding of Bashi and Domholdt is that, at
least in the state of Indiana, where their data come from, there is great diver-
sity in the use of supportive personnel. No issue has a more direct impact on
the daily life of therapists than the delegation of tasks within the clinical setting.
If physical therapy practitioners and researchers do not collectively address this
topic, others will. Then we may find ourselves working within a health care
system in which reimbursement rates and staffing patterns are predicated on
the use of personnel in ways that we find inappropriate.

Jules M Rothstein, PhD, PT
Editor

LIABILITY AWARENESS

by Rita Arriaga, PT, MS

Stories From the Front—Part One: Supervision

A real-life scenario illustrates some basic risk-management principles.

Last year, *PT* ran a three-part Liability Awareness series that adapted actual cases from the APTA-endorsed professional liability insurance claims history and discussed what risk-management techniques could have been used to reduce risk. APTA continues the series with this first of three case studies.

The following scenario presents a common concern in today's clinics. Daily, physical therapists face pressures to maximize cost-effectiveness in clinical practice. Utilization of support personnel to assist in delivery of patient care services has long been a strategy employed by PTs to enhance efficiency. We must make certain, however, that risk-management considerations are always included in training, supervising, and utilizing aides.

As you read the scenario, consider the following questions:

❖ What are the elements in this scenario that increase the PT's risk of professional liability?

❖ What risk-management techniques could have been used to reduce that risk?

A 40-year-old woman injured her back in a fall at work 1 week prior to seeing her physician. She was referred for treatment—specifically, therapeutic exercises for a lumbar strain—at a physical therapy clinic across the hall.

Although the physical therapy clinic was extremely busy that day, the PT wanted to initiate treatment right away, so the PT reviewed the physician's referral but performed no history, examination of the patient, or evaluation. The PT then instructed the physical therapy aide, who was a well-respected and trusted employee, to teach the patient a standard exercise routine that had been developed by the clinic for patients with lumbar strain and was described on a printed handout. The patient voiced no complaints about the exercises to the aide, who entered a note in the patients chart that was co-signed by the PT and scheduled a return appointment for 3 days later.

At the second visit—the day of the incident—the PT conducted and documented the examination and evaluation that he had postponed from the initial visit. He inquired about the patient's response to the exercise program that she had been instructed in by the aide, but he did not actually observe her performing the exercises.

After providing the patient with education in posture and body mechanics, the PT instructed the aide to bring the patient to the gym and add exercises to her program, including the leg press. The aide was told to follow the standard low back exercise gym program and progression that the clinic used for patients with similar complaints. The PT did not remain in the gym during the patient's exercise session but was in an adjacent treatment room with another patient.

As he had done many times before, the aide independently adjusted the exercise machines and guided the patient in their use. He told the patient to perform several repetitions of each exercise.

The patient appeared to have no problems with the first two exercises, but, after finishing the leg press exercise, she complained immediately of increased back pain. The aide applied ice to the patient's back but did not get the therapist because the patient indicated that the pain had subsided. The patient left the clinic without seeing the PT. The aide's co-signed note in the chart only indicated that the patient had performed the exercises and that ice had been applied to her back.

The patient did not return for her next scheduled appointment at the clinic. Instead, she consulted her physician, who subsequently diagnosed a herniated disc.

The patient brought a claim against the PT for negligence. The patient believed that she had been improperly instructed in the use of the equipment by the aide, who was not properly trained or supervised.

Now, turn the page for commentary on this scenario from a risk-management perspective, including a table summarizing risky elements and strategies to address them.

> **The PT did not remain in the gym during the patient's exercise session but was in an adjacent treatment room with another patient. The aide independently adjusted the exercise machines and instructed the patient in their use.**

> The information presented here is not to be interpreted as specific legal advice for any particular provider. Personal advice can only be given by personal legal counsel, based on applicable state and federal law.

LIABILITY AWARENESS

The PT did not perform an examination and evaluation of the patient's condition, and he did not render a diagnosis and prognosis before intervention was initiated.

A PT must always follow the elements of patient management as described in the *Guide to Physical Therapist Practice* to ensure appropriate and individualized treatment planning. The initial examination, evaluation, and diagnosis must occur before the PT initiates or delegates any intervention. According to APTA's House of Delegates' *Diagnosis by Physical Therapists* (HOD 06-95-12-07), "Prior to making a patient management decision, physical therapists shall utilize the diagnostic process in order to establish a diagnosis for the specific conditions in need of the physical therapist's attention."

Therapeutic exercises, a physical therapy intervention, were initiated by the aide, who was left to determine the equipment adjustment and exercise parameters on his own.

APTA's *Position on Physical Therapy Aides* (HOD 06-99-11-13) states that an aide is limited to tasks "that do not require clinical decision-making of the physical therapist or the clinical problem-solving of the physical therapist assistant" and that aides "may function only with continuous on-site supervision by the physical therapist, or, where allowable by law or regulation, the physical therapist assistant." As directed in the House of Delegates' *Position on Physical Therapy Interventions* (HOD-16-99-10-12), *physical therapy interventions* are to be provided only by PTs or by physical therapist assistants under the direction of the PT.

The PT did not adequately document the initial patient visit or the follow-up care.

APTA's House of Delegates' *Position on the Authority for Physical Therapy Documentation* states that "physical therapy examination, evaluation, diagnosis, prognosis, and intervention shall be documented, dated, and authenticated by the physical therapist who performs the service....Other notations or flow charts completed by support personnel are considered a component of the documented record but do not meet the requirements of documentation in, or of, themselves."

The PT did not provide specific follow-up at the same visit to assess the patient's response to the exercise routine and did not observe the patient performing the exercises.

A PT should assess the patient before he or she leaves the clinic to determine his or her response to or the outcome of the treatment. This is particularly important when a new intervention is initiated.

The aide did not report the incident to the PT.

Any and all adverse incidents, including patient feedback, should be reported to the PT immediately. The PT should then examine the patient before the patient leaves the clinic, carefully documenting findings.

Physical therapy intervention should always include an examination, evaluation, diagnosis, and prognosis. Regardless of whether an adverse incident ensues, a PT who fails to perform the elements of patient management when providing care is putting his or her status as a professional on the line.

Utilization of support personnel should occur only within the limitations of state statute and regulation and the policies and positions outlined by the American Physical Therapy Association. Support personnel should be aware of the limits of their independent decision-making in patient care. Support personnel also should be trained to take appropriate action when incidents occur, such as alerting the PT when a patient has an unusual complaint or response to treatment. Remember, PTs retain professional liability for care rendered under their supervision. *PT*

Rita Arriaga, PT, MS, is Assistant Clinical Professor in the Graduate Program of Physical Therapy, Department of Physical Therapy and Rehabilitation Science, University of California at San Francisco, and is a member of APTA's Committee on Risk Management Services and Member Benefits.

Suggested Readings

Arriaga, R. Stories from the front—part one: delegation. *PT—Magazine of Physical Therapy.* 1998;6(7):27-28.

Arriaga, R. Stories from the front—part two: utilization of support staff. *PT—Magazine of Physical Therapy.* 1998;6(9):31-32.

Arriaga, R. Stories from the front—part three: practice across state lines. *PT—Magazine of Physical Therapy.* 1998;6(10):31-32.

Guide to Physical Therapist Practice. Alexandria, Va: American Physical Therapy Association; 1999.

Pearls for Physical Therapists. Alexandria, Va: American Physical Therapy Association; 1997.

liability*awareness*

by Rita Arriaga, PT, MS

Stories From the Front—
Part One: PTAs and Safe Practice

A real-life scenario illustrates some basic risk-management principles.

In each of the past 2 years, **PT** has published a three-part Liability Awareness series that has adapted cases from the APTA-endorsed professional liability insurance claims history and has examined what risk-management techniques could have been used to reduce risk. APTA picks up the series this month with this first of three case studies.

> A review of the PTA's documentation showed that his notes in the record did not mention the patient's sensory impairment and were unclear about how long the hot packs were actually kept on the patient's knee.

The following scenario illustrates the need for both physical therapists (PTs) and physical therapist assistants (PTAs) to take responsibility for safe practice and addresses the liability they face if they fail to do so.

As you read the scenario, consider these questions:

❖ What are the elements in this scenario that increase the PT's and the PTA's liability risk?
❖ What risk-management techniques could have been used to reduce that risk?

This case involved a PT who supervised a hospital's physical therapy department as an independent contractor and a PTA who was a member of the hospital's staff. One of the patients being treated at this facility was a 75-year-old woman who previously had a left CVA (cerebrovascular accident) and who subsequently injured her right knee in an accident at her home. The PT performed an examination of the patient and gave an evaluation of her findings. She diagnosed pattern 4F in the *Guide to Physical Therapist Practice* (Impaired Joint Mobility, Motor Function, Muscle Performance, and Range of Motion Associated with Localized Inflammation).

The planned intervention on the day of the incident was heat, to be followed by mobility exercises. The PT verbally directed the PTA to administer hot packs to the patient's right knee, and the PTA did so. The PT was not with the PTA during the application of the packs.

After applying the heat, the PTA went to check on another patient. The original patient was left unattended for 45 minutes. By the time the PTA removed the hot packs, the patient—who had moderate sensory impairment secondary to her stroke and did not realize she was being burned—had sustained second-degree burns on the medial

aspects of her knee.

The patient brought claims against the PT and the hospital for negligence, stating that she also believed that the PTA who applied the hot packs was negligent and failed to sufficiently monitor her. She further claimed that she had been left unattended for an entire hour.

A review of the PT's documentation demonstrated that she had clearly noted the sensory loss in the patient's right leg and had indicated a heightened need for monitoring the application of thermal agents. The PT acknowledged, however, that she had not verbally communicated these factors—the sensory impairment and the need for increased monitoring—to the PTA.

A review of the PTA's documentation, meanwhile, showed that his notes in the record did not mention the patient's sensory impairment and were unclear about how long the hot packs were actually kept on the patient's knee or whether the patient was monitored during the heat application.

Now, turn the page for commentary on this scenario from a risk-management perspective, including a table summarizing risky elements and strategies to address them.

The information presented here is not to be interpreted as specific legal advice for any particular provider. Personal advice can only be given by personal legal counsel, based on applicable state and federal law.

❖　　❖　　❖

Do you have risk-management questions or concerns? Insights into what PTs need or want to know will help APTA's efforts to educate members about the types of incidents occurring in the workplace and about appropriate risk-management techniques. Contact Jennifer Baker, Director of APTA Insurance and Member Benefit Services, at 800/999-2782, ext 3145 or via e-mail at jenniferbaker@apta.org.

liabilityawareness

The PT failed to verbally communicate to the PTA the patient's sensory impairment or the need for increased monitoring of the hot packs.

While the PT properly documented the impairment and the need for heightened monitoring, she should have stated both things explicitly to the PTA. The APTA House of Delegates' position on *Direction and Supervision of the Physical Therapist Assistant* (HOD 06-00-16-27) states, "The physical therapist is directly responsible for the actions of the physical therapist assistant related to client/patient management." It further states, "Direction and supervision are essential in the provision of quality physical therapy services" and "the physical therapist remains responsible for the physical therapy services provided when the physical therapist's plan of care involves the physical therapist assistant to assist with selected interventions."

The PTA failed to follow the instructions in the PT's documentation, and failed to monitor the application of the hot packs.

Standard 5 of the APTA House of Delegates' Standards of *Ethical Conduct for the Physical Therapist Assistant* (HOD 06-00-13-24) states that PTAs "shall achieve and maintain competence in the provision of selected physical therapy interventions." Standard 6 states that PTAs "shall make judgments that are commensurate with their educational and legal qualifications as a physical therapist assistant." In failing to either read or heed the PT's documented instructions, and in leaving the patient unattended for an extended period, the PTA displayed neither competence nor good judgment..

The PTA provided insufficient documentation.

The APTA Board of Directors' Guidelines for Physical Therapy Documentation (BOD 03-00-22-54) state that documentation of each visit/encounter shall include "identification of specific interventions provided, including frequency, intensity, and duration as appropriate."

PTs retain professional liability for care rendered under their supervision. First, the PT is responsible for ensuring the competency and skill of all support personnel, including PTAs, that he or she supervises. It is assumed that the PT in this case was familiar with the experience and abilities of the PTA and chose to delegate an intervention (hot packs) that she felt was within this particular individual's capabilities to administer.

Secondly, in this particular situation, it was the PT's responsibility to clearly communicate to the PTA the patient's sensory impairment and the need for increased monitoring of the hot packs application.

The PTA, however, also shoulders some of the responsibility for this unfortunate incident. The use of hot packs in treatment (including parameters for application and monitoring) is within the scope of the basic patient care skills of a PTA. His failure to read or heed the written information in the PT's documentation and his failure to properly attend to the patient resulted in the burns and prompted the claims against the PT and the hospital. 🅟🅣

Rita Arriaga, PT, MS, is an Assistant Clinical Professor in the Graduate Program in Physical Therapy and the Director of Rehabilitation Services at the University of California, San Francisco, and chairs APTA's Committee on Risk Management Services and Member Benefits. She can be reached at 415/476-3453 or via e-mail at arriaga@itsa.ucsf.edu.

Suggested Readings

American Physical Therapy Association. Board of Directors policies. Available at www.apta.org/governance/governance_5/BODpolicies.

American Physical Therapy Association. Ethics and legal issues in physical therapy. Available at www.apta.org/PT_Practice/ethics_pt.

American Physical Therapy Association. House of Delegates policies. Available at www.apta.org/governance/HOD/governance_10.

Guide to Physical Therapy Practice. *Phys Ther.* 2001;81:in press.

Pearls for Physical Therapists. Alexandria, Va: American Physical Therapy Association; 1997.

liability awareness
by Rita Arriaga, PT, MS

Stories From the Front—
Part Two: Communication and Use of Personnel

A real-life scenario illustrates some basic risk-management principles.

For the fourth straight year, **PT** is featuring a three-part Liability Awareness series presenting cases adapted from the APTA-endorsed professional liability insurance claims history. This year's series began last month with a scenario that illustrated the need for physical therapists (PTs) to manage risks up front in an effort to avoid burns, and to respond immediately and appropriately should burns occur in order to minimize health consequences and professional liability. The following scenario spotlights liability issues in two areas: communication with other health care practitioners and direction and supervision of personnel.

As you read the scenario, consider these questions:

❖ What elements increase the PT's liability risk?
❖ What risk-management techni-ques could have been used to reduce that risk?

This case involved a 53-year-old man who sustained a significant tear to his rotator cuff while playing baseball. He underwent surgical repair and was given a referral for physical therapy. The referral was to begin passive range of motion 3 times per week for 2 weeks, then initiate a supervised home program of active exercise for 2 weeks, and Thera-Band® resistance for internal and external rotation every other day for a month. Two weeks after surgery, he had his first physical therapy visit in a sports medicine clinic that was managed by an athletic trainer.

During the first visit, a PT performed an initial examination/evaluation of the patient. The patient reported that he already had been performing several exercises (pendulum, dowel, and pulley) at home. The patient also told the PT that he had been participating in sports activities even though his physician had advised him to discontinue those activities following surgery.

Because the patient had been performing range of motion exercises at home on his own for the preceding two weeks, the PT immediately initiated the "week 3' exercises, which included a program of active exercise that included bicep and tricep exercises and shoulder flexion and abduction. The variety of therapeutic exercise, including the addition of free weights, and the number of repetitions gradually were increased during the next 2 weeks of physical therapy.

On the final scheduled visit to the PT, the patient performed all his exercises as previously outlined. The PT then asked the athletic trainer (who also was the clinic manager) to complete the intervention while the PT attended a meeting in another part of the facility. The PT told the athletic trainer to stretch the patient's shoulder and then put ice on it. During the stretching, the patient told the athletic trainer that he was experiencing severe pain in his arm. The patient also heard a popping noise in his shoulder. The athletic trainer responded that he was breaking down scar tissue and stated, "No pain, no gain." The athletic trainer then put ice on the shoulder.

When the PT returned, the patient told her about his pain and said his arm had been stretched farther than it ever had been before. The PT told the patient to ice the shoulder at home several times during the remainder of the day and to return the following day. The patient returned the next day and said he still was in pain. The PT applied heat, then initiated the exercises, but the patient could not perform them to the same extent as previously, secondary to pain. The PT told the patient to schedule an appointment with his physician.

The patient saw his physician the next day. The physician performed an arthrogram that revealed a reinjury to the repaired site. A second surgery repaired the rotator cuff.

The man sued the sports medicine clinic, charging that inadequacies by the PT in the areas of direction and supervision led to reinjury of the rotator cuff.

Now, turn the page for commentary on this scenario from a risk-management perspective, including a table summarizing factors that created risk and some of the APTA standards, policies, positions, and guidelines that specifically address them.

The information presented here is not to be interpreted as specific legal advice for any particular provider. Personal advice can be given only by personal legal counsel, based on applicable state and federal law.

liability awareness

The PT did not appropriately communicate with the referring physician.

The PT herself should have communicated directly with the physician, in keeping with *Standards of Practice for Physical Therapy* ("The physical therapy practice collaborates with all disciplines as appropriate") and *Professional Practice Relationships* (HOD 06-94-35-46; "APTA endorses a collaborative, collegial practice relationship between physical therapists and all other health care providers").

The PT may have demonstrated poor professional judgment in asking support personnel to perform stretching with a patient who was only a few weeks post surgery for a rotator cuff tear. In any event, the PT asked inappropriate staff to perform the stretching.

Principle 4 of the *Code of Ethics* (HOD 06-00-12-23) states that, "A physical therapist shall exercise sound professional judgment." Regarding the use of inappropriate staff, a number of APTA policies and positions apply. *Provision of Physical Therapy Interventions and Related Tasks* (HOD 06-00-17-28) states that PTs are "the only professionals who provide physical therapy interventions," that PTAs are "the only individuals who provide selected physical therapy interventions under the direction and at least general supervision of the physical therapist," and that physical therapy aides perform "tasks"—defined as "activities that do not require the clinical decision making of the physical therapist" or "the clinical problem solving of the physical therapist assistant." The appropriate roles of the PT and PTA also are spelled out in *Consumer Protection in the Provision of Physical Therapy Services: Qualifications of Persons Providing Physical Therapy Services* (HOD 06-01-20-20). Regarding the violation of state law in this case, among the *Standards of Practice for Physical Therapy* (HOD 06-00-11-22) is the statement, "The physical therapist complies with all the legal requirements of jurisdictions regulating the practice of physical therapy."

The PT departed in the midst of a patient visit to attend a meeting.

Beyond the fact that the PT should not have assigned an intervention to a physical therapy aide in the first place, *Provision of Physical Therapy Interventions and Related Tasks* states that tasks related to patient/client management "may only be performed by the aide under the direct personal supervision of the physical therapist or, where allowable by law, the physical therapist assistant." It further states that direct personal supervision "requires that the physical therapist or, where allowable by law, the physical therapist assistant, be physically present and immediately available to direct and supervise," and that "direction and supervision is continuous." Also, in failing to comply with state law requiring continuous PT supervision of physical therapy aides, the PT did not meet *Standards of Practice for Physical Therapy's* mandate that "the director of the physical therapy service ensures compliance with local, state, and federal requirements."

The PT in this case exposed herself to risk in a number of ways.

For one thing, the PT clearly did not appropriately communicate with the referring physician before or after the incident. There could be concern that the PT deviated from the physician's treatment plan by initiating active exercise immediately and progressing quickly to the use of free weights. The PT did this based solely on the patient's report that he already had been doing 2 weeks of passive exercise, but she did not transmit this information to the physician in order to determine if the patient had been instructed to perform these exercises at home.

Also, when the patient admitted to engaging in sports activity, a prudent risk-prevention action would have been to communicate this deviation from medical advice to the physician to clarify the appropriateness of proceeding with the original treatment progression. Finally, the PT instructed the patient to contact the physician after the incident, but because injury occurred in the clinic the PT would have been wise to have contacted the physician directly to ensure expeditious and correct transmission of the information.

The PT may have demonstrated poor professional judgment in asking another level of personnel to perform stretching on a patient who was only a few weeks post surgical repair of a tear in the rotator cuff. As stated in *Direction and Supervision of the Physical Therapist Assistant* (HOD 06-00-16-27), it is the PT's responsibility to determine when "the expertise and decision making capability of the physical therapist requires the physical therapist to personally render physical therapy interventions." Among the factors the PT must consider in making that determination are "patient/client criticality, acuity, stability, and complexity" and "liability and risk management concerns." Based on those factors alone, a strong case can be made that the PT should have performed the stretching herself or should at least have provided more direction to the athletic trainer.

A related behavior that created risk was the fact that the PT asked inappropriate support staff to perform the stretching intervention. According to APTA documents, anyone who is not a PT or a PTA is considered a physical therapy aide, and aides, such as the athletic trainer in this case, can perform only "designated tasks." Although the athletic trainer in this case also was the clinic manager, any managerial role he plays does

continued on page 26 ▶▶▶

liability awareness

not extend to the provision of patient care. Also, investigation revealed that, in this scenario, state law concurred with APTA policy on this point, meaning the PT was in violation of state law in directing the athletic trainer to perform the stretching.

A final behavior that created risk was the very action that precipitated the PT's inappropriate assignment of the intervention—the PT's departure in the midst of a patient visit to attend a meeting. APTA documents state that physical therapy aides must receive direct personal supervision from the PT, which was not the case in this scenario. Furthermore, investigation revealed that the PT was in violation of her state law that mandated that physical therapy aides be under the continuous supervision of a PT. **PT**

Rita Arriaga, PT, MS, is an Associate Clinical Professor in the Graduate Program in Physical Therapy and the Director of Rehabilitation Services at the University of California, San Francisco, and is a former chair of APTA's Committee on Risk Management Services and Member Benefits. She can be reached at 415/476-3453 or arriaga@itsa.ucsf.edu.

Suggested Readings

American Physical Therapy Association. Board of Directors policies. Available at www.apta.org/ governance/governance_5/ BODpolicies. Accessed November 29, 2001.

American Physical Therapy Association. Ethics and legal issues in physical therapy. Available at www.apta.org/ PT_Practice/ethics_pt. Accessed November 29, 2001.

American Physical Therapy Association. House of Delegates policies. Available at www.apta.org/governance/ HOD/governance_10. Accessed November 29, 2001.

A Normative Model of Physical Therapist Professional Education: Version 2000. Alexandria, Va: American Physical Therapy Association; 2000.

Guide to Physical Therapist Practice. 2nd ed. *Phys Ther.* 2001;81:9-744.

Risk Management for Physical Therapists: A Quick Reference. Alexandria, Va: American Physical Therapy Association; 2001.

Do you have risk-management questions or concerns? Insights into what PTs need or want to know will help APTA's efforts to educate members about the types of incidents occurring in the workplace and about appropriate risk-management techniques. Contact Jennifer Baker, Director of APTA Insurance and Member Benefit Services, at 800/999-2782, ext 3145, or jenniferbaker@apta.org.

liabilityawareness
by Rita Arriaga, PT, MS

Stories From the Front, Part III:
Supervision, Judgment, and the Physical Therapist Assistant

A real-life scenario illustrates some basic risk-management principles.

PT's Stories From the Front series, featuring cases adapted from the claim files of the APTA-endorsed professional liability insurance plan, kicked off its fifth year in June with a risk scenario that centered on a patient with a complex medical history who had undergone rehabilitation following rotator cuff surgery.[1] That was followed in July by a case in which a patient's history of diabetes was a complicating factor in managing rehabilitation of a torn ligament.[2] In this, the third and final column in this year's series, the focus is a physical therapist assistant's (PTA) judgment and actions in a situation in which the PTA is insufficiently supervised by a physical therapist (PT). As you read the following scenario, consider these questions:

❖ What elements increased the PTA's—and the PT's—liability risk?

❖ What risk-management techniques could have been used to reduce that risk?

This case involved a 60-year-old man who underwent an uncemented total hip arthroplasty. After an unremarkable 5-day stay at an acute care hospital he was discharged with a referral for home physical therapy. Upon discharge, the attending physician wrote a discharge note instructing the patient to start home physical therapy and begin ambulation using "toe-touch weight-bearing." The discharge note was transmitted to the home health care agency but stated "weight-bearing as tolerated." The agency subcontracted physical therapy

services to a physical therapy private practice that referred the patient to a home care PT. That PT completed an initial examination and evaluation of the patient and developed a plan of care. He determined that a PTA who also was an employee of the private physical therapy practice could carry out the physical therapy interventions for the patient.

The written physical therapy plan of care did not document whether the hip prosthesis was cemented or uncemented, nor did it record specific limitations to the patient's weight-bearing status on his affected leg. There was no indication in the written record that the PT had even read the hospital discharge referral with its incorrectly translated information. Because the plan of care contained no specific information regarding the type of prosthesis used, the PTA elected to follow a care progression that she felt was consistent with that of a cemented hip. While she started the patient at toe-touch weight-bearing on the affected leg, over the next 3 weeks she progressed him to minimal and then partial weight-bearing.

By the end of the first 6 weeks of therapy, the PTA had progressed the patient to full weight-bearing without an assistive device and had him performing pivot transfers on the affected leg. In total, she saw the patient in his home 3 times a week for 3 months. Although the patient complained of continuous soreness and swelling during that period, there was no indication in the written record that the PTA dis-

cussed the patient with the supervising PT or that the PT ever treated or reassessed the patient after his initial visit. The referring physician did follow up with the patient, seeing him periodically during the physical therapy process, but gave no written indication that the patient was progressing abnormally. The physician discharged the patient from physical therapy to a home exercise program 3 months after physical therapy had been initiated.

When nearly 6 months of independent home exercise had passed with no improvement in prosthesis adherence, the physician became concerned. A year after his initial surgery, the patient had to undergo a second arthroplasty. The second prosthesis became infected, however, necessitating a third surgery. The physician was of the opinion that the initial weeks of aggressive weight-bearing progression in physical therapy was the underlying cause of the failure of the initial prosthesis. Thus, the PTA was alleged to have contributed to the patient's prolonged pain and suffering through three surgeries, regardless of those surgeries' outcome. The PTA's insurance had to contribute more than $75,000 toward settlement of the case.

What went wrong in this scenario? What strategies could the PTA have employed to prevent or limit her risk? What important reminders for PTs does this case pose?

Now, turn the page for a commentary on this scenario from a risk-management perspective and a listing of relevant APTA policies, guidelines, and resources.

Although technically subordinate to others whose actions contributed to the negative outcome in this case, the PTA was held separately accountable for her clinical decisions and activities. There were several times during the patient's plan of care when the PTA could have taken steps to manage her own risk, regardless of the PT's actions. Her first opportunity was when she was given a plan of care that did not provide specifics regarding the nature of the prosthesis (cemented or uncemented) or weight-bearing status. While it is true that the hospital provided incorrect discharge information to the home health agency when making the physical therapy referral, the supervising PT failed to make note in the physical therapy record of his initial evaluation of any information (incorrect or not) regarding prosthesis type or weight-bearing status. The PTA should have recognized that these two details are integral to carrying out a safe and appropriate intervention for a patient who has undergone a total hip arthroplasty. Before proceeding, the PTA immediately should have contacted the supervising PT to ascertain the missing information.

Second, the PTA added to her risk with the weight-bearing progression she carried out with the patient. The education of a PTA includes knowledge of common conditions that are amenable to physical therapy intervention, including post-operative rehabilitation for total joint arthroplasties. Therefore, the PTA in this case should have been familiar with the expected progression of rehabilitation activities following total hip replacement surgery. Specifically, progressing from toe-touch to partial to full weight-bearing without an assistive device and allowing pivot transfers on the operated leg would be considered inappropriate for this patient. It is not a progression that should be carried out without the direction of the supervising PT. In the absence of clear-cut initial weight-bearing status, the PTA made a risky decision about weight-bearing progression that was beyond her scope of work and then carried out this progression independently, without consultation with the supervising PT and despite the patient's complaints of continuous soreness and swelling. Sound risk management dictated that the PTA should have consulted with the supervising PT before she progressed the patient as rapidly as she did.

Third, the PTA carried out a prolonged rehabilitation program without any reassessment by or documentation of periodic consultation with the supervising PT regarding the patient's treatment plan. Even though the PT failed to communicate on a regular basis with the PTA and thus was not up to speed on the patient's status and progress, the PTA should have been cognizant of her own responsibility to ensure that appropriate and adequate supervision by the

liability awareness

Relevant APTA Policies, Guidelines, and Resources

❖ **APTA Standards of Ethical Conduct for the Physical Therapist Assistant (HOD 06-00-13-24) and Guide for Conduct of the Physical Therapist Assistant** Standard 3 of the *Standards of Ethical Conduct* states: "A physical therapist assistant shall provide selected physical therapy interventions only under the supervision and direction of a physical therapist." The *Guide for Conduct*, a resource for interpreting the *Standards of Ethical Conduct*, further states that a PTA "shall provide only those physical therapy interventions that have been selected by the physical therapist" (Standard 3.1B); "shall not perform examinations or evaluations, interpret data, determine diagnosis or prognosis, or establish or alter a plan of care" (Standard 3.1E); and "shall have regular and ongoing communication with the physical therapist regarding the patient's/client's status" (Standard 3.1G). Also relevant to this case is Standard 4 of the *Standards of Ethical Conduct*, which states, "A physical therapist assistant shall comply with laws and regulations governing physical therapy," and Standard 4.1 ("Supervision") in the Guide for Conduct, which states, "A physical therapist assistant shall know and comply with applicable law. Regardless of the content of any law, a physical therapist assistant shall provide services only under the supervision and direction of a physical therapist." Additional guidance is provided by standards 5 and 6 of the *Standards of Ethical Conduct*, which state, respectively, that a PTA "shall achieve and maintain competence in the provision of selected physical therapy interventions" and "shall make judgments that are commensurate with his/her educational and legal qualifications as a physical therapist assistant." The *Guide for Conduct*'s Standard 5.1 ("Competence") further states that the PTA "shall provide interventions consistent with his/her level of education, training, experience, and skill." The *Guide for Conduct*'s Standard 6.2 ("Patient Status Judgments") states that a PTA "participates in patient status judgments by reporting changes to the physical therapist and requesting patient reexamination or revision of the plan of care."

❖ **APTA Code of Ethics (HOD 06-00-12-23) and APTA Guide for Professional Conduct** These two documents respectively set forth principles for the ethical practice of physical therapy and interpret those principles. Particularly relevant to this case and the actions of the supervising PT is Principle 4 of the *Code of Ethics*, which states, "A physical therapist shall exercise sound professional judgment," and principles 4.1E, 4.2A, and 4.2B of the *Guide for Professional Conduct*, which state, respectively, that "a physical therapist shall establish the plan of care and shall provide and/or supervise and direct the appropriate interventions"; "the supervising physical therapist has primary responsibility for the physical therapy care rendered to a patient/client"; and "a physical therapist shall not delegate to a less qualified person any activity that requires the unique skill, knowledge, and judgment of the physical therapist."

❖ **Risk Management for Physical Therapists: A Quick Reference** This resource includes step-by-step tips on how to mitigate a potential claim. A description and ordering information are available on APTA's Web site (www.apta.org). Click on "Online Shopping."

❖ **APTA core documents, policies, and positions** are available on APTA's Web site. Click on "About APTA" for the links.

professional provider was maintained throughout the course of treatment. In the absence of a scheduled reassessment by the PT, the PTA should have initiated contact with him and arranged for a reevaluation of the patient by the PT. At a minimum, the PTA should have reported regularly to the PT on the patient's progress and should have documented those interactions in the patient's record. Good risk management by supportive personnel includes being proactive in ensuring compliance with legal, ethical, and professional supervisory expectations.

One final note: Although this case summary emphasizes risks taken by the PTA, obviously the PT should have followed up with the PTA he was supervising regarding the patient's status. The PT ultimately is responsible for the patient's care and should perform all examination and evaluation procedures. **PT**

Rita Arriaga, PT, MS, is an Associate Clinical Professor in the Graduate Program in Physical Therapy and the Director of Rehabilitation Services at the University of California, San Francisco, and is a former chair of APTA's Committee on Risk Management and Member Benefits. She can be reached at 415/476-3453 or arriaga@itsa.ucsf.edu.

References

1. Arriaga A. Stories from the front: documentation and complex medical history. *PT—Magazine of Physical Therapy*. 2003;11(6):25-26,28.
2. Arriaga A. Stories from the front, part II: complex medical history and communication. *PT—Magazine* of Physical Therapy. 2003; 11(7):23-25.

Do you have risk-management questions or concerns? Insights into what PTs need or want to know will help APTA educate members about the types of incidents occurring in the workplace and about appropriate risk-management techniques. Contact Jennifer Baker, Director of APTA Risk Management and Member Benefit Services, at 800/999-2782, ext 3145, or jenniferbaker@apta.org.

LIABILITY AWARENESS

by Rita Arriaga, MS, PT

Stories From the Front—Part One: Delegation

A real-life scenario illustrates some basic risk management principles.

I'n this month's Liability Awareness column, *PT* presents the first of three scenarios adapted from actual cases from the APTA-endorsed professional liability insurance claims history. The following scenario illustrates a common concern in today's clinic: appropriate delegation and supervision. Currently, the number of claims against physical therapists insured through APTA's program related to this issue is rising.

As you read the scenario, consider the following questions:

1) What are the elements in this scenario that increase the PT's risk of professional liability?

2) What risk management techniques could have been used to reduce that risk?

❖   ❖   ❖

A 60-year-old woman underwent an open reduction internal fixation (ORIF) with plate and screws for a tibial fracture she had sustained in a fall. She had a medical history of other fractures and of osteoporosis. Following her surgery, she was referred to an outpatient physical therapy clinic for rehabilitation.

The PT performed the evaluation and developed a plan of care that included both range-of-motion (ROM) and strengthening exercises for the patient's lower extremity and general conditioning exercises. The treatment program was carried out in the gym area of the facility.

After the initial treatment, the PT provided no further direct care to the patient. A certified athletic trainer (ATC) who worked in the clinic carried out the exercise program and documented the patient's

> ## During the second week of treatment after removal of the hardware, a loud "pop" was heard as the ATC performed PROM exercises for the patient's knee.

progress in the clinic record. The PT did review the records after each treatment, cosigned each treatment note, and discussed the patient's case with the entire staff during weekly clinic rounds.

Six weeks after initiating treatment, the patient's hardware was surgically removed, and the patient was then sent back to the physical therapy clinic to resume rehabilitation. There was no re-evaluation by the PT; the patient's rehabilitation continued as it had been before her surgery, with the ATC as the primary provider of care, performing passive and active ROM and strengthening exercises with the patient twice a week.

During the second week of treatment after removal of the hardware, a loud "pop" was heard as the ATC performed passive ROM exercises for the patient's knee, but there were no immediate complaints of increased pain or changes in ambulatory capacity. However, the patient awoke the next day with swelling and pain on weight bearing. Subsequent tests by the patient's surgeon revealed a new tibial fracture.

The patient believed her new fracture was the direct result of poor treatment follow-up by the PT. She stated that she had been misled by the clinic, and that she had assumed that the ATC was a PT because she was only treated by the ATC and never spoke with the evaluating PT after her first visit. The patient brought a claim against

the PT for negligence, and the PT's professional liability insurance policy responded, settling the claim out of court because the opinion of the expert witness favored the plaintiff.

❖   ❖   ❖

Now, turn the page for commentary on this scenario from a risk management perspective, including a table summarizing risk elements and strategies to address them.

LIABILITY AWARENESS

Risky Elements

The patient had a perception that the ATC was a "PT" and claimed that she did not see the evaluating PT after the first visit.

The PT depended on the judgment of support personnel regarding progress and appropriateness of care plan.

The PT did not directly supervise the care provided by the ATC. (A cosignature on treatment notes or discussion of a case during rounds is not direct supervision of patient care.)

There was a significant change in the patient's status (operative hardware removal) without a re-evaluation by the PT.

Postoperative passive ROM was delegated to the ATC.

An incident that occurred during treatment (the "pop" during passive ROM) was not immediately reported to the PT.

There was no referral to the patient's physician or surgeon in light of that incident.

Strategies for Risk Reduction

The evaluating PT should obtain the patient's informed consent at the first visit, involving the patient in treatment goal setting and care planning and introducing and clearly identifying the titles and roles of all staff who will work with the patient. The evaluating PT should make specific contact with the patient at each visit.

There should be regular, periodic re-evaluation by the PT to assess the patient's progress and the continued appropriateness of the treatment plan, with careful documentation of that re-evaluation.

The PT should provide some element of direct care at each treatment session, either by re-evaluating or providing treatment. The PT should carefully document the patient's status and any changes in the care plan, including the continued involvement and role of support personnel and other caregivers. PTs must be sure that they are providing appropriate supervision of support personnel in accordance with their state practice acts.

The PT should perform a re-evaluation at a patient's first visit after surgery, carefully documenting status changes and any modifications in the care plan.

A PT, rather than support personnel, should be the one to provide the more "risky" procedures requiring specific expertise and professional judgment.

Any adverse incident should be reported immediately to the PT, and the PT should examine the patient before the patient leaves the clinic, carefully documenting any findings.

When an incident occurs, unintended, undesirable events could be mitigated by referring the patient back to his or her physician, or by the PT calling the physician for an immediate consultation. (This was especially true in this case in light of the patient's past medical history and recent hardware removal.)

Although no one is immune from a lawsuit, there are ways to reduce the risk that a patient will sue a PT for negligence. It can happen to you, no matter how competent you are. Supervision and delegation are an integral responsibility of the practicing PT. As such, it is important for the PT to monitor the activities of support personnel in accordance with his or her state practice act and to maintain regular contact with the patient that includes two-way communication. In addition, the PT may want to be sure that the facility in which he or she practices has policies and procedures in place to ensure that all caregivers are maintaining appropriate standards of patient care. This will reduce the likelihood that a patient will file a negligence claim against all providers in the treatment plan. *PT*

Rita Arriaga, MS, PT, is Assistant Clinical Professor in the Graduate Program in Physical Therapy, University of California at San Francisco, and is a member of APTA's Committee on Risk Management Services and Member Benefits.

The information presented here is not to be interpreted as specific legal advice for any particular provider. Personal advice can only be given by personal legal counsel, based on applicable state and federal law.

Liability Awareness

by Rita Arriaga, MS, PT

Stories From the Front—Part Two

A real-life scenario demonstrates some important risk-management principles.

In this month's Liability Awareness column, *PT* presents the second of three scenarios adapted from actual cases from the claims history files of APTA's endorsed professional liability insurance carrier. The following sequence of events portrays a situation that can be worrisome for today's PTs: proper utilization of assistive and supportive health care personnel by PTs who contract with skilled nursing facilities (SNFs).

As you read the scenario, consider the following questions:

1) What are the elements in this scenario that increase the PT's risk of professional liability?

2) What risk management techniques could have been used to reduce that risk?

❖   ❖   ❖

A PT contracted with a local SNF to provide physical therapy services as needed. She did not work with a physical therapy aide or physical therapist assistant. The PT had worked daily with a 70-year-old patient during the 6 days since his transfer to the SNF. He had been transferred to the SNF after a 4-day acute care hospital stay following surgery for an elective total hip replacement due to severe osteoarthritis. The patient's ambulatory ability had improved enough that, on the previous day, the PT had cleared him to begin walker ambulation with the nursing staff. On the 6th day after the patient's transfer, the PT asked the nursing assistant assigned to the patient to bring him to the physical therapy treatment room. The nursing assistant pushed the patient in a

wheelchair to the hallway just outside of the treatment room doorway, then locked the chair, got a walker, and began walking the patient into the room.

The PT saw the patient and the nursing assistant coming into the room and began watching so that she could observe the patient's gait pattern. At the same time, the PT overheard the nursing assistant tell the patient to turn the foot and toes of his leg a bit more inward so he wouldn't "walk like a duck."

As the patient took a step on the leg that had been operated on, the PT hastened forward to correct foot placement. Suddenly, the patient reported sharp hip pain and his leg started to collapse. The nursing assistant caught the patient before he could fall to the floor. The PT joined the nursing assistant and together they were able to seat the patient back in the wheelchair. A few moments after being seated, the patient regained his composure and reported no significant discomfort.

The PT decided to cancel the patient's physical therapy treatment in order to allow him to rest. She asked the nursing assistant to return the patient to his room and advised her to inform the nursing supervisor about the near fall.

The following day, the PT again asked the nursing assistant to help the patient walk to physical therapy. However, the patient again reported hip pain with the attempt to ambulate. At that time, the nursing supervisor made the decision to call the patient's physician, who subsequently determined that the patient's hip had partially dislocated. The patient eventually was discharged home, but only after a significantly lengthened SNF stay.

Ultimately, the patient believed that the incident causing his dislocation occurred because the PT had failed to ensure that the nursing assistant had been properly trained prior to asking her to assist him with ambulation. He filed a claim with the PT's professional liability insurance, alleging negligence.

❖   ❖   ❖

What strategies could have prevented or mitigated this situation? Turn the page for commentary on this scenario from a risk management perspective, including a table summarizing risk elements and strategies to address them.

Risky Elements

The PT assigned ambulation duties to a member of the nursing staff without adequate assurance of that nursing assistant's knowledge of precautions, standards of care, and protocols for common diagnoses and surgeries.

The PT did not report the adverse occurrence directly to the nursing supervisor and did not write up an incident report.

The PT did not document in the physical therapy record the incident or the decision to cancel treatment following it.

The following day, the PT did not perform a reassessment of the patient before asking the nursing assistant to ambulate the patient to physical therapy.

Strategies for Risk Reduction

The PT should participate in nursing in-service training and orientation of new staff to standards of care and critical care pathways that involve the PT as part of the patient care team. This participation should be documented by the PT. In addition, the PT should ensure that the facility's critical paths and care plans delineate the expected participation and care standards of each member of the health care team, including nursing staff. The PT should carefully document care plans and clearly delineate which patient activity levels are appropriate for each member of the team to provide. The PT should indicate clearly that the patient is safe for nursing-assisted ambulation.

The PT should take the time to seek out and speak with the nursing supervisor. In this way, the PT also can ensure that there is follow-up with the patient's physician. The PT should be sure that a complete incident report has been written up by both the physical therapy department and the SNF.

The occurrence should be documented in the physical therapy treatment record (as distinct from the incident report). Documentation should include the reason for cancellation of physical therapy treatment, the verbal report to the nursing supervisor, and the plan to contact the physician.

Following any unforeseen occurrence or change in status, the PT should perform and document a physical therapy reassessment of the patient's status. The reassessment was particularly critical in this case because the patient's referring physician had not performed a physical exam following the incident.

In order to reduce the risk that a patient might file suit alleging negligence against a PT, the PT's verbal and written communications with other members of the health care team must clearly designate the responsibilities that are expected of each caregiver. If an incident that later may be questioned does occur, a PT must take the initiative to verbally report the incident to the appropriate supervisor(s) and members of the health care team. Additionally, the PT must prepare a complete written incident report and also document the incident in the physical therapy treatment record. However, as Scott[1] pointed out in a Liability Awareness column on incident reporting, PTs should not refer to the incident report in the treatment entry, as the incident report is considered a business document unrelated to patient treatment.

Clear communication and careful documentation can help avert both the unpleasantness and further personal and legal complications that may result from the filing of a negligence claim against a PT. PT

Rita Arriaga, MS, PT, is Assistant Clinical Professor in the Graduate Program in Physical Therapy, University of California at San Francisco, and is a member of APTA's Committee on Risk Management Services and Member Benefits.

1. Scott RW. Incident reports: protecting the record. (Liability Awareness.) *PT—Magazine of Physical Therapy.* 1996;4(9):24-25.

The information presented here is not to be interpreted as specific legal advice for any particular provider. Personal advice can only be given by personal legal counsel, based on applicable state and federal law.

Pro Bono Services

Guidelines: Pro Bono Physical Therapy Services
HOD G06-93-21-39

In an effort to meet the physical therapy needs of society, the American Physical Therapy Association (APTA) encourages its members to render pro bono physical therapy services. A physical therapist may discharge this responsibility by:

- Providing professional service at no fee or at a reduced fee, to persons of limited financial means.

- Donating professional expertise and service to charitable groups or organizations.

- Engaging in activities to improve access to physical therapy.

- Offering financial support for organizations that deliver physical therapy services to persons of limited financial means.

I N   P R A C T I C E

By Ronald W Scott, JD, LLM, PT

"For the Public Good"

*The physical therapy profession could take the lead among health care
professions in adopting guidelines for pro bono service.*

When professional service is provided *pro bono publico* (L., "for the public good"), it is provided either at a reduced fee or free of charge, depending on the recipient's need. For the professionals who participate in pro bono activity, the benefits are both intangible and tangible. A profession's public image is enhanced when its members have a strong commitment to public service. Both personal and collective satisfaction results when professionals respond to a compelling human need for their profession's services. In addition, business goodwill enhances profit, a network is created among colleagues performing similar services, and professional associations and governmental entities provide technical and administrative assistance that ensures the overall success of pro bono efforts.[1]

Regardless of these benefits, the *ethical and legal responsibility* to treat patients who do not have the means to pay a standard fee is an area of concern and confusion to physical therapy clinicians and managers alike. The professional health care literature offers few guidelines on pro bono obligations.

In Search of a Model for Pro Bono Service

Of all the professions, the legal profession may have the most extensively documented history of pro bono expectations and requirements. In fact, pro bono activity in the United States traditionally has focused on the legal profession. Many of the pro bono concepts used by the legal profession may be directly transferred to physical therapy and other health care professions.

The legal profession has a centuries-old commitment—albeit an informal one not necessarily practiced by the majority of attor-

"A client's ability to pay ... may require a less charge, or even none at all.... In fixing fees, it should be remembered that the profession is... not a mere money-getting trade."

—*Canons of Professional Ethics, American Bar Association, 1908; Canon 12.*

neys—to provide legal services to people who cannot afford them. In the 20th century, this altruistic goal has been formalized into a canon of ethics in the American Bar Association's (ABA) *Canons of Professional Ethics,* 1908[2]; *Model Code for Professional Responsibility,* 1969[3]; and *Model Rules of Professional Conduct,* 1983.[4] Although the original *Canons of Professional Ethics* indicated that pro bono service was mandatory, the more recent model codes, which have been codified by state bar associations as definitive codes of conduct, label attorneys' pro bono service an "ethical obligation" rather than a "legal obligation."

In Rule 6.1 of the *Model Rules of Professional Conduct,* the ABA established the following professional standard for attorneys:

A lawyer should render public interest legal service. A lawyer may discharge this responsibility by providing professional services at no fee or a reduced fee to persons of limited means or to public service or charitable groups or organizations, by service in activities for improving the law, the legal system or the legal profession, and by financial support for organizations that provide legal services to persons of limited means.[3]

The nonbinding Comment to the rule expounded on the foundational ethical principle by stating:

Every lawyer, regardless of professional prominence or professional work load, should find time to participate in or otherwise support the provision of legal services to the disadvantaged. The provision of free legal services to those unable to pay reasonable fees continues to be an obligation of each lawyer as well as the profession generally.[3]

A Rocky History of Commitment

At the National Conference on Access to Justice in the 1990s, held in June 1989 in New Orleans, Louisiana, Lardent[5] sketched the rocky history of attorney commitment to pro bono activity, emphasizing that current pro bono involvement was meeting only 20% of the legal needs of the underprivileged. She cast much of the blame on professional attorney associations, which she believed had failed 1) to take the lead in institutionalizing pro bono service as an expectation of legal professionals, 2) to integrate pro bono programs and establish normative standards and assessment criteria, and

3) to offer technical assistance to volunteers. She also pointed out that several state bar associations were considering mandating pro bono service by the attorneys licensed in those states.

Some state courts (and the federal court system) have experimented with requiring attorneys licensed in a jurisdiction to provide minimally intrusive pro bono service in that jurisdiction. One justification for this requirement is the argument that because attorneys have a virtual monopoly in practicing their profession, they owe a public duty to represent, at a reduced rate or free of charge, people who are poor. Another justification is based on the belief that representation of all clients before the courts is an ethical, professional, and social responsibility.[6]

> **"The rendition of free legal services to those unable to pay reasonable fees [is] an obligation of every lawyer, but the efforts of individual lawyers are often not enough to meet the need. Thus it has been necessary for the profession to institute additional programs to provide legal services.... Every lawyer should support all proper efforts to meet this need for legal services."**
>
> —*Model Code of Professional Responsibility, American Bar Association, 1969; Ethical Considerations 2-25.*

In 1992, the Florida Bar Association enacted a regulation that comes very close to mandating universal pro bono work. The regulation established the expectation that Florida-licensed attorneys will perform at least 20 hours of voluntary pro bono service annually or make a cash contribution of $350 to help fund legal services for indigents, and requires each attorney to report his or her pro bono service to the state each year. This regulation has been endorsed by the Florida Supreme Court, the state's highest court.[7]

The Health Care Professions and Pro Bono Service

With 37 million Americans uninsured or underinsured for health care and a quarter of the population over age 65 living below the poverty line,[8] there is a tremendous need for pro bono health care in this country. Some of that need is being met by individuals and groups; however, major health care professional associations and state or federal administrative agencies have offered few pro bono guidelines. The American Medical Association has no formal policy on pro bono expectations, and a MEDLINE search of the professional literature showed only one resource on pro bono health care—a letter to the editor published in *American Family Physician*, urging tax breaks for physicians who provide free medical care for people who are needy.[9]

Legislators and policy makers have created various incentives to encourage health care professionals to engage in pro bono activity. Several states, including Arizona and South Carolina, provide a type of "good Samaritan" immunity from malpractice liability for health care professionals performing pro bono service. This immunity protects the health care provider from liability as long as the provider's conduct (even if it is adjudged legally negligent) does not constitute gross negligence or reckless conduct. The American Tort Reform Association is lobbying for similar protection nationwide as an incentive to encourage pro bono participation among health care professionals.[10]

Some legislators, perhaps most notably Representative Ron Wyden (D-OR), support statutes relieving malpractice insurance premiums for the nation's 2,000 federally funded health care clinics now treating indigents. Under these statutes, the clinicians in these facilities would be treated as federal employees and therefore would be personally immune from malpractice liability. Under the Federal Tort Claims Act, the federal government would be vicariously liable for mal-

Pro Bono Services: A Professional Responsibility

APTA's Massachusetts Chapter proposed a motion to the 1992 House of Delegates that called for adoption of an Association position on pro bono physical therapy services. Due to time constraints, the motion did not make it the floor for consideration. Because of the large numbers of physical therapy practitioners who donate their time and services to patients and not-for-profit organizations, this motion will come forward at the 1993 House of Delegates.

The motion, as proposed, stated that:

A physical therapist engaged in the practice of physical therapy should render pro bono physical therapy service. A physical therapist may discharge this responsibility by: providing professional service at no fee or at a reduced fee, to persons of limited financial means; or donating professional expertise and service to charitable groups or organizations; or engaging in activities to improve access to physical therapy; or offering financial support for organizations that deliver physical therapy services to persons of limited financial means.

According to APTA President Marilyn Moffat, PT, PhD, FAPTA, who throughout her career has been dedicated to community service, "The object of APTA is to meet the physical therapy needs of society. We have a professional obligation to meet these needs for all segments of society, and that includes the millions of Americans who are in need of health care but who have limited means to pay for it."

"The legal profession cannot remain a viable force in fulfilling its role in society unless its members receive adequate compensation for services rendered.... Nevertheless, persons unable to pay all or a portion of a reasonable fee should be able to obtain necessary legal services, and lawyers should support and participate in ethical activities designed to achieve that objective."

—*Model Code of Professional Responsibility,*
American Bar Association, 1969; Ethical Considerations 2-16.

practice settlements and judgements against these clinicians.[11]

Fear of Malpractice Claims

Fear may prevent many health care professionals from providing pro bono service—fear that patients with low incomes are more likely to have adverse treatment outcomes because of poor baseline health, fear that patients with low incomes are more likely to sue than are other populations. Federal government studies have reached differing conclusions on whether the level of litigiousness is related to income status; however, a 1991 Maryland study concluded that obstetric patients who were Medicaid-eligible were no more likely than women in the general population to file claims for negligence against health care providers.[12]

Measures must be taken to dampen fears of malpractice claims. One measure might be to create an exception to the reporting requirements of the National Practitioner Data Bank. Designed to serve as a resource for verifying the accuracy of information provided by applicants to health care positions, the Data Bank currently requires "hospitals, health care institutions, Boards of Medical Examiners, professional societies of medical doctors, dentists, 'other health care practitioners...,' and malpractice payment entities" to report malpractice actions.[13] An exception to these requirements would exclude those cases in which services were rendered

pro bono—unless the conduct of the provider constitutes gross negligence or reckless conduct.

Even without the protections described above, however, health care professionals treating patients who are indigent can take affirmative steps to limit their exposure to the risk of malpractice claims, such as maintaining effective communication and rapport with the patient and thoroughly documenting services rendered.[14]

A Larger Social Responsibility

All professional associations should closely study the model established by the legal profession for pro bono service and consider developing similar policies regarding their members' participation in minimally intrusive pro bono service. State agencies licensing primary health care providers—including physicians, physical therapists, dentists, chiropractors, and other health care professionals—should consider administrative regulations that codify licensed professionals' pro bono obligations as part of a larger social responsibility. In addition to establishing pro bono policies, professional associations and state licensing bodies also must take responsibility for integrating pro bono efforts across all disciplines, providing continuing education, networking, and administrative and other support for volunteers who give selflessly of their time. Professional corporations, practice groups, and individual providers also may

consider incorporating pro bono policies into their practices or publicizing already-existing programs to encourage and give guidance to others.*

Pro bono service should be an expectation (but never a requirement) of all professionals to whom the state has granted an exclusive license to practice a profession for profit. The tangible and intangible benefits—to individual professionals, associations, administrative licensing agencies, and society as a whole—are limitless. 𝒫𝒯

Ronald W Scott, JD, LLM, PT, is a major in the Army Medical Specialist Corps and is a physical therapist and legal advisor at Brooke Army Medical Center, San Antonio, Tex.

References

1. Lardent EF. Recruitment and retention of volunteer attorneys. In: The Resource: A Pro Bono Manual. Chicago, Ill: American Bar Association, 1983: 7-10.
2. Canons of Professional Ethics. Chicago, Ill: American Bar Association; 1908.
3. Model Code of Professional Responsibility. Chicago, Ill: American Bar Association, 1969.
4. Model Rules for Professional Conduct. Chicago, Ill: American Bar Association, 1983.
5. Lardent EF. Pro Bono in the 1990s: The uncertain future of attorney volunteerism. In: The Proceedings of the National Conference on Access to Justice in the 1990s—New Orleans, June 9-11, 1989: 425-439.
6. Krieger M. Lecture notes, "Professional Responsibility." University of San Diego School of Law, San Diego, CA; 1983.
7. Florida goes halfway in pro bono program. *The National Law Journal.* 1992;14(27):6.
8. US Census Bureau, Statistical Abstract, 110th ed. Washington, DC: Government Printing Office; 1990.
9. Berger M. Tax breaks for physicians providing free medical care. *Am Fam Physician.* 1992;45:2485.
10. Good Samaritan laws sought for health workers. *PT Bulletin.* 1990;5(23):3,38.
11. Relief Sought for Clinics' Malpractice Costs. *PT Bulletin.* 1991;6(30):5.
12. Mussman MG, Zawistowich L, Weisman CS, et al. Medical malpractice claims filed by Medicaid and non-Medicaid recipients in Maryland. *JAMA.* 1991;265:2992-2994.
13. Fraiche D. Peer review and the data bank. *Clinical Management.* 1992; 12(3):14-17.
14. Scott RW. *Health Care Malpractice: A Primer on Legal Issues.* Thorofare, NJ: SLACK, Inc; 1990.

The ABA/ACCI Corporate Counsel Pro Bono Guide (American Bar Association, Chicago, Ill, 1990: 4, 21-26) provides a general outline on how to set up a corporate pro bono program and specifically highlights programs established by Xerox Corporation, ALCOA®, and AETNA. An integral part of a corporate or group practice pro bono program at any level is the indemnification of the participants by the corporation through payment of the volunteers' malpractice insurance premium and the contractual promise to cover any deductible incurred.

Liability Protection: What PTs Should Know

Before physical therapists can begin volunteering at the Fourth Street Clinic (see page 48), they must fill out an application, complete with two professional references and copies of their license and certification. "We send the applications to the Utah Health Department, pay $1, and enroll each volunteer in the state's insurance program," says Allan Ainsworth, PhD, Fourth Street Clinic Director. "This is done regardless of the liability insurance a volunteer may individually carry because it outguesses any problems that might arise and better protects the volunteers as well as the clients."

Protecting volunteers is a priority at the Fourth Street Clinic, but not every physical therapist donating services is lucky enough to receive this type of protection. With the growing numbers of uninsured and low-income people in this country, there is a great need for pro bono work. However, major health care professional associations and state and federal administrative agencies have offered few pro bono guidelines Where does this leave the physical therapist who is interested in volunteering, but is concerned about malpractice claims?

According to Ronald W Scott, JD, PT, OCS, Associate Professor, Department of Physical Therapy, School of Allied Health Sciences, University of Texas Health Sciences Center, San Antonio, Tex, physical therapists who donate their services should refer to an attorney with specific concerns, but he says it is important to remember that when volunteering services, a physical therapists's code of ethics, mode of practice, compliance with state practice acts, and standards of care are the same as with paid services.

"Physical therapists should check their professional liability insurance before volunteering professional services, whether it is at a homeless shelter, a fitness clinic, a posture screening, or a telephone hotline," says Barbara A Melzer, PhD, PT, Chair of APTA's Committee on Risk Management Services and Member Benefits. "If your employer holds your liability insurance, you may only be covered for services performed within the workplace. If you hold your own insurance policy, you may be protected for all services you perform, whether it is inside or outside your place of employment, as long as those services fall within the definition of physical therapy services covered by the policy."

Melzer also suggests checking your state laws because some states provide limited (does not apply to gross negligence) protection from civil liability specifically for physical therapists performing services without compensation. In addition, physical therapists only needing insurance coverage for pro bono services can purchase part-time liability protection.

Disability Legislation

Americans With Disabilities: Role of the American Physical Therapy Association in Advocacy, Promotion, And Accommodation
HOD P06-04-12-12 (Initial HOD 06-76-17-44)

People with disabilities share the same rights as all other individuals to have access to and opportunities for full economic, social, and personal development. The American Physical Therapy Association (APTA) shall advocate for full inclusion of people with disabilities in all aspects of community life and within the profession of physical therapy. As the Association that represents physical therapists who are the experts in the analysis of human movement, performance, and function, APTA should seek ways to promote education regarding the Americans with Disabilities Act (ADA) Accessibility Guidelines as well as implementation of the ADA.

APTA shall comply with the requirements of the ADA for all APTA-sponsored events, including conferences, continuing education, and meetings, providing for accessibility or reasonable accommodations for people with disabilities.

Non-Discrimination
HOD Y06-98-14-06 (Initial HOD 06-84-18-76)

The American Physical Therapy Association (APTA) prohibits preferential or adverse discrimination on the basis of race, creed, color, sex, gender, age, national or ethnic origin, sexual orientation, disability or health status in all areas including, but not limited to, its qualifications for membership, rights of members, policies, programs, activities, and employment practices.

The APTA Board of Directors shall include this reference in any published statement on non-discrimination.

This policy is not intended to prohibit the need for affirmative action in areas related to race, color, sex, gender, national or ethnic origin, and disability or health status, as outlined in the policy, Affirmative Action (HOD P06-98-14-05).

Affirmative Action
HOD P06-98-14-05 (Initial HOD 06-81-12-42)

The American Physical Therapy Association (APTA) is committed to serving the needs of all people who require physical therapy and to meeting the needs of all its members. As noted in its policy, Non-Discrimination (HOD Y06-98-14-06), APTA "prohibits preferential or adverse discrimination on the basis of race, creed, color, sex, gender, age, national or ethnic origin, sexual orientation, disability or health status in all areas."

The Association's stand against "preferential or adverse discrimination" does not negate the need for APTA to act affirmatively for certain classes of people, identified by race, color, sex, gender, national or ethic origin, or disability or health status. APTA supports the planning and implementation of comprehensive Affirmative Action programs.

Research Report

Responses Within Nonfederal Hospitals in Pennsylvania to the Americans With Disabilities Act of 1990

Background and Purpose. This study described responses within nonfederal hospitals in Pennsylvania to the Americans With Disabilities Act of 1990 (ADA). Subjects. The target population consisted of all 277 nonfederal hospitals licensed by the Pennsylvania Department of Health and Department of Public Welfare. Methods. Questionnaires were mailed to the 270 chief administrators for the 277 hospitals. Results. One hundred seventeen questionnaires (43.3%) were returned. More facilities had trained their managers regarding the ADA versus their nonmanagerial employees. Overall, 80.3% of the hospitals had an ADA committee or coordinator. Fifty-four percent of the respondents reported that job accommodations cost less than $500. Approximately 45% of the participants cited that the percentage of new construction costs spent to increase accessibility in their hospitals was less than 4.9%. More complaints and legal matters were received by facilities regarding the employment provisions of the ADA rather than the accessibility provisions. Conclusion and Discussion. The results suggest that hospitals need to monitor ADA-related expenses, more employee training is needed to ensure the ADA's success, and more representation is needed on hospital committees by rehabilitation personnel and individuals with disabilities. [Jones DL, Watzlaf VJM, Hobson D, Mazzoni J. Responses within nonfederal hospitals in Pennsylvania to the Americans With Disabilities Act of 1990. *Phys Ther.* 1996: 76:49–60.]

Key Words: *Disability, Hospital, Legislation, Rehabilitation.*

Dina L Jones

Valerie JM Watzlaf

Douglas Hobson

Jane Mazzoni

The Americans With Disabilities Act of 1990 (ADA) was enacted on July 26, 1990 (Public Law 101–336).[1] This comprehensive law prohibits discrimination against individuals with disabilities in the areas of employment, public services, public accommodations, and telecommunications. With an estimated 43 million individuals with disabilities in America,[2] the ADA is regarded by many observers as the most important civil rights legislation in the last quarter of a century.[3]

Physical therapists have a responsibility to keep abreast of current issues and legislation in the health care environment. With the ADA, physical therapists can perform an important role in the act's implementation and success.

A "disability" under the ADA is defined as one of the following[1]:

1. A "physical or mental impairment that substantially limits one or more of the major life activities of such individuals." Speaking, breathing, walking, seeing, and learning are examples of vital activities necessary for daily living.

2. A "record of such an impairment." This record protects those individuals who have recovered from a physical or mental impairment.

3. "Being regarded as having such an impairment." This definition applies to those who are mistakenly perceived to have a disability, or those who have a physical or mental impairment that does not appear to limit major life activities.

Disorders such as speech and hearing impairments, cerebral palsy, blindness, multiple sclerosis, and mental retardation are considered disabilities under the ADA. Short-term impairments or conditions such as pregnancy, sprained ligaments, or fractures are not regarded as disabilities.

Title I of the ADA applies to employers with 15 or more employees, including health care facilities. The law mandates that individuals with disabilities may not be discriminated against in employment practices such as hiring, training, distribution of benefits, or promotions. An employer must accommodate a worker's disability unless it can be proven to pose a hardship (ie, requiring substantial difficulty or expense). Examples of "reasonable accommodation" include modified work schedules, raised or lowered furniture, and adaptive equipment.

Employers are prohibited from making inquiries to determine whether an applicant has a disability. An employer may, however, inquire about an applicant's ability to perform "essential" job tasks. A medical examination may be required, but only after an offer of employment has been made to an applicant and only if all new employees are subject to the same examination. Job descriptions that outline the essential and nonessential functions of a job should assist in determining whether reasonable accommodations are necessary.

The ADA does not mandate that an applicant with a disability who can perform the essential functions of the job (with or without accommodation) should be hired over an applicant without a disability. The person who is best qualified for the job should be hired.

DL Jones, PT, is Coordinator of Education, Physical Therapy Department, University of Pittsburgh Medical Center, Montefiore University Hospital, 200 Lothrop St, Pittsburgh, PA 15213 (USA) (DLJST4@vms.cis.Pitt.edu); Clinical Assistant Professor, Department of Physical Therapy, University of Pittsburgh, 101 Pennsylvania Hall, Pittsburgh, PA 15261; and a doctoral student, Graduate School of Public Health, University of Pittsburgh. She was a master's degree candidate, School of Health and Rehabilitation Sciences, University of Pittsburgh, at the time the study was conducted. Address all correspondence to Ms Jones at the first address.

VJM Watzlaf, PhD, RRA, is Assistant Professor, Health Information Management Department, School of Health and Rehabilitation Sciences, University of Pittsburgh.

D Hobson, PhD, is Associate Professor and Director of Rehabilitation Technology Program, School of Health and Rehabilitation Sciences, University of Pittsburgh.

J Mazzoni, RRA, is Assistant Professor, Health Information Management Department, School of Health and Rehabilitation Sciences, University of Pittsburgh.

This study was presented at the Annual Conference of the Pennsylvania Physical Therapy Association; November 4–6, 1994; Philadelphia, PA.

This study was approved by the University of Pittsburgh Institutional Review Board for Psychosocial Research (IRB #93291).

This study was supported in part through funding received from the SHRS Research Development Fund, School of Health and Rehabilitation Sciences, University of Pittsburgh.

This article was submitted May 31, 1995, and was accepted August 15, 1995.

Title II of the ADA applies to public services. State and local governments may not discriminate against individuals with disabilities, and must provide accessible facilities. Furthermore, public transportation systems must offer services that are accessible to individuals with disabilities.

Public hospitals are not required to make structural changes if other methods can be utilized to achieve accessibility.[4] New construction and alterations to current facilities must be accessible to individuals with disabilities in both public and private hospitals.[4]

Public accommodations, and services operated by private entities, must increase accessibility in the most integrated setting to comply with Title III of the ADA. Businesses such as hotels, hospitals, restaurants, and theaters must allow "full and equal enjoyment" of their goods and services to individuals with disabilities. Architectural and communication barriers must be removed where removal can be readily achieved and accomplished without undue burden.

Examples of Title III changes in health care facilities include allowing access to service animals,[5] providing sidewalk curb cuts,[5] transporting patients or employees in accessible vehicles,[6] and supplying television captioning devices for individuals with disabilities.[6] Furthermore, hospitals and nursing homes must make 10% and 50% of their rooms, respectively, accessible to individuals with disabilities under Title III.[7]

Regarding qualified interpreters, public hospitals must honor an individual's auxiliary aide and service of choice unless the hospital can prove that effective communication can be achieved via another method.[4] Private hospitals are not required to give primary consideration to the aide of choice, but are encouraged to work with the individual to determine an effective method of communication for both parties.[4]

Title IV seeks to bridge the gap between impaired telephone users and the general population. Interstate and intrastate telecommunication relay services must be provided for individuals with hearing or speech impairments. Title V of the ADA contains miscellaneous provisions, including the recovery of attorneys' fees and the exemption of homosexuals, transvestites, and compulsive gamblers from the term "disabled."

Consequently, hospitals, as both employers and places of public accommodation, are responsible for complying with Titles I, II, and III of the ADA. A hospital, for example, may be held liable for discrimination if the hospital participates in a job fair that is physically inaccessible to individuals with disabilities.[4] In one instance, two rehabilitation facilities were included in a lawsuit filed by five individuals with disabilities. The plaintiffs claimed that they were discriminated against when they attended a conference sponsored by the two

facilities at a hotel that did not have accessible rooms.[8] The organizations all settled by agreeing to hold future conferences in accessible facilities.[9]

According to McGarry,[10] the role of physical therapists in the ADA requires (1) a professional obligation to have an understanding of the ADA; (2) the ability to identify environmental obstacles and assist in finding reasonable, cost-effective accommodation options; (3) acting as "gatekeepers" by referring patients with complaints of limited accessibility to the appropriate hospital or community resources; and (4) providing services in combination with occupational therapists and vocational rehabilitation specialists to create the most accessible environment possible.

Regarding Title I, physical therapists may assist employers with quantifying essential job functions and performing functional capacity evaluations (FCEs) as needed. In addition, therapists can educate employers as to how individuals with disabilities can perform job tasks differently but still produce the desired outcomes.

Physical therapists may assist with Title III compliance by consulting with hospital architects. Therapists can tour the facilities and provide recommendations for improved accessibility based on their knowledge of space and endurance requirements to negotiate wheelchairs or to ambulate with assistive devices.

Furthermore, Frieden[11] notes that two thirds of working-age persons with disabilities desire to work but are unable to find a job due to discrimination. This population may represent a heretofore untapped resource. Consequently, physical therapists can serve an important role in helping individuals with disabilities return to work. Physical therapists also often have the first opportunity to inform people with disabilities, especially those with newly acquired disabilities, of their rights and responsibilities under the law (Michael Graham, National Association of Rehabilitation Facilities; personal communication; February 28, 1991).

A primary concern in the implementation of the ADA is the expense for employers and operators of public accommodations to comply with the law. The financial implications of implementing the ADA have frequently been labeled "significant." For example, the American Hospital Association predicts that the cost of implementing the ADA over the next decade will be between $20 billion and $40 billion.[12] There is a scarcity of data, however, to support or criticize these claims.

Several sources state that most job accommodations can be achieved at less expense than some expect.[13-15] Statistics from the Job Accommodation Network reveal that 69% of suggested accommodations cost less than $500 and 50% cost less than $50.[15] Of those accommodations, 31% can be made at no cost.[16] For example, from 1978 to 1992, the average cost per job accommodation at Sears, Roebuck and Co was $121.42.[17] Twenty-eight percent of the accommodations cost less than $1,000, and 69% were achieved at no cost.[17]

Similar optimism may apply to Title III and the public accommodation provisions. Some of the lower cost estimates in the literature range from 0.5% to 5% of total construction costs as the additional costs necessary to comply with the ADA.[18–20]

The Congressional Budget Office estimated the cost of the ADA as $31 million for each fiscal year 1994 and 1995.[1] This figure reflects the responsibility of organizations such as the Equal Employment Opportunity Commission (EEOC), the US Department of Transportation, the Architectural and Transportation Barriers Compliance Board, the Office of Technology Assessment, the US Department of Justice, and the Federal Communications Commission to determine the needs of individuals with disabilities, prescribe regulations, and provide requisite enforcement mechanisms.

The potential for the ADA to create a tremendous number of lawsuits due to the law's imprecise language remains a major concern. The law fails to provide explicit details defining terms such as "reasonable," "undue hardship," and "effective." As a result, the courts will be responsible for deciding the details of the ADA on a case-by-case basis.

The EEOC estimated a 20% increase in general work load, or approximately 12,000 additional cases per year, once the ADA took effect.[21] As of January 1993, the agency was receiving close to the predicted 1,000 Title I complaints per month, but expected a higher rate in the future.[22] By the end of 1994, almost half of the complaints received were related to employment discharges.[22,23] The second most frequent charge involved failure to provide reasonable accommodation.[22,23] In one case,[23] a nurse was restricted from lifting greater than 11.34 kg (25 lb) due to knee surgery. The Office of Civil Rights decided that the nurse was a "qualified individual with a disability" but that reasonable accommodation could not be made because lifting more than 11.34 kg was an essential function of her position.

As of January 1993, the Justice Department had received more than 1,850 Title III complaints of alleged violations.[24] The Justice Department kept approximately 1,400 of the claims for investigation, and the remaining claims were referred to other agencies.[21]

Most of the ADA literature focuses on interpretation of the law or prediction of the potential impact in terms of cost and litigation. Little literature exists regarding the actual outcome of the law. This dearth of information is plausibly due to the short time period that has elapsed since the passage of the ADA.

Two studies have examined the "awareness" of the ADA. A 1991 Louis Harris Survey revealed that only 18% of the general public was aware that a law to protect individuals with disabilities was recently passed.[25] In addition, Peter David Blanck[26] found that 68% of the 47 Oklahoma employers in his study were not aware of the passage of the ADA. All of those in the study who knew of the passage of the ADA knew that they were not required to always choose "disabled" applicants over "nondisabled" applicants.

In summary, little research has addressed the impact of the ADA, including its effect on the health care field. Thus, further study is needed. The purpose of this descriptive study was to report the responses within nonfederal hospitals in Pennsylvania to the ADA regarding the following:

1. How well the chief hospital administrators understand the ADA, including (1) the definition of "disability," (2) the proper use of preemployment medical examinations, (3) hiring requirements for applicants with disabilities versus applicants without disabilities, and (4) whether they know that alterations to existing hospital facilities must be accessible to individuals with disabilities.

2. Efforts at organizational education and compliance, including (1) the nature of educational training provided for management and employees, (2) whether a committee has been established to address the requirements of the ADA, (3) whether any individuals with disabilities are a member of the committee, and (4) whether any physical therapists are a member of the committee.

3. The financial impact on facilities to comply with the ADA, including (1) the average cost per job accommodation and (2) the estimated percentage of new construction costs spent in order to make the hospital more accessible to individuals with disabilities.

4. The number of complaints and lawsuits filed thus far regarding (1) the employment provisions and (2) the public accommodation provisions.

In the 3½ years since the passage of the ADA, it was expected that hospital administrators would be aware of and understand the ADA, and that most facilities would have implemented some form of educational training for their management staff and employees. Moreover, a substantial financial impact was not anticipated, primarily due to the recent effective dates of the ADA. Hospitals may not have had such data available at this early date. Furthermore, hospitals, as recipients of federal funds, should already comply with the Rehabilitation Act of 1973.

Finally, it was expected that fewer than a dozen complaints and few or no lawsuits had been filed since the ADA took effect. Although the ADA recently became effective, such a study would prove useful in determining the status of the preceding issues and providing baseline data for future studies.

The "chief hospital administrators" were chosen for the study because they more than likely have a greater impact on ADA-related issues within an organization than, perhaps, a director of human resources. In addition, the chief administrators should be familiar with the effects of both the employment and public accommodation provisions of the ADA. Examples of a "chief hospital administrator" included an executive director, a president, an administrator, a chief operating officer, a chief executive officer, or a superintendent.

Method

Subjects

The target population consisted of all 277 nonfederal hospitals (with 270 chief administrators) in Pennsylvania that were licensed by the Pennsylvania Department of Health and Department of Public Welfare. Because the ADA does not address federal facilities, 9 federal hospitals were removed from the original population of 286 hospitals. The list of Pennsylvania hospitals was obtained from the *Directory of Pennsylvania Hospitals*,[27] published by the State Health Data Center of the Pennsylvania Department of Health (Harrisburg, Pa).* The reporting period for the data in the directory was July 1, 1990, through June 30, 1991. The latest addenda to the directory were on October 12, 1993.

The scope of the study extended only to Pennsylvania because resources were not available to accurately survey the entire United States. In addition, Pennsylvania had a representative sample of all types of hospitals in the United States (Helen Heidelbaugh, Hospital Association of Pennsylvania; personal communication; July 28, 1993).

The population hospitals were categorized by number of licensed beds (Tab. 1). The following bed ranges were chosen: (1) 1 to 250, (2) 251 to 500, (3) 501 to 750, and (4) ≥751 beds. The hospitals ranged from a 6-bed for-profit dental hospital to a 1,515-bed nonprofit general and psychiatric medical center. When the addenda to the directory indicated that a merger had occurred between two or three hospitals, the number of beds at each institution were combined into one number for the study. Information regarding the number of persons employed at each facility was not contained in the directory.

The directory used 11 categories to classify the hospitals by type of service provided (Tab. 1). In four instances, two types

*These data were supplied by the State Health Data Center of the Pennsylvania Department of Health, which specifically disclaims responsibility for any analyses, interpretations, or conclusions.

Table 1.
Demographic Characteristics of Hospitals

Demographic Characteristic	Target Population of Facilities (N=277)	Participating Facilities (N=117)
Number of licensed beds (%)		
1–250	66.0	60.7
251–500	25.9	29.1
501–750	6.1	5.1
≥751	1.4	2.6
Unknown	0.7	2.6
Types of service (%)		
General	72.9	68.4
Psychiatric	13.7	16.2
Obstetrics/gynecology	0.4	0.9
Eye	0.4	0.9
Rehabilitation	6.5	6.8
Children's	1.8	1.7
Alcoholism	1.1	0.9
Oncology	0.4	0.9
Geriatric	0.4	0.9
Podiatric	0.4	0.0
Dental	0.4	0.0
Unknown	0.4	1.7
General and rehabilitation	0.7	0.0
General and psychiatric	0.7	0.9
Form of control (%)		
Nonprofit	87.0	83.8
Profit	7.6	5.1
State	4.7	8.5
Unknown	0.7	2.6

of service (such as general and psychiatric) were combined for the study due to mergers between hospitals. The directory also classified the hospitals by form of control, that is, the type of organization legally responsible for the operation of the hospital (Tab. 1). Information on form of control was necessary because hospitals that were controlled by a religious organization were exempt from Title III of the ADA.

Instrumentation

A 23-item questionnaire was developed by the principal investigator (DLJ) focusing on how well chief hospital administrators understand the ADA's provisions, efforts at organizational education and compliance, and the financial and legal impact on hospitals to comply with the ADA (Appendix). Whereas most of the questions had multiple-choice options, a few of the education questions allowed participants to choose more than one response. Several open-ended questions were provided in the legal and demographic sections. Comment sections were included throughout the questionnaire where appropriate.

The first part determined the administrators' understanding of the ADA definition of "disability." The respondents had to decide which of 16 conditions listed are considered disabilities under the ADA. This part of the survey was followed by

Table 2.
Demographic Characteristics of Survey Participants

Demographic Characteristic	Percentage
Job title (%)	
Hospital administrators	13.7
Vice presidents	17.9
Assistant administrators	2.6
Human resources	36.8
ADA° coordinators	3.4
Other	11.1
Unknown	14.5
Educational background (%)	
High school	2.6
Undergraduate degree	26.5
Graduate degree	44.4
Postgraduate degree	21.4
Other	1.7
Unknown	3.4
Educational degrees (%)	
Hospital/health administration	12.8
Business	21.4
Human resources	9.4
Nursing	4.3
Other	38.4
Unknown	13.7
Years of hospital experience (%)	
<1	0.0
1–5	13.7
>5–10	14.5
>10	70.9
Unknown	0.9
Years at current hospital (%)	
<1	3.4
1–5	30.8
>5–10	27.4
>10	36.7
Unknown	1.7

°ADA=Americans With Disabilities Act.

two employment scenarios related to Title I, and later by a public accommodation scenario related to Title III.

The next section focused on ADA education of managerial and nonmanagerial employees, and whether a hospital had a committee established to address the requirements of the ADA. Managerial employees included those whose primary role was administrative. Those whose primary responsibilities focused on the delivery of services were considered nonmanagerial employees.

The financial section requested the average cost per job accommodation at the respondents' facilities, along with the percentage of total new construction costs spent on increasing accessibility for individuals with disabilities. In the legal segment, participants were asked to comment on the nature and number of any complaints and legal matters regarding the employment and accessibility provisions.

The final section dealt with demographic information, including the title, educational background, and hospital experience of the individual completing the survey. Participants were then given the opportunity to request a summary of the results of the study.

Prior to its distribution, the instrument was examined by six individuals for clarity, content, and length. These individuals were (1) one former hospital administrator; (2) three current chief hospital administrators representing general, psychiatric, and rehabilitation hospitals; (3) one ADA specialist; and (4) one academic professor with published research on the ADA. Suggested revisions were made to finalize the survey instrument. For example, "not applicable" and "do not know" options were added to several questions to increase accuracy. Reliability testing of the survey instrument was not, however, conducted.

Procedure

In January 1994, the questionnaires were sent with a cover letter to the 270 chief administrators. The names of the administrators were obtained from the American Hospital Association's *1993 Guide to the Health Care Field.*[28] Hospitals were given 2 weeks to respond. The survey instrument was mailed one additional time to nonrespondents. In addition, phone calls were placed to facilities to encourage completion of the survey. The target response rate was 50%.

Data Analysis

The data were compiled and analyzed with assistance from the University of Pittsburgh Office of Measurement and Evaluation of Teaching. The frequency of response and percentage of respondents were calculated for each question.

For the 16 potential disabilities, the mean number of correct scores and standard deviation were calculated. In addition, three one-way analyses of variance (ANOVAs) were performed to determine whether a relationship existed between the respondents' understanding of the ADA definition of "disability" and their (1) educational background, (2) number of years of hospital experience, or (3) number of years employed at the current facility.

Educational level was defined as undergraduate, graduate, and postgraduate. The number of respondents with high school-level education was small (2.6%); therefore, this category was eliminated from the analysis. The number of years of hospital experience and number of years at the current facility were defined as: <1 year, 1 to 5 years, >5 years to 10 years, and >10 years. The number of participants with less than 1 year of hospital experience (0.0%) and the number of participants with less than 1 year of employment at the current facility (3.4%) were low and, therefore, were eliminated from the analyses.

If a significant difference was found, a Scheffé *post hoc* comparison procedure was performed to determine where the differences were. All statistical tests of significance were conducted at the .05 level.

Results

Demographic Characteristics

One hundred seventeen individuals in nonfederal hospitals in Pennsylvania responded to the survey, for a response rate of 43.3%. Ninety-four of the participants (80.3%) requested a summary of the results. Despite the less than anticipated response rate, the respondents were representative of the population of all nonfederal hospitals in Pennsylvania. The participating facilities were similar to the population hospitals in terms of size, type of service, and form of control (Tab. 1).

Table 2 presents the demographic characteristics of the respondents by job title, educational background, educational degree, years of hospital experience, and years at current hospital. Sixteen of the surveys (13.7%) were completed by hospital administrators. These 16 respondents had the following titles: Administrator, Executive Director, President, Chief Operating Officer, Chief Executive Officer, and Superintendent. The survey was most frequently completed by human resources personnel.

Understanding of the ADA

Sixty-five percent of the participants first learned about the ADA through their "professional association or literature." The second most frequently chosen response was the "news media" (14.5%).

Table 3 demonstrates how the respondents replied to each of the 16 conditions examining their understanding of the definition of disability. The most frequently missed item was current alcohol abuse. Approximately 36% of the respondents mistakenly believed that current alcohol abuse is considered a "disability" under the ADA.

A knowledge of disabilities score was computed as the number of correct answers on the set of 16 items. Overall, the scores ranged from 6 to 16, with a mean score of 13.36 (SD=2.30). Twenty-seven of the 115 respondents (23.5%) answered all 16 of the items correctly. Fifty-four percent of the respondents scored at least 14 correct answers.

An ANOVA revealed a relationship ($P=.0000$) between educational level (undergraduate, graduate, or postgraduate) and the number of correct answers on the knowledge scores (undergraduate mean=14.13, graduate mean=13.46, and postgraduate mean=11.48). The Scheffé *post hoc* comparison procedure showed that the scores of the graduates and undergraduates were higher than the scores of the postgraduates. An ANOVA also revealed that there was no

Table 3.
How Well the Respondents Understand the Americans With Disabilities Act Definition of "Disability"

Condition	Answered Correctly (%) (n=115)	Answered Incorrectly (%) (n=115)
Fractured elbow[a]	80.0	20.0
Multiple sclerosis	97.4	2.6
Blindness	99.1	0.9
Former drug use	68.7	31.3
Sprained ankle[a]	80.9	19.1
Cancer	76.5	23.5
Current alcohol abuse[a]	64.3	35.7
Organic brain syndrome	80.9	19.1
Diabetes	79.1	20.9
Pregnancy[a]	69.6	30.4
Cerebral palsy	96.5	3.5
Homosexuality[a]	93.0	7.0
Mental retardation	90.4	9.6
Compulsive gambling[a]	81.7	18.3
Deafness	97.4	2.6
Human immunodeficiency virus	80.9	19.1
$\bar{X}=13.36$		
SD=2.30		

[a]Condition is not considered a "disability" under the Americans With Disabilities Act.

relationship between number of years of hospital experience ($P=.3926$) or number of years employed at the current facility ($P=.1102$) and the knowledge scores.

The employment scenario question asked, "Under the ADA, when should a preemployment medical examination be performed?" One hundred five of the participants (89.7%) responded correctly that the examination should be performed after an offer of employment has been extended to an individual.

The next scenario examined how well the respondents knew the hiring requirements for individuals with disabilities versus individuals without disabilities. One hundred nine of the participants (94.8%) answered correctly that they are required to hire "whoever is best qualified for the job" under the ADA.

The respondents also demonstrated how well they understood one of the Title III accessibility requirements (question 14). One hundred two participants (97.1%) in hospitals not affiliated with religious groups answered correctly that hospital renovations must be accessible to individuals with disabilities.

Table 4.
Average Cost Per Job Accommodation Since Implementation of Title I of the Americans With Disabilities Act on July 26, 1992

Category	Percentage^a
$0–50	35.4
$51–200	10.6
$201–500	8.0
$501–1,000	2.7
≥$1,001	5.3
Do not know	38.1

^{a}n=113.

Organizational Education and Compliance

Approximately 91% of the respondents reported that managerial training had occurred in their facilities. Only 44.0% of the respondents, however, indicated that their nonmanagerial employees had received ADA training. Regarding the type of training that was received by management, the most frequent type of training was conducted by the organization and held on site. For nonmanagerial employees, the most frequent form of training was provided through written literature. Specific examples of training included viewing an ADA videotape and incorporating the ADA into new employee orientation.

Efforts at organizational compliance were determined by how many facilities had a committee established to address the requirements of the ADA. Forty-three of the 116 respondents (37.1%) reported having such a committee. The most frequently cited size of the committee was 6 to 10 members. Twenty of the committees included individuals with disabilities as members. Twenty-three of the committees included physical therapists. Fifty-one of the respondents reported having an ADA coordinator instead of a committee. Overall, 94 of the 117 hospitals (80.3%) had an ADA committee or ADA coordinator.

Financial Impact

Table 4 shows the average cost per job accommodation for employees with disabilities since the implementation of Title I on July 26, 1992. Fifty-four percent of the respondents reported that job accommodations cost less than $500. Thirty-eight percent of the participants did not know the average cost per job accommodation in their facility. Specific examples of job accommodations included one facility spending $2,500 for hearing devices for multiple employees, a different facility spending $2,000 for an electric scooter for two employees, and another facility being able to provide flexible work hours as needed.

Besides job accommodation costs, the ADA poses additional construction costs to ensure accessibility for individuals with disabilities. Table 5 shows the percentage of total new

Table 5.
Percentage of Total New Construction Costs Spent in Hospitals Not Affiliated With Religious Groups to Increase Accessibility under Title III of the Americans With Disabilities Act

Category	Percentage^a
0.0%	13.9
<1.0%	12.9
1.0%–4.9%	17.8
5.0%–9.9%	3.0
≥10.0%	3.0
Do not know	49.5

^{a}n=101.

Table 6.
Legal Impact of the Americans With Disabilities Act (ADA)

	Title I Employment Provisions (n=117)	Title III Accessibility Provisions (n=117)
Facilities that reported at least one ADA complaint	23 (19.7%)	6 (5.1%)
Facilities that reported at least one ADA legal issue	21 (17.9%)	5 (4.3%)

construction costs spent in hospitals not affiliated with religious groups to increase accessibility under Title III. Approximately 45% of the respondents reported that the percentage of new construction costs spent to increase accessibility in their facility was less than 4.9%. Almost 50% of the participants did not know the answer.

Legal Impact

The final section of the survey addressed complaints and legal matters related to Titles I and III of the ADA (Tab. 6). Twenty-three of the 117 facilities (19.7%) reported having received at least one employment complaint. Only one respondent commented on the nature of a complaint. In this instance, the hospital had received a complaint from an "employee claiming a disability handicap when he only had a short-term injury." Twenty-one facilities (17.9%) reported at least one legal matter regarding employment. One facility reported an EEOC claim of discrimination under the ADA due to an employee "being laid off from a position." Another hospital reported one legal matter where promotion was the issue.

Moreover, six of the facilities (5.1%) claimed receiving at least one accessibility complaint (Tab. 6). Some of the complaints were that the "trays and silverware needed to be made accessible," that the distances from the "disabled parking spaces to the medical office building entrance" were too far, and that not all of the entrances to a facility were accessible. Furthermore, a complaint was even received at one institution stating that there were "too many disabled parking spaces." Five hospitals (4.3%) reported at least one legal issue regarding the accessibility provisions of the ADA.

Discussion

Demographic Characteristics

Our target response rate was 50%. Although only 43.3% of the hospitals responded, the participating hospitals were representative of the population of all nonfederal hospitals in Pennsylvania (Tab. 1).

This study was one of the first to examine initial responses to the ADA. Why was the response rate not higher? Some plausible explanations are (1) that hospital personnel are too busy to handle extra tasks such as completing surveys, regardless of content; (2) that due to the complex organizational structure of hospitals, the survey could have been delegated to other personnel, such as human resources staff, or to those whose responsibilities do not require knowledge of the ADA; (3) that hospital personnel may not be familiar enough with the ADA to fully realize its probable effect on their facilities; or (4) that ADA-related issues may not have surfaced yet in some nonfederal hospitals in Pennsylvania.

Understanding of the ADA

The respondents scored high on the three scenario questions regarding understanding of the ADA (89.7%, 94.8%, and 97.1% correct answers, respectively). In particular, the high score (94.8% correct) on the hiring requirements scenario supports Blanck's findings—all of the Oklahoma employers in his study who knew of the passage of the ADA knew that they were not required to always choose "disabled" applicants over "nondisabled" applicants.[26]

The study participants also were asked to decide which of the 16 conditions listed in Table 1 are considered "disabilities" under the ADA. A perfect score of 16 correct answers was achieved by 23.5% of the participants. The understanding of the ADA definition of disability was not affected by the number of years of hospital experience of the respondents nor the number of years employed at their current facility. Educational background, however, made a difference in how accurately the respondents replied to the question. Furthermore, graduates and undergraduates had higher scores than did postgraduates.

The finding that respondents with an undergraduate or graduate level of education outperformed respondents with a postgraduate level of education appears to be counterintuitive. Knowledge generally is expected to increase with further education. Only recently, however, has information about the ADA been incorporated into the curricula of academic programs. Therefore, respondents to the survey most likely gained their knowledge of the ADA through nonacademic sources such as their hospital or professional association or the news media.

Organizational Education and Compliance

Most facilities have trained their management team. Why is the training rate much lower for employees? Resources such as time and cost certainly are factors. Most likely, the types of training that were received were among the least expensive options. Perhaps, as the impact of the ADA becomes apparent in the future, employers will weigh the costs and benefits of employee education. After all, employees shape a visitor's initial impression of a facility.

Furthermore, slightly over three quarters of the facilities had either an ADA committee or ADA coordinator. This number could be higher considering the comprehensive provisions of the ADA. In addition, more representation is needed on the committees by rehabilitation personnel and individuals with disabilities. There also is the possibility that ADA-related activities were occurring within the institutions but the person completing the survey was not aware of them.

Financial Impact

The conclusions in this study support some of the lower cost estimates found in the literature. For instance, the job accommodation findings seem consistent with statistics from the Job Accommodation Network, which revealed that 69% of suggested accommodations cost less than $500.[15] Regarding new construction costs, the results of this study are similar to estimates in the literature that range from 0.5% to 5%.[18-20]

Thus far, the financial impact of the ADA does not appear to be noteworthy. Some reasons for this apparent low financial impact are that some hospitals are not tracking costs associated with the ADA; the ADA only recently became effective and, therefore, it may be too early to judge the final impact; and many hospitals, as recipients of federal funds, already comply with the Rehabilitation Act of 1973, the statutory predecessor of the ADA.

Although the financial implications of the ADA appear to be low, the study revealed that 38.1% of the respondents did not know the average cost per job accommodation and 49.5% did not know the percentage of new construction costs spent to increase accessibility in their facilities. How may hospitals assess the financial impact of the ADA if the actual costs are unknown?

One possible explanation for the high number of "do not know" responses on the questionnaires relates to the various job responsibilities of those individuals completing the survey. Future studies might further inquire about the nature of the participants' job responsibilities. It is hoped that this study will aid in encouraging hospitals to monitor their ADA-related activities and expenses.

Legal Impact

The legal impact of the ADA is more difficult to determine because the literature does not provide a measurable standard against which to judge its importance. In addition, it is difficult to obtain such information due to the nature of the topic. Not all respondents who reported complaints or legal matters specified the number of such occurrences. Furthermore, few comments were received regarding the nature of these matters. One pattern, however, is evident—more complaints and legal matters were received by facilities regarding the employment provisions of the ADA than were received regarding the accessibility provisions.

Limitations

The limitations of the survey included the following: (1) Hospitals may not be collecting data on the cost of complying with the ADA; (2) if a hospital had a large number of complaints or a lawsuit was filed against the hospital, the respondent may not admit this in the survey; (3) hospital administrators generally delegate tasks such as completing surveys to other hospital personnel; (4) persons completing the survey may not have been aware of all ADA-related activities at their facilities; and (5) this study examined Pennsylvania hospitals, and how the results relate to other hospitals has yet to be determined.

Future Studies

It is hoped that this study has provided useful baseline data for future studies. Additional research could include (1) expanding this study to determine regional or national differences in the ADA, (2) examining the impact of the ADA in the private health care sector, (3) a longitudinal study of the ADA to determine its future impact, and (4) determining the impact of the ADA from the perspective of individuals with disabilities.

Conclusion

The signing of the ADA on July 26, 1990, signified a major step toward equal opportunity, rights, and access for all Americans with disabilities. Former President George Bush "likened the ADA of 1990 to the dismantling of the Berlin Wall as a symbol of freedom for a once oppressed people."[7]

As rehabilitation providers, physical therapists should participate in ADA activities. Physical therapists can be proactive and volunteer to join, or create, ADA committees within their facilities. Their expertise in creating accessible environments for individuals with disabilities should prove invaluable.

In addition, physical therapists can sponsor ADA training programs for employees and assist with developing reasonable accommodations for employees with disabilities. Regarding research, physical therapists have the opportunity to determine the impact of the ADA from the perspective of individuals with disabilities. Finally, as health care providers

assume an active role in ADA education and research, perhaps there will be fewer instances in which an individual is discriminated against because of a disability.

Acknowledgments

Gratitude is expressed to Peter David Blanck, PhD, JD, of The University of Iowa for his direction and Elaine Rubenstein, PhD, of the University of Pittsburgh Office of Measurement and Evaluation of Teaching for her statistical assistance. Special thanks are extended to Patrick Jones, Patricia Hutchison, Beatrice Maruca, Rosalyn Ambrose, and Danica Williams for their technical support.

References

1 Public Law 101–336. *US Code Congressional and Administrative News*. 1990; codified at 42 USC secs 12101–12213.

2 Marcotte P. New disabilities law: business must accommodate handicapped employees. *ABA Journal*. 1990;76:21–22.

3 Susser PA. The ADA: dramatically expanded federal rights for disabled Americans. *Employee Relations Law Journal*. 1990;16:157–176.

4 Pearle M. Hospitals ask about the ADA. *Health Texas*. 1992;48:8–9.

5 Council of Better Business Bureaus' Foundation. *Access Equals Opportunity: Your Guide to the Americans With Disabilities Act*. 1992.

6 Carmack PJ. The ADA: new directions for the disabled—and hospitals. *Health Systems Review*. 1992;25:12–16, 20–22.

7 New access rules near for disabled. *Pittsburgh Press*. January 22, 1991;22:A-6.

8 Bucsko M. Access suit hits hotel, others. *Pittsburgh Post-Gazette*. July 2, 1993;66:B-2.

9 Stoffer H. Disabilities law opening doors. *Pittsburgh Post-Gazette*. February 13, 1994;67:A-1, A-7.

10 McGarry AM. Americans With Disabilities Act: compliance and implications. *The Pyramid—Section on Administration, American Physical Therapy Association*. 1993;23:3.

11 Frieden L. The Americans With Disabilities Act of 1990: Will it work? *Am J Occup Ther*. 1992;46:468–469.

12 Greater accessibility for the disabled costing hospitals billions. *Hospital Patient Relations Report*. 1992;7:1–2.

13 Berkery PM Jr. The Americans With Disabilities Act: its impact on small business. *National Public Accountant*. 1990;35:42–47.

14 Fagin AI, McAvoy JZ, Dorman AB. New federal legislation creates challenges, benefits for business. *National Law Journal*. September 3, 1990; 12:18.

15 Job Accommodation Network. *Cost of Job Accommodations*. 1987.

16 Smith RB. Reasonable accommodation. *Occup Health Saf*. 1992;61:4.

17 Blanck PD. Communicating the Americans With Disabilities Act transcending compliance: a case report on Sears, Roebuck and Co. *The Annenberg Washington Program*. 1994:12.

18 Barton HM. Accessibility key to compliance under ADA. *Tex Med.* 1992;88:32–35.

19 Post NM. Still dazed by the disabilities act. *Engineering News-Record.* 1992:28–30,32.

20 Hunsicker JF. Ready or not: the ADA. *Personnel Journal.* 1990;69:81–86.

21 Kemp EV Jr. EEOC gears up for the Americans With Disabilities Act: a message from the chairman. *Federal Bar News and Journal.* 1992;39:37–38.

22 EEOC developments: more disability charges have been filed than estimated, General Counsel says. *Bureau of National Affairs.* 1993;11:124.

23 Mirone JA. Reasonable accommodation in disability law. *PT—Magazine of Physical Therapy.* 1995;3:68–69.

24 Sanborn R. A quiet birthday. *National Law Journal.* 1993;15:1,42.

25 National Organization on Disability. *Willing to Act: Highlights of the 1991 Louis Harris Survey of Americans' Attitudes Toward People With Disabilities.* 1991:1–20.

26 Blanck PD. The emerging work force: empirical study of the Americans With Disabilities Act. *Journal of Corporation Law.* 1991;16:693–803.

27 Directory of Pennsylvania Hospitals. Harrisburg, Pa: State Health Data Center, Pennsylvania Department of Health; 1991:1–9.

28 *1993 Guide to the Health Care Field.* Chicago, Ill: American Hospital Association; 1993.

Appendix.

Americans With Disabilities Act (ADA) of 1990 Survey With Emphasis on Nonfederal Hospitals in Pennsylvania

Please indicate answers to the following questions by placing an "x" in the box beside the best answer, or by writing in the answer where appropriate. Feel free to provide comments where appropriate. All responses will be kept strictly confidential.

1. How did you first learn about the ADA?
   - ☐ Through the hospital
   - ☐ School
   - ☐ News media (television, radio, magazine)
   - ☐ Professional association/literature
   - ☐ Church
   - ☐ Family
   - ☐ Friend
   - ☐ An individual with a disability
   - ☐ An organization that represents individuals with disabilities
   - ☐ Other, please specify:_____

2. For each of the conditions below, please mark those that you consider a disability under the ADA:
   - ☐ Fractured elbow
   - ☐ Multiple sclerosis
   - ☐ Blindness
   - ☐ Former drug use
   - ☐ Sprained ankle
   - ☐ Cancer
   - ☐ Current alcohol abuse
   - ☐ Organic brain syndrome
   - ☐ Diabetes
   - ☐ Pregnancy
   - ☐ Cerebral palsy
   - ☐ Homosexuality
   - ☐ Mental retardation
   - ☐ Compulsive gambling
   - ☐ Deafness
   - ☐ Human immunodeficiency virus

3. Under the ADA, when should a preemployment medical examination be performed? (Check only one)
   - ☐ Before an offer of employment has been extended to an individual
   - ☐ After an offer of employment has been extended to an individual
   - ☐ It does not matter when the examination is performed
   - ☐ Do not know

4. John and Paul have applied for the same pharmacy position at a local hospital. Both applicants have similar levels of education, work experience, and skills necessary to perform the job. Paul discloses that he has a disability and would require some assistance to perform the main tasks of the job. John could perform all the tasks by himself. Under the ADA, who are you required to hire? (Check only one)
   - ☐ John
   - ☐ Paul
   - ☐ Whoever is best qualified for the job
   - ☐ Do not know

5. Have your managers received any training with regard to the ADA?
   - ☐ Yes
   - ☐ No
   - ☐ Do not know
   a. If no, do you have plans for training in the future?
   - ☐ Yes
   - ☐ No
   - ☐ Do not know
   - ☐ Not applicable
   b. How was the training provided (or how will it be provided)? (Please check all that apply)
   - ☐ Conducted by the organization and held on site
   - ☐ Conducted by an external agency but held on site
   - ☐ Conducted by an external agency but held off site
   - ☐ Other, please specify:_____
   - ☐ Not applicable, no training has been or will be provided
   c. If training has already occurred, what percentage of your managers have received such training?
   - ☐ 1%–25%
   - ☐ 26%–50%
   - ☐ 51%–75%
   - ☐ 76%–100%

6. Have your nonmanagerial employees received any training with regard to the ADA?
   - ☐ Yes
   - ☐ No
   - ☐ Do not know
   a. If no, do you have any plans for training in the future?
   - ☐ Yes
   - ☐ No
   - ☐ Do not know
   - ☐ Not applicable
   b. How was the training provided (or how will it be provided)? (Please check all that apply)
   - ☐ Written literature
   - ☐ Facility wide in-service(s)
   - ☐ Departmental in-service(s)
   - ☐ Other, please specify:_____

(continued)

Appendix. *(continued)*

☐ Not applicable, no training has been or will be provided

c. If training has already occurred, what percentage of your employees have received such training?

☐ 1%–25%
☐ 26%–50%
☐ 51%–75%
☐ 76%–100%

7. Does your facility have a committee established to address the requirements of the ADA?

☐ Yes (Answer questions 8–10)
☐ No (Go to question 11)
☐ Do not know (Go to question 12)

8. How many members are included on the committee?

☐ 1–5
☐ 6–10
☐ 11–15
☐ 16–20
☐ ≥21
☐ Do not know

9. Are any individuals with disabilities a member of the committee?

☐ Yes
☐ No
☐ Do not know

If yes, how many?

☐ One
☐ Two
☐ Three
☐ Four
☐ Five
☐ >Five
☐ Do not know

10. Are any physical therapists a member of the committee?

☐ Yes
☐ No
☐ Do not know

11. If there is no committee, do you have a person designated as an ADA coordinator?

☐ Yes
☐ No
☐ Do not know
☐ Not applicable (there is a committee)

12. What has been the average cost per job accommodation for employees with disabilities in your facility since July 26, 1992? Examples of job accommodations include purchasing special equipment, modifying work duties, or rearranging work schedules to assist individuals with disabilities.

☐ $0–$50
☐ $51–$200
☐ $201–$500
☐ $501–$1,000
☐ ≥$1,001
☐ Do not know

Comments:

13. Is your facility governed by a religious organization?

☐ Yes
☐ No

If yes, skip to question 16

14. A local hospital is converting its "D" wing from a maternity unit to a medical-surgical unit. Under the ADA, must the renovations be accessible to individuals with disabilities?

☐ Yes
☐ No
☐ Do not know

15. What percentage of total new construction costs have been spent on making your hospital more accessible to individuals with disabilities

starting from the following dates:

—January 26, 1992, for public hospitals?
—January 26, 1993, for private hospitals?

☐ 0%
☐ <1%
☐ 1%–4.9%
☐ 5%–9.9%
☐ ≥10%
☐ Do not know

16. Are you aware of any complaints from employees or hospital clients/families under the ADA regarding:

a. Employment procedures in your hospital (such as hiring, firing, promotion, or training procedures)?

☐ Yes
☐ No

If yes, please specify the number of complaints:_____
Comments:

b. The accessibility of your hospital (skip this question if your hospital is governed by a religious organization)?

☐ Yes
☐ No

If yes, please specify the number of complaints:_____
Comments:

17. Are you aware of any legal matters/situations brought by an employee or client of your hospital under the ADA regarding:

a. Employment procedures in your hospital?

☐ Yes
☐ No

If yes, please specify the number of situations:_____
Comments:

b. The accessibility of your hospital (skip this question if your hospital is governed by a religious organization)?

☐ Yes
☐ No

If yes, please specify the number of situations:_____
Comments:

18. Please mark the approximate percentage of sources of reimbursement for your hospital (note: total should equal 100%):

Private pay	_____%
Medicare	_____%
Medicaid	_____%
Private insurance	_____%
Charity care	_____%
Other	_____%

19. Title of individual completing the survey:_____

20. Educational background of individual completing the survey (please check the highest level attained):

☐ High-school diploma
☐ Undergraduate degree   Major:_____
☐ Graduate degree   Major:_____
☐ Postgraduate degree   Major:_____
☐ Other: _____   Major:_____

21. Number of years of hospital experience of individual completing the survey:

☐ <1 year
☐ 1 year–5 years
☐ >5 years–10 years
☐ >10 years

22. Number of years employed at current facility:

☐ <1 year
☐ 1 year–5 years
☐ >5 years–10 years
☐ >10 years

23. Would you like to receive a summary of the results of the study?

☐ Yes
☐ No

Thank you for your time and effort.

A D A

Q&A

by John A Mirone

QUESTION: *How do we identify the requirements for graduation from academic programs in a way that is nondiscriminatory to students with disabilities?*

This column debuts with what may be one of the most practical and intriguing—and one of the most difficult—questions related to the Americans with Disabilities Act (ADA). *How do we identify the requirements for graduation from academic programs in a way that is nondiscriminatory to students with disabilities?* This is a question that not only should concern the world of academics but the world of practice, because those requirements help shape the next generation of practitioners. The case example used to illustrate the graduation requirements dilemma focuses on whether a student should be required to demonstrate a patient transfer as part of those requirements.

The Process

The process of identifying requirements for graduation from academic programs involves three basic steps: 1) identifying the knowledge and skills required to competently practice at the entry level, 2) establishing a curriculum that reflects those competencies, and 3) publishing—before making admissions decisions—graduation requirements that are fully consistent with the curriculum (and therefore, as explained below, with job requirements).

Generic knowledge and skills. Identifying the knowledge and skills required to competently practice at the entry level is easier said than done. At a minimum, there must be a description of generic knowledge and skills. Education programs and students have a kind of "implied contract" holding that, upon graduation, students will have the skills necessary to practice. To ensure that students will have those skills, educators who have experi-

This is a question that not only should concern the world of academics but the world of practice, because those requirements help shape the next generation of practitioners.

ence with entry-level practitioners in clinical situations must reach a consensus regarding these generic competencies.

Establishing a curriculum. A general consensus regarding generic knowledge and skills required for safe and effective practice is the best case scenario for establishing a legally and morally defensible curriculum. Because of that consensus, graduation from an accredited program ensures that entry-level practitioners have command over the minimum competencies required for practice. It is reasonable to assume that requirements reflecting generally agreed-upon generic competencies will be relatively easily defended against charges of discrimination. It may be argued, for example, that the ability to physically demonstrate a patient transfer is not a generic requirement—but that the *cognitive skills* related to patient transfer are a generic requirement.

Teaching generic competencies required for safe and effective entry-level practice is considered only the *minimum* starting point;

academic programs are expected to instruct beyond the generic competencies. Whatever is required, however, should be clearly related to the practice of physical therapy. There is no *one standardized* job for a physical therapist or physical therapist assistant, and individual education programs cannot be expected to prepare all students for all possible jobs. A degree of uniqueness, then, is reasonable and appropriate.

According to case law regarding the adjudication of cases under the Rehabilitation Act of 1973 (a logical starting point for predicting what will happen when ADA cases go to court), academic programs have been granted some degree—but not an unlimited amount—of discretion regarding what they teach and require. It is impossible to know whether the requirement that students must physically demonstrate a patient transfer would be upheld in court. A central issue would be the degree to which the requirement is job-related. On the one hand, some jobs may require that therapists physically transfer patients (eg, small physical therapy departments without physical therapy aides and certain home care settings). On the other hand, assigning a physical therapist assistant or physical therapy aide the task of physically transferring patients (termed "job restructuring" under ADA) may be considered a *reasonable accommodation* in other situations (eg, larger physical therapy departments that have many therapists or that have physical therapist assistants or physical therapy aides).

Publishing graduation requirements consistent with the curriculum—and job requirements. The need for publishing articulate program requirements cannot be overemphasized. The best case scenario is as follows:

• All critical clinical skills necessary to practice physical therapy effectively and safely are incorporated into the curriculum.

- Published requirements to complete the program reflect those clinical skills.

It is possible, however, that a clinical skill necessary to safely and effectively practice physical therapy may not be covered by the curriculum. In such a case, because the skill is not part of the curriculum, the skill obviously cannot be made a requirement to *complete* the curriculum. *In this context,* any one of the following actions would be considered discriminatory under the law:

1. Denying admission on the basis of the belief that the applicant would not be able to demonstrate the skill.

2. Denying admission on the basis of the belief that the applicant will not get a job. *This issue is irrelevant to the application decision.*

To emphasize this last point: It is a myth that admissions decisions can be based on a judgment that the individual with a disability will not be able to get a job. *The only relevant decision is whether an applicant can meet graduation requirements.* If it becomes apparent that the requirements to complete a program do not include critical skills,

> It is a myth that admissions decisions can be based on a judgment that the individual with a disability will not be able to get a job.

it would be appropriate to revise requirements for admission—*before* the next round of admissions. When faced with whether to admit a person with a disability into an academic program, a decision maker may have no intent to discriminate and may be interested only in public protection; however, "discovering" a new requirement (which is not reflected in the curriculum) is both legally risky and unethical.

To Avoid Discrimination and Ensure Critical Skills

Many academicians recognize the following two moral obligations: 1) to protect the public and 2) to make admissions decisions, without discriminating against persons with disabilities, on the basis of the student's ability to meet fair and reasonable academic requirements. Not articulating in advance reasonable requirements of the academic program, however, may compel the program by law to admit a student who will not be able to perform truly essential skills necessary for public protection. What is the best advice? Revisit academic requirements and make certain that 1) requirements are fair, reasonable, and nondiscriminatory and that 2) critical skills necessary for competent performance have not been assumed or neglected. *PT*

A PRACTICAL APPLICATION OF THE ADA

by Kim Osborne, PT ↝ *photographs by Patti Hogue*

One PT manager's story

My private practice in rural New Mexico had grown rapidly during its first 5 years, with four physical therapists and one occupational therapist treating outpatients. We also were contracting to provide services to a small hospital, the local school system, nursing homes, and home health agencies. We had just finished a ribbon-cutting ceremony, an open house, and a dance to commemorate the opening of a new facility. As I toured the facility, I casually mentioned to my administrative assistant that "one day" I expected to have someone in a wheelchair on my staff. I was proud the new building was accessible.

With the echoes of celebratory words and music still fresh in my ears, I was unprepared for the telephone call I received the next morning. That "one day" had arrived sooner than I expected it would.

Willie Stubblefield, a new graduate who had been a staff physical therapist for only 6 weeks, was lying in the intensive care unit in halo fixation (Fig 1). Twenty-four hours after dancing and celebrating with all of us, he had been in a motor vehicle accident and had sustained fractures of the right facets of C3 and C4. He had been wearing a seatbelt at the time of the accident; how-

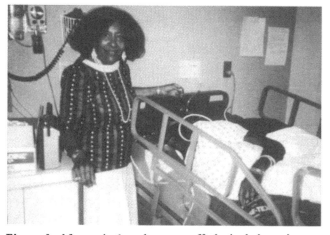

Figure 1. After only 6 weeks as a staff physical therapist, new graduate Willie Stubblefield (above, with his mother) was lying in the intensive care unit in halo fixation. "I let him know that no matter what the outcome of his current situation, he had a job waiting for him," says Kim Osborne, PT.

ever, even before the emergency medical team arrived on the scene, he knew he had no sensation from his chest downward.

I had my first opportunity to speak with Willie 36 hours after the accident. In typical physical therapist fashion, he was certain he would return to work by the end of the week! I also had the opportunity to let him know that no matter what the outcome of his current situation, he had a job waiting for him. I never paused to consider the ramifications of this promise. I had been preaching to the local businesses for years about the positive aspects of returning an injured worker to the job; now it was my turn to be a trailblazer and set an example for the community.

Willie's recovery period included a fusion of the cervical spine with an acute care hospital stay of 1 month and a rehabilitation stay of 6 months. He took an additional 4 months to recuperate at home. During his recuperation, he successfully passed his professional licensure examination. He returned to work 11 months after his injury.

Early the same year Willie was injured, the Americans with Disabilities Act (ADA) was signed into law. Because in my business the total number of employees was less than 25, we technically did not have to meet the requirements of the law until July 1994. Nonetheless, Willie's case illustrates a practical application of the ADA. I now had before me a "qualified individual with a disability"[1] seeking employment in a job that traditionally is physically demanding. With residual spastic quadriplegia, Willie met the ADA criterion of having a "physical impairment" in one or more "major life activities,"[1] qualifying him as an individual protected under the ADA.

The first step toward bringing Willie back to work included determining "essential functions of the job."[1] On his first day back at work, Willie and I reviewed the job description he had signed the year before. We found that, if we accommodated his needs, he would be able to fulfill all job requirements. This fact was a tribute to an outcome-oriented job description and our willingness to make reasonable accommodations.

Figure 2. A door-handle extension was needed to allow access in and out of the hospital department in which Willie was working.

"On their orientation day, I casually mentioned to two relatively new staff PTs that one of our PTs is quadriplegic," says Kim Osborne (right, red shirt). *"They rushed home to look at the all-staff photo—they hadn't even noticed he was in a wheelchair! That's when I knew that Willie had become totally integrated into our staff."*

ates,[2] in 50% of cases, costs of "reasonable accommodation" are trivial (ie, under $50) (Tab 1). We found this to be true. In the first year of his employment postinjury, a total of $10 was spent to accommodate Willie's needs. A door-handle extension ($5) was needed to allow access in and out of the hospital department in which Willie was working (Fig 2). Four cinderblocks ($1.25 each) were placed under his desk to accommodate the height of his wheelchair (Fig 3).

Many potential problems were solved at no expense by suggestions from Willie. I feared he would have difficulty using a dictaphone, for example. He solved the problem by using his tongue to turn the dictaphone on and off (Fig 4). Other adjustments included using a universal cuff to write (Fig 5) and unique ways to dial the telephone and use the computer (Figs 6, 7). A "mouse" was purchased to allow more efficient computer access; another employee also uses a mouse on a regular basis because of personal preference. We currently are investigating the use of a word prediction software program to speed Willie's typing time.

Because of the time constraints of his attendant, we adjusted his work schedule so that he would begin 1 hour later than the other therapists.

After 1 year of employment, we worked with Willie and the New Mexico Department of Vocational Rehabilitation to obtain an adapted van, which was his year-end raise and not a reasonable accommodation. He now is able to drive independently between home and the clinic.

"Hidden Costs"

There have been other, "hidden" costs associated with Willie's employment; however, these have been minor when com-

Outcome-Oriented Job Description

Outcome-oriented statements in a job description are worded to focus on the desired *end result* rather than on *how* that result is accomplished. The outcome-oriented job description may require, for example, that the physical therapist *perform accurate measurements of muscle strength in patients with varied neuromuscular and musculoskeletal disorders* rather than specifying that the physical therapist will *perform manual muscle testing,* or it may require that the therapist *perform goniometric measurement of joint range of motion* rather

than specifying that the therapist will *hold the goniometer and align the axis of rotation and lever arms to measure joint range of motion.*

Reasonable Accommodations

As reported by Berkeley Planning Associ-

Figure 3. Four cinderblocks were placed under Willie's desk to accommodate the height of his wheelchair. Figure 4 (middle). Willie solved the problem of how to use the dictaphone by using his tongue to turn the dictaphone on and off. Figure 5 (bottom). Willie uses a universal cuff to write at his desk.

pared with his contributions.

The state of New Mexico requires continuing education credits to maintain licensure; Willie needed an attendant to accompany him to these courses. For one fiscal year, the costs associated with this attendant were $420. On several occasions, his attendant for these courses was a technician employed by my practice. This strategy resulted in increasing the pool of knowledge among my staff (Tab 2).

Willie was denied enrollment in the company medical insurance plan because of his preexisting condition. *However, the Equal Employment Opportunity Commission's (EEOC) regulations expressly require employers to give employees with disabilities "equal access" to whatever health insurance or other benefits coverage the employer provides to other employees.*[3] We fortunately were able to obtain insurance coverage for him through a state-sponsored high-risk pool. This type of insurance costs $60 per month more than for employees of similar age who do not represent a "high risk."

There are other overhead costs involved in hiring an employee with a disability that have been absorbed by our "system." In this respect, however, I feel that few differences among my employees exist. I am speaking here of time spent by support staff obtaining van modifications, scheduling special travel arrangements, and assisting with expense reports. Other employees have similar benefits of employment depending on their needs: An employee may obtain assistance from the accountant for completion of tax forms, for example.

The Benefits

The benefits of Willie's employment have been many. He has successfully managed a hospital physical therapy department in a 250-bed hospital for 20 months. Before the hospital contracted with my business to have Willie cover the department, the hospital had been without a physical therapist for 8 months. Most patients naturally are curious but afraid to ask about Willie in his wheelchair. Many times their questions are answered by the colleagues who serve as Willie's "hands" during working hours.

Many patients have reported that working with Willie has helped them minimize their own condition and move forward with their lives. When patients have a therapist with a disability, they have a therapist with an empathetic ear—and who knows better than someone in a wheelchair what works best for seating needs?

The Process of Acceptance

Willie's acceptance by his coworkers and patients has been an evolving process. As with all work relationships, busy days can create stress. Adding a disability to the equation can add to that stress. There have been some difficult moments; for example, a physical therapy aide complained to the hospital administration that he was being required to do "more work" as a result of the reasonable accommodations made on Willie's behalf. This situation, however, was no different from any other situation involving employee relations: Open communication and education are the best answers.

Tax Benefits

My business qualified for benefits through the Targeted Jobs Tax Credit (Title 26, Internal Revenue Code, Section 51). This

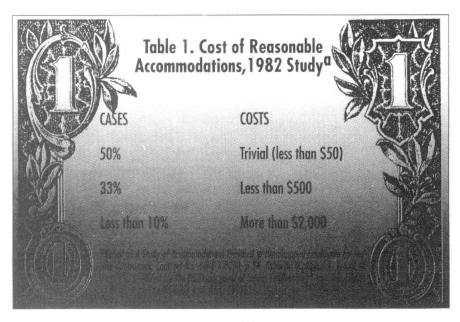

Table 1. Cost of Reasonable Accommodations, 1982 Study[a]

CASES	COSTS
50%	Trivial (less than $50)
33%	Less than $500
Less than 10%	More than $2,000

law applies to new employees with disabilities. We were able to receive a tax credit in the amount of 40% of the first $6,000 of Willie's first-year wages. (There is no credit after the first year of employment.) For an employer to qualify for the credit, a worker must have been employed for at least 90 days or have completed at least 120 hours of work for the employer. The Targeted Jobs Tax Credit currently is defunct; however, it may soon be restored.

There are other tax incentives that may be of interest to those hiring or serving people with disabilities, such as the Tax Deduction to Remove Architectural and Transportation Barriers to People with Disabilities and Elderly Individuals (Title 26, Internal Revenue Code, Section 190) and the Disabled Access Tax Credit (Title 26, Internal Revenue Code, Section 44). Section 190 allows deductions for "qualified architectural and transportation barrier removal expenses." Also eligible for the deduction are expenses incurred as a result of making a facility or public transportation vehicle connected with a trade or business more accessible and usable by individuals with disabilities.

The Disabled Access Tax Credit is available to "eligible small businesses" in the amount of 50% of "eligible access expenditures" for the taxable year that exceed $250 but do not exceed $10,250. "Eligible small businesses" are those businesses that had either a) $1 million or less in gross receipts for the preceding tax year or b) 30 or fewer full-time employees during the preceding tax year. "Eligible access expenditures" are expenses paid or incurred by an eligible small business to enable that small business to comply with applicable requirements under the ADA. These expenditures include amounts paid or incurred:

i) for the purpose of removing architectural, communication, physical, or transportation barriers that prevent a business from being accessible to or usable by individuals with disabilities;

ii) to provide qualified readers, taped texts, and other effective methods of making visually delivered materials available to people with visual impairments;

iii) to provide qualified interpreters or other effective methods of making aurally delivered materials available to individuals with hearing impairments;

iv) to acquire or modify equipment or devices for individuals with disabilities; or

v) to provide other similar services, modifications, materials, or equipment.[4]

My experience with Willie has led me to take an even stronger stand when advocating return to work for injured patients. It has only strengthened my conviction that people with disabilities are capable of playing a critical role in the workforce. The ADA provides another tool for therapists and people with disabilities in their quest for success in the workplace. *PT*

Kim Osborne, PT, is President, Therapy Services Associates PC, Lovington, NM. Osborne gave a presentation on her experience with implementing the ADA at a joint instructional course—ADA: Practical Application and the Physical Therapist's Role, cosponsored by APTA's Private Practice Section and Orthopaedic Section—held before APTA's 1993 Combined Sections Meeting in San Antonio, Tex.

References

1 The Americans with Disabilities Act, 1990. Washington, DC: US Department of Justice, Civil Rights Division; 1990.

2 Collignol F, Vencill M, Barker L. A study of accommodations provided to handicapped employees by federal contractors, Contract No. J-9-E-1-0099, p. 29, Table 6a. Prepared for the US Department of Labor, Employment Standards Administration. Berkeley Planning Associates; 1982.

3 Ogletree, Deakins, Nash, Smoak, & Stewart, Attorneys at Law. *Americans with Disabilities Act: Employee Rights and Employer Obligations.* New York, NY: Times Mirror Magazines Inc, Books Division; 1992.

4 Harrison M, Gilbert S, eds. *ADA Handbook.* Beverly Hills, Calif: Excellent Books; 1992.

Figures 6 and 7. Willie has found a unique way to dial the telephone and use the computer.

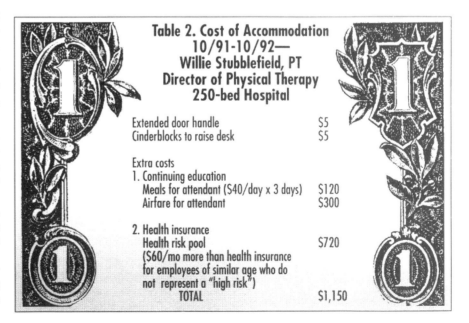

Table 2. Cost of Accommodation 10/91-10/92—Willie Stubblefield, PT Director of Physical Therapy 250-bed Hospital

Extended door handle	$5
Cinderblocks to raise desk	$5
Extra costs	
1. Continuing education	
Meals for attendant ($40/day x 3 days)	$120
Airfare for attendant	$300
2. Health insurance	
Health risk pool	$720
($60/mo more than health insurance for employees of similar age who do not represent a "high risk")	
TOTAL	$1,150

A D A

by John A Mirone

UESTION: *Does the Americans with Disabilities Act (ADA) compel affirmative action?*

One of the most popular and pervasive myths about the ADA is that it is affirmative action for people with disabilities.

With regard to employment or admission to academic programs, the ADA does *not* require:

Selection of an individual because he or she is disabled. Eager advocates for people who are disabled may unintentionally—and wrongly—lead others to believe that selection of a candidate is *forced because* that candidate has a disability.

Selection of a less-than-qualified individual because he or she is disabled. Assuming that the employer is using fair and defensible standards, an employer is not obligated to hire a typist who can type only 50 words per minute when the essential functions of the job require 65 words per minute. However, if an employer rejects a candidate who is disabled because the candidate does not meet the 65-words-per-minute standard and the employer later hires a person who is able-bodied and types only 50 words per minute, that employer may be subject to charges of discrimination. Similar analogies can be made regarding standards for admission into academic programs. *Fair and defensible standards need not be lowered.*

Selection of an individual who is not the most qualified person for the position. What if, in the above case, both candidates had met or exceeded the 65-word-

Many myths exist regarding the ADA. Most will be demystified over time as case law clarifies the regulations. Some can be dispelled today—through a better understanding of the ADA's *intent*.

per minute requirement? The employer would have been free to hire the person *most qualified* for the position, whether he or she was able-bodied or disabled.

Selection of a candidate for admission to an academic program when that candidate is disabled and meets minimum basic criteria for admission (eg, minimum Scholastic Achievement Test scores) but has an overall ranking—assuming fair and defensible criteria for admission—that exceeds the number of available positions. A program is not obligated to admit an individual who is disabled when that individual is ranked #20 among candidates and only 10 slots are available.

The technical accuracy of the above information does not imply that an employer or an

academic program cannot or should not voluntarily institute an affirmative action program. There are a number of good reasons for voluntary affirmative actions:

- Physical therapists and physical therapist assistants are members of a profession that advocates for persons with disabilities; the profession therefore should support affirmative action.

- Previously established policies that could be construed as discriminatory should be reversed. Even if an employer or program is *not* guilty of discrimination in a technical sense, there still may be financial and public relations costs when the employer or program is *perceived* as being discriminatory. Affirmative action programs may help limit these costs and time-consuming defensive actions.

- Affirmative action can be a legal strategy for employers or academic programs that are facing or are likely to face charges of discrimination. Voluntary corrective actions may be considered signs of "good faith," which may prevent needless legal action or reduce penalties if an employer or university is found to be guilty of discrimination.

Question: *Did the framers of the ADA intend the act to be a lawyers' employment and retirement fund in disguise?*

According to one myth about the ADA, the framers purposely wrote the act in a confusing and ambiguous way and predicted that the act would result in an enormous amount of litigation. According to the framers, the *intent* was for the ADA to be:

- Clear and unambiguous when possible
- Fair
- Flexible when appropriate
- Not likely to result in an enormous amount of adversarial, conflictual litigation

Clarity, flexibility, and smooth cooperation cannot necessarily be achieved simultaneously. The ADA basically prohibits discrimination against persons with disabilities and requires that employers, state and local governments, and businesses make reasonable accommodations for persons with disabilities. What factor, then, most typically determines whether there will be litigation? Agreement—or lack of agreement—that particular accommodations are "reasonable."

The term "reasonable" is used as a flexible and fair qualifier. The idea behind this term is that only reasonably fair accommodations—at reasonable costs—are obligatory. Universities, for example, are not expected to go out of business to make accommodations. Establishing rigid rules about costs, however, would not take into consideration the contextual and situational factors. That is, what is reasonable for one academic program could be devastating for another. For the framers of the ADA, the solution to this dilemma was to ask *only* for reasonable accommodations.

Furthermore, the framers of the ADA explicitly state that the process of determining what is reasonable should entail communication between business and academic decision makers and applicants with disabilities. Yes, some litigation is inevitable; but reasonable persons acting in good faith can be expected, generally speaking, to develop reasonable solutions to problems.

The ADA *is* clear and unambiguous in that it is intended to prevent discrimination. Many specific requirements also are unambiguous; for example, the act contains much specific information regarding the technicalities of architectural requirements, such as the height of control panels, the amount of clearance for maneuvering in doorways and shower stalls, and the angle of curb ramps.

Although the ADA was not intended to be a litigation bonanza for lawyers, the inescapable fact is that the ADA is *law* and ADA problem solvers therefore are likely to be *lawyers*. And (as lawyers frequently persuade us) the law typically is too tricky or dangerous for amateurs to handle. If one party to a negotiation involves a lawyer in the proceedings, for example, the other party must do the same. Regardless of how a dispute is resolved or how long the resolution takes, lawyers must be consulted; the more complex and ambiguous the issues, the more *often* lawyers are likely to be employed. Why have a law, then? We as a society need more than voluntary guidelines to support our common goal of eliminating discrimination against people with disabilities. *PT*

A D A

CASE LAW
by John A Mirone

Cook v State of Rhode Island

A landmark court case survives an appeals ruling—
and rattles the foundation of disability law.

Bonnie Cook previously had worked for several years at the Ladd Center, a Rhode Island facility for patients with mental retardation. In 1988, she again sought employment at that facility; however, the Center did not hire her, believing that doing so would pose a hazard to residents. The Center argued that because Cook weighed more than 300 lb, she would not be able to evacuate patients during an emergency. Cook brought suit, arguing that she was unfairly discriminated against because of her disability—obesity.

Cook brought her case before a state administrative board, whose findings were not in her favor. A Rhode Island affiliate of the American Civil Liberties Union then represented her in further court action. She brought suit in the US District Court (*Cook v State of Rhode Island*, 1990) and was awarded $100,000 in compensatory damages by a federal jury.

The defendant, the Rhode Island Department of Mental Health, decided to appeal the decision—and a panel of judges issued a landmark ruling that is expected to have a profound effect on disability law. Although this particular case was filed under the Rehabilitation Act (Section 504), it is expected that the resulting case law will have a powerful impact on suits brought under the Americans with Disabilities Act (ADA).

What Qualifies as a Disability?

It was clear why the Ladd Center did not rehire Cook: her obesity. The crucial legal question was *whether Cook was covered by disability law and therefore entitled to protection and recourse.*

Any one of the following three criteria qualifies a person as having a disability under either the ADA or the Rehabilitation Act: 1) a mental or physical *impairment that substantially limits* one or more major life activities (eg, working), 2) a *record* of such an impairment, or 3) being regarded as having an impairment (ie, the *perception* of a disability, even if the perception is incorrect).

Cook therefore could have argued that she was covered because obesity is an impairment or because she was *regarded* as having an impairment—even though her obesity was *not* an impairment and the perception that she had an impairment was incorrect.

Is obesity an impairment? Under the ADA, obesity usually is not covered because it is a disability only in rare circumstances. That is, obesity does not normally *"substantially limit"* a major life activity.

There are some cases, however, in which obesity may constitute a disability. Under the ADA, a physical impairment is any physiological condition that affects any one of several bodily systems, including the digestive and the endocrinal. It therefore could be argued that obesity is a covered disability *when obesity is the manifestation of a physiological disorder.*

The *really* interesting point in the Cook case was that the appeals panel did not reach its judgement based on the definition of her obesity as a disability. *The panel decided that the evidence indicated Cook's obesity was perceived as a disability by the defendant.* In other words, Cook did not have to prove she actually had a disability. She had only to demonstrate that the defendant regarded, perceived, or thought of her as disabled!

The Essential Finding: To Whom Does It Apply?

The essential finding, upheld on appeal, was that a *proven perception* of disability qualifies for protection and recourse under disability law, even in the absence of evidence that a disability actually exists.

Although the case was filed under the Rehabilitation Act, the finding certainly will precipitate many suits under the ADA. The appeals panel ruling was specific to an employment setting; however, the ruling about what qualifies for coverage under the ADA will be broadly pertinent (eg, to state licensure, services offered to the public, education program admissions).

The Cook case raised—but did not answer—an interesting question regarding qualification for a disability under the law. The defendant argued that because Cook's obesity was the result of *voluntary* actions, it did not constitute a disability. The Equal Employment Opportunity Commission (EEOC) argued *for* Cook, stating that neither the ADA nor the Rehabilitation Act requires consideration of the *cause* for disability. The EEOC considers it relevant that the disability may have been exacerbated by voluntary behavior.

Undoubtedly, the question of "voluntariness" will be raised in many future cases. If it is decided that disability as a result of voluntary behavior disqualifies a person for coverage under the ADA, the implications will be profound. Spinal cord injury as the result of a skiing (voluntary) accident, for example, might not qualify as a covered disability. And what about heart disease as a result of smoking? *PT*

John A Mirone is Associate Director of APTA's Department of Practice.

ADA CASE LAW

by John A Mirone

Reasonable Accommodation in Disability Law

The EEOC relates that approximately 25% of ADA complaints filed relate to employers' alleged failures to provide reasonable accomodation.

As the number of claims filed under the Americans with Disabilities Act (ADA) grows, it is becoming increasingly likely that employers will be sued for failure to provide reasonable accommodation for their employees' disabilities. The Equal Employment Opportunity Commission (EEOC) reports that approximately 25% of the ADA-related complaints filed with its office as of December 1994 specifically related to alleged failures to provide reasonable accommodation (Table).

According to the ADA, reasonable accommodation may include but is not limited to the following[1]:

- Making existing facilities readily accessible and useable by persons with disabilities.
- Restructuring jobs, modifying work schedules, or reassigning an employee to a vacant position.
- Acquiring or modifying equipment or devices.
- Adjusting or modifying examinations, training materials, or policies.
- Providing qualified readers or interpreters.

An employer is required to make reasonable accommodation for an employee's disability unless such accommodation would pose an "undue hardship"—defined as significant difficulty or expense in light of 1) the nature and cost of the accommodation, 2) the financial resources of the employer, 3) the type of operation of the employer, and 4) the impact on the operation of the facility.

In some cases, courts have decided in favor of employers, which indicates either that no reasonable accommodation for a specific employee's disability existed or that accommodation requested by an employee exceeded the definition of "reasonable."

Courts also have dismissed charges against employers on procedural grounds (eg, failure of an individual with a disability to notify his or her employer of the disability or failure to exhaust administrative procedures before filing a complaint with the EEOC).

In other cases, courts have decided in favor of employees. Employers increasingly are finding that it may be a serious—and costly—error to insist that an employee be "100%" before returning to work (because the implication is that reasonable accommodation for a disability is not a topic for discussion). Another potentially serious mistake is for an employer to offer accommodation based on a diagnostic category or on the *type* of disability an employee has. It must be remembered that reasonable accommodation is based on an *individualized* analysis of the essential requirements of a job and the employee's ability to meet them.

Under Title I of the ADA, the EEOC is responsible for investigating and attempting to resolve charges of employment-related violations in the private sector. Title II of the ADA pertains to employment practices of state and local governments, and charges of violations are investigated by the Office of Civil Rights (OCR) of the US Department of Justice. Employees are free to seek remediation through private court action if the OCR or the EEOC decides not to file a lawsuit on the individual's behalf. Charges of "failure to provide reasonable accommodation" also may be filed under a variety of federal or state disability laws, some of which may allow a jury to decide the penalty.

Penalties for an employer's failure to provide reasonable accommodation for a disability may be severe—whether or not the case is subject to a claim under the ADA. An employee may be entitled to various remedies, including hiring, promotion, reinstatement, or back pay or other remuneration. Employees also may be entitled to compensation for mental anguish or inconvenience.

The cases described below fall into that vast "gray area" in which it is not immediately clear whether accommodations requested by an individual are in fact "reasonable." In cases such as these, there typically is room for debate. Both of the cases below relate to the issue of modified or "lighter" duty.

Orange County Department of Education (CA), 5 NDLR, 388 (OCR 1994)

A nurse who worked with students with disabilities injured her knee and had surgery for the condition. Several weeks later, a physician documented that she was able to return to work, specifying, however, that this included a restriction against lifting more than 25 lb. The nurse's employer refused her request for modified duty, and the nurse filed a complaint with the OCR.

The OCR determined that, because the nurse's knee injury affected her ability to perform a "major life activity"—lifting more than 25 lb—the nurse qualified as an individual with a disability. The next step was to determine whether lifting more than 25 lb was an essential requirement of that particular nurse's position in that specific setting. The OCR decided that it was and ruled that a reasonable accommodation could not be made through reassignment of responsibilities or through job modification. Furthermore, the

OCR ruled that if the nurse continued working with students with disabilities, she would present a risk to herself and the students. She was not a "qualified individual with a disability," and thus the employer had not violated the ADA by failing to provide reasonable accommodation.

Based on this case, could the OCR or the EEOC decide that a physical therapist with a lifting restriction is not a qualified individual with a disability and that his or her employer does not have to provide job modifications or reassignment of responsibilities? Not necessarily. The court might decide in favor of the employer in certain cases (eg, the therapist performs home care without another therapist or physical therapist assistant, and lifting more than 25 pounds is an essential function of his or her position) and in favor of the therapist in other cases (eg, the therapist works in a department in which there are other therapists or therapist assistants to whom lifting duties could be reassigned).

Howell v Michelin Tire Corporation, 5 NDLR, 290 (Ala 1994)

An employee filed a claim charging that his employer had violated the ADA by failing to provide accommodation for his known disability. The employee had a clearly documented condition (hip dysplasia). He had been working for the employer for several years. When his condition deteriorated, he requested accommodation for his disability in the form of "lighter duty." His employer denied the request.

The employee pursued compensatory and punitive damages, requesting a jury trial. His employer asked the court to dismiss the claim. The court denied the employer's request, upholding the employee's right to a jury trial to seek compensatory and punitive damages. The judge stated that it was not absolutely clear who would win the case; for example, it had not yet been established whether the employer could have provided reasonable accommodation without undue hardship. The court did offer observations in favor of the employee, however, noting that other employees with disabilities had been assigned "lighter duty," which constituted evidence that this alternative may have been available for the employee in question. (The case has not yet been decided; in cases

such as this, it is likely that the employer will choose to settle out of court.)

In this case, the employer apparently made no attempt to accommodate the employee in question and thereby increased the chances that the employee could sue successfully for damages in a jury trial. It would have been prudent for the employer to reevaluate its position when faced with the combination of punitive damages and a jury trial because such a situation may result in penalties that are more severe than the cost of providing the accommodation. It may have been somewhat disconcerting for this employer to realize that a record of providing accommodation for some employees with disabilities could later be used *against* the employer in a case in which the same accommodation was not granted to another employee.

Although the increasing number of ADA claims may force employers to more closely examine the issue of reasonable accommodation for their employees' disabilities, the reality is that case law will not define what is a reasonable accommodation for any specific condition, diagnosis, or disability. Investigation and resolution of ADA complaints absolutely require an individualized, case-by-case analysis to identify a reasonable accommodation—or to determine whether a reasonable accommodation exists at all. This analysis typically includes assessment by qualified health professionals, and physical therapists may find their expertise in this area increasingly in demand.

John A Mirone is Director, Federation of State Boards of Physical Therapy, Arlington, Va. He previously was APTA staff liaison to APTA's Task Force on the ADA.

References

1   Equal employment opportunity for individuals disabilities; final rule (29 CFR 1630). *Federal Register.* July 26, 1991;56:12.

Table. Cumulative ADA Charge Data as of December 31, 1994

ADA Violations Most Often Cited

	Number	Percent of Total[a]
Discharge	20,171	50.5
Failure to provide reasonable accommodation	10,264	25.7
Hiring	4,364	10.9
Harassment	4,294	10.8
Discipline	2,947	7.4
Layoff	2,069	5.2
Benefits	1,576	3.9
Promotion	1,495	3.7
Rehire	1,472	3.7
Wages	1,385	3.5
Suspension	910	2.3

[a] List adds up to more than 100% because individuals can allege multiple violations.

Impairments Most Often Cited

	Number	Percent of Total[b]
Back impairments	7,799	19.5
Neurological impairments	4,824	12.1
Emotional/psychiatric impairments	4,569	11.4
Extremities	2,934	7.3
Heart impairments	1,833	4.6
Diabetes	1,437	3.6
Substance abuse	1,416	3.6
Hearing impairments	1,231	3.1
Vision impairments	1,148	2.9
Blood disorders	1,054	2.6
HIV (subcategory of blood disorder)	729	1.8
Cancer	970	2.4
Asthma	714	1.8

[b] List is incomplete; percentages therefore do not add up to 100%.

Source: Office of Program Operations, Equal Employment Opportunity Commission's Charge Data System National Data Base.

Capitol Watch

IDEA Legislation — A Positive for PT and Children with Disabilities

by Pamela Phillips
APTA Senior Lobbyist

Since enactment of Public Law 94-142, the Education for ALL Handicapped Children Act of 1975, the quality of life for children with disabilities has improved dramatically. Before enactment of this ground-breaking law, 1 million children with disabilities were excluded from school, and many were housed in institutions. Today, one of the basic goals of the Individuals with Disabilities Education Act (IDEA), which is part of the Education for ALL Handicapped Children Act, has largely been met: Children with disabilities have equal access to education. Without educational opportunities afforded to children with disabilities under IDEA, a large portion of our population would be uneducated and unemployed.

One of the many issues that the 104th Congress is reviewing is the reauthorization of IDEA. Not only does this civil rights law provide funding for special education, but it also includes funding for related services (including physical therapy) for children with disabilities throughout the United States. The current cost-cutting climate in Congress could have had the following results for IDEA: funding cuts, block grants to the states, and/or the elimination of related services.

APTA's Section on Pediatrics and APTA's Government Affairs Department have worked together to prevent this from happening by meeting with House and Senate members on the appropriate subcommittees and their staffs and by working with other associations and coalitions, such as the American Occupational Therapy Association and the Consortium for Citizens with Disabilities.

A 1995 document, "Section on Pediatrics —APTA Recommendations on the Reauthorization of the Individuals with Disabilities Act," prepared by the Section and distributed to Congressional and staff members recommends:

• Continued identification of physical therapy in Part B of the Act as a related service for children and youths with disabilities and as a primary service in Part H (currently proposed as Part

Pamela Phillips

C) for infants and toddlers with disabilities.

• Maintenance of the "highest standard" requirement for physical therapy, including state licensure for physical therapists and proper training and supervision of paraprofessionals (licensed physical therapist assistants, physical therapy aides, and classroom associates).

• Increased emphasis on the systematic monitoring of student progress toward identified outcomes. Not only would services to individual students improve, but the research base for future decision-making regarding effective and efficient service delivery also would be enhanced.

• Modification of the current definition of disability in IDEA to a functional definition similar to the definition used in Section 504 of the Rehabilitation Act and the Americans with Disabilities Act. Limitations in both academic and nonacademic areas should be included in the definition, and life activities should be defined to include all areas affecting learning, including mobility and self-care skills.

• Most importantly, the Section believes that the funding of IDEA should be increased to strengthen the following achievements:

• Employment rates of individuals with disabilities have increased dramatically. Fifty-seven percent of youths with disabilities are competitively employed within 5 years of leaving school.

• The costly institutionalization of children with disabilities has dropped drastically. Just over 1% of children with disabilities now require institutionalization.

• The drop-out rate of students with disabilities has declined significantly.

Action on IDEA has been pushed into 1996, the second session of the 104th Congress, despite the fact that IDEA was scheduled for reauthorization in 1994. In order for the program to continue, Congress approved extension until lawmakers have

time to "mark up" or review the proposed bills line by line. This session, Congress worked on the Contract with America and budget issues.

The House subcommittee succeeded in producing two drafts of legislation, which APTA and the Pediatrics Section reviewed. The Section said it was "pleased to see the continued inclusion of the major components of IDEA. New elements, such as mediation, architectural barriers, and increased reference to and involvement of parents reflect careful consideration and community input." Suggested changes were mainly technical. They include:

• Ensuring that the utilization of paraprofessionals is consistent with state laws and regulations.

• Including related services in the definition of special education.

• Including related service personnel in the Individualized Education Program if they were involved in the evaluation or provided services to the child.

The second House draft reflected the first two of these suggested changes.

By mid-November, the Senate subcommittee was still drafting a bipartisan bill. It requested that APTA submit comments before the draft was created; recommendations similar to those distributed to the House subcommittee members were submitted. In addition, the Senate held a number of hearings in which many of the witnesses mentioned the benefits of related services such as physical therapy.

Another important part of IDEA is the amount of money allocated for this program by the House and Senate Appropriations Committees. This money directly affects not only the important services that physical therapists provide to children with disabilities, but critical physical therapy education programs as well.

By mid-November, the House had completely eliminated all discretionary funding under IDEA for both "Early Childhood Education" and "Special Education Personnel Development." The Senate has recommended continued funding at 1995 levels—$25.2 million to fund IDEA's Early Education Program and $91.3 million to fund IDEA's Special Education Personnel Development Program. The two bills must go to a joint conference committee and are likely to be vetoed by President Clinton as part of the Labor–Health and Human Services–Education Appropriations bill. Members of APTA's grass-roots network, PTeam, were asked to write letters to their members of Congress in support of the Senate version.

APTA members, particularly those who work in pediatrics, are encouraged to contact representatives and senators in support of reauthorization of IDEA to ensure continued identification of physical therapy as a related service for children and youths in Part B and as a primary service in Part H (proposed as Part C) for infants and toddlers under IDEA.

A D A   L A W
by   M a r g o t   M i l l e r ,   P T

Serving as an Expert

PTs increasingly find themselves called on to provide expert opinions on ADA cases, in the workplace and in court. This unique position requires a thorough understanding of both ADA law and the responsibilities of an expert.

itle I of the Americans with Disabilities Act (ADA) prohibits discrimination against qualified individuals with disabilities in any term or condition of employment.[1] Under the ADA, employers must conduct objective, job-related testing that is individualized and specific to determine a qualified applicant or employee's ability to perform the essential functions of a job.

This requirement presents an opportunity for physical therapists. Because PTs possess a special expertise in evaluating musculoskeletal deficits and determining individuals' functional abilities, they frequently are called on to render expert opinions in ADA cases in the legal arena and the employment setting.

ADA Outside the Courtroom

PTs frequently are asked by employers to confirm or deny a match between an applicant or employee and a particular job. The PT's activities in this arena include such things as analyzing a job, writing a functional job description, developing preemployment screens, identifying reasonable accommodations for employees with disabilities, and developing and conducting functional capacity testing and job-specific testing that complies with ADA guidelines and ensures that the civil rights of persons with disabilities are not violated.

PTs also have an important role to play in determining whether a case has applicability under the ADA. Through careful analysis and evaluation of an individual's strengths and limitations, PTs are able to identify an individual's disability and determine *whether that disability interferes with that individual's ability to perform a major life activity* (a defining prerequisite for protection under the ADA).

Employers sometimes ask PTs for expert opinions on whether an individual poses a *direct threat* in the workplace. A direct threat is a significant risk to the health or safety of the individual or of others that cannot be reduced or eliminated through reasonable accommodation (eg, through a modification of policies, practices, or procedures). The ADA protects only *qualified* individuals with disabilities: If an individual is unable to safely perform the essential functions of a job even with reasonable accommodations, he or she is not a qualified individual. Under the ADA, employers are obligated to make fair, reasonable accommodations that will enable qualified individuals with disabilities to perform the required job activities. ADA is the embodiment of the idea that fair, defensible standards need not be lowered to provide employment opportunities to persons with disabilities.

The PT's role in evaluating whether an individual's employment constitutes a direct threat involves a number of steps: After determining whether the individual's disability substantially limits one or more major life activities, the PT must identify any *specific* risks posed by that individual in a particular job and determine whether the risks can be eliminated or reduced through reasonable accommodation. If they cannot, a direct threat is confirmed, and the PT would conclude that the job isn't appropriate for that person. If the risks can be eliminated or reduced, the PT's role is to identify appropriate and reasonable accommodations, which might include restructuring the workplace environment, rearranging the work or the worksite, or using specific adaptive equipment.

The following case illustrates the PT's role in determining whether an applicant or employee represents a direct threat in the workplace.

An employee had been off of work for 8 weeks because of exacerbation of multiple sclerosis symptoms. The employee's physician determined that the employee's strength, endurance, and coordination had improved, but the employee's balance continued to be problematic, and he had to use a cane most of the time. The employee believed that he was ready to return to work, but the employer didn't agree, expressing a fear that the employee could lose his balance and fall on the production floor. A PT was called in to assess the situation.

The PT first gave the employee a 2-day functional evaluation to objectively document his balance abilities with and without the cane and to evaluate his balance during functional activities, including lifting and carrying, walking on a level surface, and stair climbing. The PT obtained a job description from the employer and compared the employee's cur-

rent abilities with the critical demands of his job. She concluded that there was a match between the employee's abilities and his job, but some question remained about his ability to navigate the work floor. The employee reported that the floor typically was cluttered and that the walking aisles were extremely narrow. In addition, he stated that waste product usually was thrown on the floor and picked up at the end of the day.

The PT recommended a site visit to evaluate the employee in his work environment. She determined that the employee had no difficulty navigating the work floor using a cane and was able to walk around the waste product. However, to eliminate the possibility of any employee slipping on the waste product, the PT recommended that the employer provide containers for waste product. The employer did so, and the employee successfully returned to productive work.

This three-step approach replaced the employer's subjective perceptions and unsubstantiated fears with factual evidence regarding the employee's abilities.

PTs On the Witness Stand

PTs sometimes find themselves called on to apply the same expertise they apply in workplace ADA determinations in the courtroom—as expert witnesses in ADA cases. Certainly, ADA cases aren't the only kinds of cases in which the PTs may be called to the witness stand: PTs frequently serve as witnesses in cases involving Workers' Compensation. How different is the PT's role in an ADA case from the PT's role in a Workers' Compensation case?

According to Melanie Ellexson, MBA, OTR, FAOTA, Assistant Vice President and Executive Director of the STEPS Industrial Clinics, Schwab Rehabilitation Hospital, Chicago, Ill, and Barbara Kornblau, JD, OTR, CIRS, CCM, DAAPM, an attorney specializing in ADA cases, there's a big difference. In a typical Workers' Compensation case, the PT serves as a *fact* witness, relating the specifics of an individual's physical abilities and limitations to specific job tasks. As a fact witness, the PT's testimony is based on his or her involvement in the case. According to Ellexson and Kornblau, the issue in such cases typically is whether an individual's residual problems from injury or illness would prevent him

or her from performing a particular job. The employer does not have an obligation to make reasonable accommodations.

In an ADA case, however, the PT is asked to testify as an *expert* witness, which is different from a fact witness in that the PT is called in after the fact to offer an opinion based on his or her expertise, in a case that he or she would not necessarily have been involved with otherwise. The specifics of the PT's testimony are related not only to an employee or applicant's ability to perform the essential functions of a job, but also to that individual's ability to perform the job *with or without reasonable accommodations.*

Claude Peacock, MEd, LPC, Director of the Rehabilitation and Employment Institute of Alabama, has served as an expert witness on a number of cases. According to Peacock, before serving as an expert witness, a PT first must be knowledgeable about the ADA. Peacock recommends the technical assistance manual developed by the Equal Employment Opportunity Commission (EEOC)[2] as a good source for the kind of information about ADA that PTs who serve as expert witnesses will need. He also encourages PTs to become familiar with ADA decisions that have already been rendered.

Peacock emphasizes that documentation of objective findings—without speculation—is critical in ADA cases. In addition, he advises that a reasonable accommodation plan should be based on a holistic profile of the individual, including academic and vocational aspects as well as physical aspects. He cautions, however, that PTs on the witness stand must stay within their area of expertise—the physical accommodations—and avoid entering into vocational aspects. Peacock recommends that PTs work together with other professionals (eg, psychologists, physicians, and occupational therapists) to develop the necessary profile of the individual.

Helene Fearon, PT, also has served as an expert witness in a number of ADA cases, including the case described below.

A woman with limited eyesight applied for a job. She was presented with a job description and was told that women were not considered for employment because the work was considered too heavy. The woman told the employer that she believed that she would be able to do the work,

but she was not hired. She filed suit under the ADA, claiming that she had been denied employment because of her limited eyesight.

Fearon was called as an expert witness to investigate how the job description had been developed. In performing a functional analysis of the job, she identified the essential functions and critical demands of the job, which included frequent lifting and carrying of 75 lb or more. It was during this process that the plaintiff had to agree that, in fact, she did not have the physical capability to perform the primary job duties and that therefore, she was not a qualified individual with a disability. Neither gender discrimination nor discrimination based on the woman's limited eyesight were issues. Had the employer utilized preemployment screening early on, the above scenario probably would not have occurred.

PTs today are in a unique position to have a positive impact on the resolution of ADA cases. Whether they are serving as expert witnesses in ADA court cases, working as primary therapists for individuals with disabilities who are preparing to return to work, or assisting employers in ensuring that the process of matching employees to jobs is in compliance with the law, PTs play a critical role in ensuring that Americans with disabilities are provided the same opportunities as Americans without disabilities.

Margot Miller, PT, is Director of National Programs at Isernhagen and Associates Inc, Duluth, Minn. She has 15 years of experience in work injury management and functional evaluation of the injured worker.

The author wishes to thank Melanie Ellexson, Barbara Kornblau, Claude Peacock, Helene Fearon, and Barbara Larson, OT, Director, Health Dimensions Industrial Program, Cambridge, Minn, for their time and interest in this article.

References

1   Americans with Disabilities Act of 1990. 42 USC §12112.
2   Equal Employment Opportunity Commission. *A Technical Assistance Manual on the Employment Provisions (Title I) of the ADA.* Washington, DC: EEOC Office of Communications; 1992.

A D A   L A W
by Laurie Johnson, PT

Preemployment Screening

*Under the ADA, PTs can help ensure that job applicants' disabilities
do not automatically disqualify them for work.*

Physical therapists have always been in a unique position to assist employers in hiring employees whose physical abilities match the physical job demands. With the advent of industrial and occupational rehabilitation programs and the passage of the Americans with Disabilities Act (ADA), opportunities in these areas have been greatly enhanced.

On July 20, 1990, the ADA was signed into law. The dates established for compliance with this landmark legislation were July 29, 1992, for employers with 25 or more employees, and July 26, 1994, for employees with 15 to 24 employees.

The ADA was passed to provide persons with disabilities both comprehensive protection from discrimination in employment and access to public services. Title I of the ADA, Employment, is meant to ensure that persons with disabilities are evaluated for employment based on their qualifications and abilities and not on stereotypes or misconceptions regarding their disabilities. Title I prohibits discrimination in all aspects of employment, including application procedures, examinations, hiring, benefits, and wages.

Employers have found themselves greatly challenged by this legislation. They now are required to identify "essential job functions," develop "functional job descriptions" and "post-offer functional medical screens," and provide "reasonable accommodations" to assist in the hiring process. PTs who work with individuals with disabilities should have

a good understanding of Title I and the protection it gives to their patients; in addition, employers will benefit from working with PTs who understand the implications of Title I in regards to hiring. PTs have a tremendous opportunity in helping employers comply with the ADA and, in so doing, select qualified applicants who can perform their jobs safely and are hired without discrimination.

ADA Definitions

Articles in the physical therapy literature[1,2] have defined some of the terms and concepts contained in the ADA. Following is a brief review of some of those definitions:

Disability is defined as a physical or mental impairment that substantially limits one or more major life activities. The definition also includes having a record of such an impairment or being regarded as having such an impairment.

An individual who is *substantially limited* in regard to the major life activity of working is significantly restricted (compared to the average person with comparable work qualifications) in performing either a class of jobs or a broad range of jobs in various classes. Inability to perform a single job is not considered a substantial limitation.

Individuals who are considered *qualified* can meet the skill, education, experience, licensure, or other such requirements of the job. A qualified individual can perform the essential functions of a job either with or without reasonable accommodations. Essen-

tial functions of jobs are not specifically defined by the ADA, rather, they are determined on a job-by-job basis by analyzing individuals' job tasks.

Reasonable accommodation is any modification or adjustment to a job or the work environment that will enable a qualified individual with a disability to participate in the application process, perform essential functions, and have employment privileges that are equal to those of an employee or applicant without a disability.

Selection of Employees

Newkirk and Maxwell[3] outlined six steps in the employee selection process:

1. Preparation and posting.
2. Pre-offer inquiry and examination.
3. Agility and drug testing.
4. Employment decision.
5. Post-offer medical examination.
6. Reasonable accommodation.

The ADA defines "pre-employment" as the time before an individual begins actual work for an employer. Within this period, the "pre-offer" period is before an offer of conditional employment has been made, and the "post-offer" period is after a conditional offer has been made but before an individual begins work.

Preparation and posting (pre-offer). To comply with the ADA, employers must provide interviewing sites that are physically accessible to all applicants. Employers also must be prepared to provide reasonable accommodation (if needed) for the application and interview process. Accommodations might include such things as sign-language interpreters, applications in Braille, or qualified readers.

During a pre-offer job interview, an employer may ask an applicant if he or she can perform essential job functions with or without accommodation. PTs can work with employers in developing functional job descriptions (FJDs) that can be used as supporting documentation of the essential job functions. It is important that these job descriptions be kept current.

An FJD developed specifically for ADA purposes must determine:

- The physical demands of the job.
- The essential functions of the job.
- Job modifications (reasonable accommodations) that could be made for an individual with a disability.

In addition, a written FJD must describe and quantify the "critical demands" of a job. As defined by Isernhagen,[4] the critical demands are those essential functions of a job that require specific physical attributes and place stress on the individual when they are performed (eg, lifting, carrying, or standing). Quantifying these critical demands is necessary to conduct post-offer examinations.

Pre-offer inquiries and examinations. Title I of the ADA states that employers may not inquire about the existence, nature, or severity of a disability and may not conduct medical examinations before determining that an applicant is qualified or before making a conditional offer of employment.[5] Adherence to this condition reduces the chance that an applicant's disability or history of disability will be used as a basis for rejection of that applicant before his or her nonmedical qualifications are evaluated.

Employers may, however, state the physical requirements of the job and ask whether the applicant can perform the essential functions of a job. The FJD assists the employer at this step. At this stage, for example, it would be acceptable for an employer to ask an applicant whether he or she:

- Can lift 50 pounds from the floor.
- Can stand for 3 hours.
- Has a driver's license.

An employer also may ask an applicant to demonstrate how he or she would perform both the essential and marginal functions of the job, with or without reasonable accommodation. If the applicant indicates that he or she will need reasonable accommodation, the employer may require the applicant to produce documentation that he or she has a disability as defined by the ADA and is therefore entitled to the accommodation.[5] If the applicant is protected by the ADA, the employer must either provide reasonable accommodation (if it does not pose an undue hardship on the employer) or allow the applicant to demonstrate how he or she would perform the job with the accommodation.

Agility tests, defined as a demonstration of simulated job-related tasks where the physiological response to the testing is not measured, are not considered medical and can be administered at any time in the hiring process to all similarly situated applicants regardless of disability.[3] However, if such tests have the effect of screening out individuals with disabilities, the employer must demonstrate that the test is job-related and consistent with business necessity and that performance of the job cannot be achieved with reasonable accommodation.[3]

The Employment Decision

An employer is not required to hire an applicant with a disability if he or she is not the most qualified applicant or if he or she is unable to perform the essential functions of the job even with reasonable accommodation. However, if a qualified applicant with a disability is not hired or given a conditional offer of employment, that decision must not be related to the disability alone.

Post-offer medical (entrance) examinations. The ADA is very specific in defining the timing and scope of medical examinations. After a conditional offer of employment, Title I allows employers to require medical examinations and make disability-related inquiries.[5] These medical examinations and inquires must be given to all applicants for jobs in the same category. Information collected through the examinations must be kept separate from other records and be treated as confidential, and the results can only be used in compliance with the ADA.

In the post-offer hiring stage, the job analysis and FJD can be used to assist the employer and PT in developing a functional medical exam. The following protocol for setting up such an exam was suggested by Miller[6]:

1. Perform a functional job analysis or review an accurate FJD. With the employer, identify the critical demands.

2. Select the functional activities to be performed, and verify with the employer that they can be performed safely at the work site.

3. Evaluate whether the selected functional activities are job-related. Involve the employer in this process.

4. Establish an evaluation protocol to include consent form, explanation, history, musculoskeletal evaluation, functional activities, scoring, and release of results.

5. Require and monitor safety during screening.

6. Involve the employer in establishing a minimum level of performance necessary to perform the critical demands.

7. Provide an evaluation summary to include:
   a. Critical demands evaluated.
   b. Minimum criteria for each critical demand.
   c. Whether critical demand was met.
   d. Recommendations to employer regarding test results (the responsibility for hiring criteria and the final hiring decision is the employer's).

If an applicant is identified as having a disability (as defined by the ADA), and the medical evaluation concludes that the applicant cannot perform the essential job functions or in performing them would cause a direct threat to him- or herself or others, the employer must be prepared to offer an opportunity for the applicant to demonstrate that he or she can perform the essential job functions with reasonable accommodation. If an applicant at the post-offer stage requests accommodation, the employer may require documentation of that individual's disability in order to assess the applicant's entitlement to reasonable accommodation.

To reject an individual from a job, the medical evaluation must support the conclusion that:

1. If employed, the applicant would pose a direct threat to the safety of himself or herself and others.

2. The applicant cannot perform the essential job functions even with reasonable accommodation.

Again, only information that is job-related or consistent with business necessity can be used to reject an individual from a job. Therefore, it is very important that the medical examinations include evaluation of the applicant's functional capacity to perform the job, and that the reports reflect the functional abilities and limitations of the individual as they relate to the job. Medical exams must be objective and must not be used with the intent of screening out qualified applicants and employees with disabilities; rather, they should be used to determine reasonable accommodation and ensure proper job placement.

The ADA offers many challenges and opportunities to persons with disabilities, employers, and PTs. If all three join together in partnership and strive to understand and comply with Title I, the challenge of identifying and employing qualified individuals with disabilities can and will be met. Proper job analysis, accurate FJDs, appropriate functional evaluations, identification of accommodations for work tasks, and matching workers to the work will result in a safer and more productive work place for all employees.

Laurie Johnson, PT, is a physical therapist and faculty member of Isernhagen and Associates, Duluth, Minn.

References

1 Connolly JB. Understanding the ADA. *Clinical Management.* 1992;12(2):40-45.
2 Miller M. Serving as an expert. *PT—Magazine of Physical Therapy.* 1995;4(2):26,28.
3 Newkirk WL, Maxwell B. *Occupational Health Services: Practical Strategies for Improving Quality and Controlling Costs.* Chicago, Ill: American Hospital Publishing; 1993.
4 Isernhagen S. Reconciling realism with reality: the Americans with Disabilities Act. *Industrial Rehabilitation Quarterly.* 1991;summer:8,14-15, 18-19.
5 *Enforcement Guidance: Preemployment Disability-Related Inquiries and Medical Examinations Under the Americans with Disabilities Act of 1990.* ADA Division, Office of Legal Counsel, Equal Employment Opportunity Commission; 1994.
6 Miller M. *The Comprehensive Guide to Work Injury Management.* Gaithersburg, Md: Aspen Publishers Inc; 1995.

Suggested Readings

Maroldo RA, ed. *The ADA's Impact on the Employment Relationship: An Explanation of Selected Employment Regulations.* Horsham, Pa: LRP Publications; 1994.
Lotito MJ, Alvarez FP, Pimental R. *The Americans with Disabilities Act: Making the ADA Work for You.* Northridge, Calif: Milt Wright and Associates Inc; 1992.
The Americans with Disabilities Act Questions and Answers. National Institute on Disability and Rehabilitation Research; 1991.
Wyrick J. Reasonable accommodation: capstone to the ADA. *Advance for Occupational Therapists.* 1992;Jan 27:8.

Capitol Watch

PTs Help Make IDEA a Reality

In June, President Clinton signed a reauthorization of the Individuals with Disabilities Education Act (IDEA) in a formal ceremony on the White House lawn. The symbolic act validated the efforts of many students, parents, teachers, school administrators, special interest groups, and professionals committed to making free and appropriate education accessible to children with disabilities.

The reauthorized IDEA is an updated version of the landmark civil rights law that was first enacted in 1975 to ensure that "all children with disabilities have available to them...a free appropriate public education which emphasizes special education and related services designed to meet their individual needs."

Physical therapists retain a vital role under the reauthorized IDEA as providers of related services. If PTs are involved in the evaluation of or provide services to the child, they may also participate in Individualized Education Programs (IEPs), the personalized plans developed by parents, teachers, counselors, and related personnel that are a cornerstone of IDEA implementation.

"The physical therapy services provided are based on the individual needs of the child," says Susan Effgen, PhD, PT, Legislative Chair for APTA's Pediatrics Section. "A child with Down syndrome might get X, whereas a child with cerebral palsy might get Y. The point is to come up with a cohesive, appropriate plan. It all comes down to what decisions are made by the student, the parents, and faculty in the IEP meetings."

Effgen and Loretta Knutson, PhD, PT, PCS, President of the Pediatrics Section, attended the IDEA signing ceremony and thanked President Clinton on behalf of concerned physical therapists. Although Knutson and Effgen officially represented the approximately 5,000 pediatric physical therapists in their Section, in a greater sense they

stood for all the physical therapists who have campaigned over the years to secure and maintain an equitable education for children with disabilities.

"Because this law affects children with disabilities and their families, it affects all of society," says Knutson. "We have an obligation to ensure that federal and state education dollars go toward the education of all children." Knutson notes that the growing number of physical therapists working in school systems increases the profession's responsibility on education issues.

Prior to IDEA, children with disabilities often were segregated into alternate schools or classrooms, were held to lower standards, and received inferior educations. "We cannot have an educational system that is defined by low expectations for any child—disabled and nondisabled," said Education Secretary Richard Riley, at the June signing ceremony.

Susan Effgen has worked on IDEA since its enactment 21 years ago. She first stood and delivered before a US Department of Education committee in 1975, when the original IDEA guidelines scantily defined physical therapy as "the treatment of atrophied muscles." She went to bat again on IDEA issues when she gave testimony at a July hearing of the Department of Education's Office of Special Education Programs (OSEP). Last spring, Effgen participated in interprofessional working groups that collaborated to craft bill language that met the satisfaction of nearly everyone involved.

"We wanted to ensure that physical therapy was still included as a related service and that the highest professional standards were maintained," says Effgen. IDEA requires that physical therapists utilized by IDEA be licensed in their state. The reauthorized IDEA also includes physical therapist assistants, who likewise must be certified or licensed in accordance with state law.

When IDEA was sunsetting 3 years ago, efforts to renew the law were impeded by budgetary problems. In a now infamous winter of discontent in Washington, the federal government shut down due to both record snows and a deadlock between the White House and Capitol Hill over proposed budgets. IDEA, which was in the works at this time, was shunted aside in the midst of federal employee furloughs and hastily drafted omnibus bills.

IDEA as it now exists resembles a version that died in the 104th Congress. But that and other reauthorization proposals were detained by the conflicting efforts of many different factions lobbying Congress. Some special interests represented teachers and school administrators, who balked at mainstreaming students and assuming high legal costs; others were special education teachers, health professionals, and civil rights activists, who sought to protect the interests of the students themselves. "It finally took someone saying 'enough is enough'," says Knutson.

The current reauthorization began in the House as HR 5, introduced by Rep Bill Goodling (R-Penn), Chair of the House Education and Workforce Committee, in January and was introduced in the Senate as S216 by Sen James Jeffords (R-Vt), Chair of the Senate Labor and Human Resources Committee.

Therapists involved with new IDEA give a lot of credit to David Hoppe, Chief of Staff to Senate Majority Leader Trent Lott (R-Miss). Last spring Hoppe, whose son has Down syndrome, organized weekly working groups of special interest representatives and other Hill staffers to help craft a piece of legislation aimed at unanimous approval. As a result, of all the votes cast on Capitol Hill, only three Representatives and one Senator opposed the bill.

Winfield Crigler, a lobbyist who worked on IDEA reauthorization for 2 years, says, "This was far outside the normal legislative process and may prove to be a model for difficult bills in the future."

Despite the Presidential seal of approval and the enactment of the revamped IDEA into law, advocates are worried about funding for the program, which has traditionally fallen far short of the federal government's obligation. "APTA has concerns about the annual federal government appropriation for IDEA, which has an obligation to provide 40% of the average cost of educating children with special needs," said Pamela Phillips, senior lobbyist for the Association. "Currently, the government is providing only 7% for the program and unfortunately, this percentage does not increase in the Clinton Administration's proposed FY 1998 budget."

Sen Judd Gregg (R-NH) has led a movement in the US House of Representatives to get Congress to assume greater fiscal responsibility for programs already in place, rather than creating new initiatives. Gregg and a contingent of lawmakers concerned about the gap in federal funding for IDEA offered an amendment to the bill calling for an increase in federal contributions over the next 7 years. The bill was withdrawn, however, when the House Appropriations Committee assured that they would increase federal contributions to IDEA over the FY 97 level.

One of the few stumbling blocks to the passage of IDEA was a provision that would have permitted the cessation of services for disciplinary reasons with little warning. Critics were fearful that such a provision could be used by school systems as a pretext to eliminate costly services to students. The compromise solution was to compel schools to institute a "behavior management plan" for the student as part of his or her IEP prior to any expulsion. "This measure makes the school take some responsibility a priori instead of post hoc," Effgen explains.

Physical therapists remain involved with IDEA. Although the public law was officially reauthorized on June 4, 1997, when President Clinton signed the bill, new rules and regulations for compliance are still pending. OSEP has deputized the nonprofit National Parent Network on Disabilities to draft consensual language for the rules and regulations, and APTA and the Pediatrics Section have submitted recommendations. APTA also testified in regard to the new IDEA regulations in Washington, DC, on July 16. When the proposed regulations are published in the *Federal Register*, all concerned parties will have a 90-day comment period, and APTA will provide comments in the proposed rules.

Knutson points out that the Pediatrics Section first published guidelines for therapists practicing in an educational environment nearly a decade ago, a document that is in the process of being reissued. "The rule of thumb is not to administer treatment that is not directly related to function," she says. Adds Effgen, "PTs working with students must constantly think about how the service they're providing relates to education, how does it help the child get from point a to point b."

Even though she recently stepped down as the Section Legislative Chair, Susan Effgen says she will continue to track IDEA activities and urge other PTs to do the same. "We must be vigilant in our role of ensuring an appropriate, quality education for our children. It's a nev-erending effort."

—Steve Davolt

ADA Case Law

by Laurie A Walsh, PT, Esq

Technical Standards in Education Programs

Federal law prohibits discrimination against qualified persons with disabilities in college admissions decisions. Here's a look at how that law is being interpreted.

Institutions of higher learning, including physical therapy education programs, frequently are uncertain about what accommodations are appropriate for them to provide for students with documented disabilities. For example, there may be questions about the technical requirements an education program can impose. This column will describe the basic legal principles involved in the use of technical standards in institutions of higher learning, with a review of statutory and case law. Although few of the reported cases or administrative decisions specifically address technical standards for physical therapy education programs, some aspects of these decisions can be extrapolated to PT and PTA education programs.

Under the Americans with Disabilities Act (ADA),[1] colleges and universities are prohibited from discriminating against qualified students with disabilities. The Rehabilitation Act of 1973[2] (specifically Section 504 of Title V) also prohibits such discrimination by institutions that receive federal financial assistance, which means that the vast majority of colleges and universities are subject to the provisions of both laws. Essentially, both laws require educational institutions to provide qualified persons with disabilities opportunities to participate in the programs and services they offer that are equal to the opportunities provided to persons without disabilities.

The ADA does not specifically address what colleges and universities must do to avoid discriminating against students with disabilities; those regulations were addressed years earlier under the Rehabilitation Act. ADA regulations do state that when the ADA grants protection equal to or less than that provided by Title V of the Rehabilitation Act, the standards of Title V shall be used. Consequently, given the relative silence of the ADA in this area, courts and administrative bodies look to the standards of the Rehabilitation Act for guidance when issues regarding alleged discriminations by colleges and universities are raised.

The Rehabilitation Act requires institutions to offer qualified students with documented disabilities appropriate academic adjustments, accommodations, or aids to enable those students to have equal educational opportunities. The implementing federal regulations[3] of the Rehabilitation Act provide some specifics as to what institutions of higher learning must do to accommodate students with disabilities. Modifications such as granting students extensions of time to complete graduation requirements, developing course substitutions, and adapting the manner in which specific courses are conducted are all specifically recognized in the *Code of Federal Regulations* as appropriate academic adjustments. The use of instructional aids, such as taped texts, interpreters, and adapted classroom equipment, also are specifically identified as appropriate.

The obligation to provide such adjustments and aids, however, is extended only to *qualified* students with disabilities. To be qualified, a student must be able to meet the academic and technical standards the institution requires for any student to be admitted into, participate in, and graduate from the program. Standards that can be shown to be essential to the program will not be considered discriminatory.[3]

The concept of academic standards is well understood; it typically refers to a student's grade point average or another specific level of academic achievement necessary for the student to gain admission or remain in good standing. A growing number of academic institutions, however, are also developing *technical standards*, additional, nonacademic requirements that a student must be able to meet to participate meaningfully in the program and, in the case of health care professional education programs, to demonstrate the skills required for safe and effective practice.

Legal Cases

Cases that address the issue of technical standards can be found both among reported court cases and among complaints addressed to the US Department of Education's Office for Civil Rights (OCR). The OCR has authority under both the ADA and the Rehabilitation Act to adjudicate complaints alleging discrimination by colleges and universities. The OCR is an administrative body whose decisions are subject to court review, just as lower court decisions may be reviewed by higher courts. As the federal agency with designated expertise in this area, however, OCR's determinations would be given a great deal of deference by a reviewing court.

Southeastern Community College v Davis.[4] No discussion of technical standards would be complete without a discussion of the leading US Supreme Court case in this area. In this case, a licensed practical nurse who had been diagnosed with a bilateral sensorineural hearing loss applied for admission to a program to obtain a degree in registered nursing. The applicant provided documentation that established that she was required to lip-read and use a hearing aid to communicate effectively, and that close personal supervision by a nursing instructor would be necessary for her to complete the clinical requirements of the program.

The nursing school denied admission. Experts they had consulted, including the executive director of the state nursing board, stated that the applicant could not safely complete the required clinical training program because of her disability. Her reliance on lipreading, for example, would make effective communication impossible during procedures that required use of surgical masks. Consequently, the nursing school had concluded that the applicant was not "otherwise qualified" under the Rehabilitation Act to participate in the program.

The applicant sued, arguing that the program could be modified to allow her to safely complete the program. According to the applicant, the program could provide her with individual supervision by an instructor when she was directly attending patients and could waive required course work where effective verbal communication was a necessity.

The applicant first sued the school in a US district court, which agreed with the school, indicating that the applicant's disability prevented her from functioning safely in either the program or her proposed profession. A circuit court of appeals reversed that decision, stating that the Rehabilitation Act required the school to consider the applicant's qualifications without regard to her hearing and to consider program modifications without regard to expense or difficulty.

The US Supreme Court, however, reversed the circuit court and rejected the applicant's arguments, laying the foundation for many of the current principles of academic accommodation and technical standards, as follows:

1. An academic program, in keeping with the regulations promulgated under the Rehabilitation Act, is free to establish technical standards essential to participation in that particular academic program. In this case, the standards involved a legitimate physical qualification: the ability to communicate orally.

2. Although the regulations require programs to make adjustments to accommodate persons with disabilities, the law does not require institutions to fundamentally alter programs or accept undue financial and administrative burdens to accommodate a student. In this case, the requested adjustments (one-on-one supervision and waiver of required aspects of clinical work) were considered by the Court to be fundamental alterations of the program.

3. A program is not required to modify its curriculum just because a student with a disability can perform effectively in some areas of practice but not in others. In this case, the Court noted that the applicant could have worked effectively in some areas of nursing practice; however, the program in question was designed to educate professionals able "to perform all normal roles of a registered nurse." According to the Court, this constituted legitimate academic policy on the part of the program, and the law did not require the program to lower its standards to admit the applicant.

Following *Davis,* the US Supreme Court clarified the issue of a federally funded program's responsibility to make modifications for persons with disabilities, stating in *Alexander v Choate*[5] that programs must analyze any requested modifications

ADA Case Law

to determine if they are reasonable adjustments. Although a program is not required to make fundamental alterations, it still must make reasonable accommodation to otherwise qualified students.

Thomas Jefferson University.[6] In this case, an individual with C-5 quadriplegia was denied admission to a medical school. The case report noted that he had "very limited use of his arms and hands" and limited sensation in "his hands, arms, legs and posterior." His grade point average and Medical College Admissions Test (MCAT) scores were sufficient to make him competitive with other applicants, but he was denied admission because of his failure to meet the school's technical standards.

Those standards required, in part, that applicants have "a) sufficient use of the senses of vision and hearing and somatic sensation necessary to perform a physical examination using palpation, auscultation and percussion; and b) the ability to learn and perform certain laboratory and diagnostic procedures." The university argued that, owing to his disability, the applicant would be unable to perform many aspects of a complete physical examination.

This was not the end of the discussion, however. The university still had to consider whether there were reasonable adjustments that would permit the applicant to meet the requirements. The only requested adjustment that would have done so was to permit a surrogate, or aide, to perform these tasks in class and laboratory experiences. The university argued that this would not be acceptable because it would be the surrogate, not the applicant, who would be learning and performing these tasks. The student brought a complaint before the OCR.

The OCR agreed that the adjustment was unacceptable because "the complainant would not be actually acquiring the skills necessary for the practice of medicine." Consequently, the OCR ruled that the applicant was not a qualified indi-

vidual within the meaning of the Rehabilitation Act, and the admission denial was upheld.

A similar case was decided by the Supreme Court of Ohio. In *Ohio Civil Rights Commission v Case Western University,*[7] a medical school applicant who had lost her vision argued that the use of an intermediary to perform such technical requirements as reading radiographs, viewing slides through a microscope, or performing the surgical rotation was a reasonable accommodation. The applicant also

ADA CASE LAW

asked whether these requirements could be waived.

In this case, the college's technical requirements were based on standards contained in the Association of American Medical Colleges' *Report of the Special Advisory Panel on Technical Standards for Medical School Admission,*[8] which stated that medical school applicants must "be able to observe a patient accurately," that "observation necessitates the functional use of the sense of vision and somatic sensation," and that "the use of an intermediary means that a candidate's judgment must be mediated by someone else's power of selection and observation." The court rejected the applicant's argument, stating that "the use of an intermediary would interfere with the student's exercise of independent judgment—a crucial part of developing diagnostic skills." The court also rejected requiring waivers, noting that the purpose of medical schools is to produce a general practitioner with "the knowledge and skills to function in a broad variety of clinical situations and to render care to a wide variety of patients."

Doherty v Southern College of Optometry.[9] This case involved a student with retinitis pigmentosa, a disorder that limited his visual field, and an unidentified neurological condition that impaired his motor skills, touch sensation, and coordination. During the student's freshman year in the 4-year optometry program at Southern College of Optometry (SCO), the college added a pathology clinical proficiency requirement for 4th-year students. The requirement set a mandatory level of clinical proficiency involving examination techniques with certain instruments. By the student's 4th year, he was unable to demonstrate the required level of proficiency, despite having been given an extra quarter to practice. The college refused to grant him a degree, and the student sued, alleging, among other things, that the college had violated the Rehabilitation Act.

The student requested a waiver of the clinical proficiency requirement as a reasonable accommodation. His argument was based on several points, including the facts that the proficiency requirement was imposed after he was admitted to the program and that the techniques and instruments in question were not widely used by optometrists in their practices.

The court denied the student's argument. The college's policy established that each school year was governed by that year's college catalog, which contained statements that changes might be necessary "from time to time" and that the catalog should not be considered a contract. The court found that, although the college could not impose retroactive requirements, it could establish additional technical standards for work not yet completed, as it had done in this case.

The court also denied that the waiver of the proficiency requirement was a reasonable accommodation. According to the court, the fact that the instruments in question were not yet widely used in clinics did not make the requirement unreasonable; the court noted that their use was increasing as more states broadened optometry practice acts to permit their use. An education program, stated the court, is free to "set standards for its program that ensure a particular level of competence in particular areas." The court noted that a program is "not required to accommodate a handicapped individual by eliminating a course requirement which is reasonably necessary to proper use of the degree conferred at the end of a course of study."

Specific to Physical Therapy

There is little in the legal literature that specifically addresses technical standards for physical therapy education programs. The case of *Blackhawk Technical College,*[10] described below, is the first legal case this author has found related to physical therapy education programs. Unfortunately, the

decision in this case is a brief letter opinion from the OCR that details few of the facts of the case—but it does address some basic points specific to physical therapy education.

A student with a right above-knee amputation sought to obtain a degree as a physical therapist assistant (PTA). The education program to which she applied had developed a list of essential job functions of PTAs that students would be required to master to complete the program successfully. The essential functions had been identified through a review of the academic research literature and with the input of an advisory board consisting of PTs and PTAs.

In this case, the essential functions at issue were "assisting patients with gait training with parallel bars and on stairs, assisting patients on crutches and patient transfer such as from a bed to a tilt table and from a mat to a wheelchair." The student admitted that she would not be able to perform those activities. Pursuant to her rights under the Rehabilitation Act, she suggested modifications in the performance of these functions (which, unfortunately, were not specifically identified in the decision). The college rejected the requested modifications, stating that they "would not deliver the therapeutic benefit for which the function is intended or would be unsafe in [their] execution." The college then advised the student that she could submit alternative modifications for review and that a place in the clinical portion of the program would be reserved for her, pending submission of acceptable modifications.

The student brought a complaint before the OCR, alleging, among other things, that the failure to modify the requirements constituted discrimination. OCR, however, dismissed her complaint; they found that the college had used an appropriate method for determining the skills necessary to the current practice of PTAs. The college also had performed what OCR considered an appropriate review of the student's requested modifications, and the OCR determined that the college's rejection of those requests was based on "legitimate concerns for the delivery of therapeutic benefit and the safety of patients." The college's refusal to admit the student to the clinical portion of the program was upheld.

As the preceding cases show, education programs may develop appropriate technical standards for students. Case law has required that those standards reflect current practice and essential functions required for safe and effective practice and that the standards not be used merely as a pretext for excluding students with disabilities. As noted in *Doherty*, schools may also identify emerging practice patterns and techniques as essential. The cases above indicate that technical requirements might

be formally adopted in the form of a technical standards document or might be established through other means, such as reference to research literature, expert testimony, and other existing program requirements.

The Blackhawk decision gives one example of what the law considers to be an appropriate method for developing the content of technical standards in physical therapy education: review of current literature and consultation with practitioners. Recent publications continue to add to the body of literature identifying essential functions in physical therapy,[11-14] and many of these resources describe specific items that might be included in technical standards.

It should be noted, however, that the Blackhawk decision involved a PTA education program. Although the basic principles regarding technical standards would

also apply to PT education programs, specific items constituting technical standards would certainly be different in the different types of programs.

Ingram[11,12] surveyed directors of accredited professional physical therapy programs in the United States on their opinions about which activities constituted essential functions in physical therapist practice. A list of specific assessment and treatment activities was generated. The study found that survey respondents tended to rank assessment procedures higher than treatment procedures. Some of the respondents implied that many treatment activities could be delegated by PTs and therefore were less essential.

There is some question whether the physical performance of certain tasks in physical therapist practice could be considered nonessential if those tasks can be dele-

ADA CASE LAW

gated.[15] We do not know how a court would treat this question; however, the argument might be made that, because a PT's practice encompasses all the tasks that are also within PTA practice, and PTAs are required to practice under the supervision of a PT, the PT should be at least as proficient as his or her subordinates in any given task. It is possible that a court could find that the ability to delegate a task does not render it nonessential. This reasoning would also be in keeping with the principle noted in *Davis* and *Ohio Civil Rights Commission* that programs educate general practitioners. Graduates would probably be expected to master, with or without reasonable accommodations, the skills needed to function within the broad scope of physical therapy practice. In any case, determination that a particular task is an essential requirement does not end the analysis. Under the law, a program must *always* consider whether a reasonable accommodation exists to meet the requirement.

Application of Standards

In the implementation of technical standards, decisions must be made on a case-by-case basis. Each student's abilities will be different, different requirements may be implicated, and different accommodations may be requested. It is important to note that there are individuals with significant disabilities, including complete blindness or quadriplegia, who have successfully completed academic programs for health care providers. A program may voluntarily choose to waive a requirement that a student is unable to fulfill because of a disability and for which no reasonable accommodation exists. The school might choose to do so because the student has other particular strengths, skills, or credentials that the school believes would enable that person to contribute to the profession despite limitations imposed by the disability. The law does not *prohibit* programs from voluntarily making fundamental alterations to accommodate a student's inability to meet all the essential requirements, but the law does not *require* those alterations.

Technical requirements should be periodically reviewed and updated. As the court noted in *Davis,*

> It is possible to envision situations where an insistence on continuing past requirements and practices might arbitrarily deprive genuinely qualified [persons with disabilities] of the opportunity to partici-

pate in a covered program. Technological advances can be expected to enhance opportunities to rehabilitate [persons with disabilities] or otherwise qualify them for some useful employment. Such advances also may enable attainment of those goals without imposing undue financial and administrative burdens on a State. Thus, situations may arise where a refusal to modify an existing program might become unreasonable and discriminatory.[4]

In addition, as the roles of PTs and PTAs continue to evolve, existing technical requirements may become obsolete, while others might need to be added. Which specific tasks are to be considered essential requirements will be determined by individual programs, according to the legitimate needs of the profession. Resources such as federal disability law, legal cases and other decisions, and expert opinion and professional literature can guide programs in the development of essential technical requirements.*PT*

....

Laurie A Walsh, PT, Esq, is Assistant Professor, Physical Therapy Program, Daemen College, Amherst, NY. She can be reached via e-mail at lwalsh@daemen.edu.

References

1 The Americans with Disabilities Act of 1990, 42 USC §§ 12101 et seq.
2 Rehabilitation Act of 1973, 29 USC §§ 791 et seq.
3 Nondiscrimination on the basis of handicap in programs and activities receiving federal financial assistance. 34 CFR §104.
4 *Southeastern Community College v Davis*, 442 US 397 (1979).
5 *Alexander v Choate*, 469 US 287 (1985).
6 *Thomas Jefferson University* (PA), 1 NDLR 229 (1990).
7 *Ohio Civil Rights Commission v Case Western University.* 666 NE2d 1376 (1996).
8 *Report of the Special Advisory Panel on Technical Standards for Medical School Admission.* Washington, DC: Association of American Medical Colleges; 1979.
9 *Doherty v Southern College of Optometry*, 862 F2d 570 (6th Cir 1988), cert denied, 493 US 810 (1989).
10 *Blackhawk Technical College.* OCR Docket No. 05942176 (1995).
11 Ingram D. Essential functions required by physical therapist and physical therapist assistant programs. *Journal of Physical Therapy Education.* 1994;8(2):57-59.
12 Ingram D. Opinions of physical therapy education program directors on essential functions. *Phys Ther.* 1997;77:37-45.
13 *Guide to Physical Therapist Practice.* Alexandria, Va: American Physical Therapy Association; 1997.
14 Commission on Accreditation in Physical Therapy Education. *Evaluative Criteria for Accreditation of Education Programs for the Preparation of Physical Therapists.* Alexandria, Va: American Physical Therapy Association; 1998.
15 Mirone J. ADA Q&A. *PT—Magazine of Physical Therapy.* 1993;1(6):39-40.

Suggested Reading

Technical Assistance Manual on the Employment Provisions (Title I) of the Americans with Disabilities Act. Washington, DC: US Equal Employment Opportunity Commission; 1992.

Automony/Collaboration/ Communication

by Rita Arriaga, PT, MS

Stories From the Front—
Part Three: Consultation

*A real-life scenario illustrates some basic
risk-management principles.*

In November, **PT** began a three-part Liability Awareness series that adapted actual cases from the APTA-endorsed professional liability insurance claims history and discussed what risk-management techniques could have been used to reduce risk. **PT** concludes the series with this final case study.

The following scenario presents a common situation in the clinic in which PTs seek advice or consultation from one another. In this particular case, the primary therapist asks a peer to see a patient and provide input regarding treatment. Although this in itself is not unusual or inappropriate, clinicians do need to be aware of related risk-management considerations.

In our desire to help each other and our patients, we cannot neglect risk-management considerations in our behaviors and actions.

As you read the scenario, consider the following questions:

❖ What are the elements in this scenario that increase the PT's risk of professional liability?

❖ What risk-management techniques could have been used to reduce that risk?

A 40-year old woman was referred to a physical therapy clinic for treatment of recurrent cervical pain, associated muscle spasms, and limited mobility affecting some functional activities. The patient was examined by a PT who learned through the subjective history that, in addition to her cervical complaints, the woman had experienced temporomandibular joint (TMJ) problems in the past. However, at the time of her physical therapy treatment, she was not undergoing any treatment for that dysfunction.

The PT initiated a course of treatment for the patient's cervical symptoms, but after 2 weeks, significant reduction in the patient's pain and improved functional mobility had not been achieved.

The therapist knew that another PT in the clinic was taking a long-term manual therapy course. Noting that the PT had a cancellation in her schedule that afternoon, he approached the other PT and asked her if she would see his patient and give him her recommendations regarding his current treatment program. The second PT gladly agreed.

The primary PT then explained to his patient that, if she concurred, he would like another therapist in the clinic to examine her. He explained that he wanted the other PT's opinion to assure himself that he had considered all possible treatment approaches to try to achieve symptom relief for the patient's cervical problem. The patient agreed, and the PT brought the consulting therapist into the treatment booth.

The primary PT quickly gave a brief description of the patient's symptoms to the consulting PT and described his intervention to date. He handed her the patient's chart and then excused himself for a few moments to talk to his next patient who had arrived for a scheduled appointment.

The consulting PT did not look at the chart. Instead, she began her own physical examination of the patient. After observing the patient's active movement of the neck and asking about symptoms, the consulting PT began gentle passive movements. During the course of this part of the examination, the patient complained of the immediate onset of jaw pain when the consulting PT moved her head.

The patient refused further examination and quickly left the clinic. It was only then that the consulting PT looked at the patient's chart and saw the notation by the primary PT that the patient had a history of TMJ problems. The primary PT, upon returning to the booth, acknowledged that he had failed to verbally advise his colleague of this pre-existing history before he asked for her consultation. His colleague, in turn admitted that she had not taken any precautions for the TMJ in her examination because she assumed the primary PT would have warned her if the patient had a history of any such problem.

The patient did not return for physical therapy treatment and, subsequently, required several TMJ surgeries. She filed a complaint, citing both therapists with malpractice and negligence in their failure to consider her TMJ history and take appropriate precautions during their examination. *Now turn the page for commentary on this scenario from a risk-management perspective, including a table summarizing risky elements and strategies to address them.*

liability awareness

The primary PT did not fully inform the consulting PT of the patient's history, including her TMJ problems.

When asking for even the most informal consultation from a colleague, it's essential to provide the other clinician with full information regarding the patient's history and your intervention to date.

The consulting PT failed to perform a thorough history of her own before applying evaluative techniques. She did not take time to review the patient's chart before she began the examination.

Even in an informal consultative situation ("Oh, by the way, do you have time to see this patient with me?"), the consulting PT must conduct a thorough subjective history before initiating any type of physical exam. Through chart review and patient interview, the consulting PT could have become aware of the patient's relevant medical history.

It is common for PTs to seek advice from one another in the clinic. In our efforts to relieve our patients' symptoms and improve their function, most of us have had the experience of seeking recommendations from a peer, frequently without prior formal arrangements. In some clinic settings, co-treatments are opportunities to both maximize the efficacy of our interventions and learn from one another. However, as this scenario illustrates, in our desire to help each other and our patients, we cannot neglect risk-management considerations in our behaviors and actions.

When asking a colleague to participate or consult in direct patient care, although you retain your role as the primary PT, you are asking your colleague to establish a patient-therapist relationship.

The primary PT carries the responsibility of fully apprising the consulting PT of his or her patient's prior and/or related medical problems. The consulting PT should be completely aware of the patient's history by performing a chart review or querying the primary PT before conducting an examination. Neither PT should make assumptions prior to conducting an examination, evaluation, or intervention.

A review of APTA documents, including the *Standards of Practice* and the *Guide to*

Physical Therapist Practice will make you aware of professional expectations in patient interactions. (PT)

Rita Arriaga, PT, MS, is Assistant Clinical Professor in the Graduate Program of Physical Therapy, University of California at San Francisco, and is a member of APTA's Committee on Risk Management Services and Member Benefits.

Suggested Readings

Arriaga R. Stories from the front—part one: delegation. *PT—Magazine of Physical Therapy.* 1998; 6(7):27-28.

Arriaga R. Stories from the front—part two: utilization of support staff. *PT—Magazine of Physical Therapy.* 1998; 6(9):31-32.

Arriaga R. Stories from the front—part three: practice across state lines. *PT—Magazine of Physical Therapy.* 1998; 6(10):31-32.

Arriaga R. Stories from the front—part one: supervision. *PT—Magazine of Physical Therapy.* 1999; 7(11):55-56.

Arriaga R. Stories from the front—part two: modalities. *PT—Magazine of Physical Therapy.* 1999; 7(12):60-61.

Do you have risk management questions or concerns? Information about what PTs need or want to know will help APTA's efforts to educate members about the types of claims occurring in the workplace and about appropriate risk-management techniques. Contact Jennifer Baker, Director, APTA Insurance and Member Benefit Services, at 800/999-2782, ext 3145 or via e-mail at jenniferbaker@apta.org.

APTA Announces Its Risk Management Toolkit

Everything you need for your risk-management reference library! The kit includes the first two publications in APTA's Professional Issues Learning Series, including both volumes of *Ethics in Physical Therapy* and both volumes of *Law & Liability,* and two copies of 25 of the risk-management brochure *Pearls for Physical Therapists.* For details on ordering, call the APTA Service Center at 800/999-2782, ext 3395 or visit the online catalog on APTA's Web site at www.apta.org.

liability awareness

by Rita Arriaga, PT, MS

Stories From the Front— Part Three: Communication with Other Health Care Providers

A real-life scenario illustrates some basic risk-management principles.

For the third year in a row, **PT** is featuring a three-part Liability Awareness series presenting cases adapted from the APTA-endorsed professional liability insurance claims history. This year's series began in January with a look at physical therapist assistants (PTAs) and safe practice[1] and continued in February with an examination of the needs and responsibilities of recent graduates of physical therapy programs.[2] This final case study in the current series highlights the need for physical therapists (PTs) to communicate with other health care providers in the interest of optimal patient care.

As you read the scenario, consider these questions:

❖ What are the elements in this scenario that increase the PT's liability risk?

❖ What risk-management techniques could have been used to reduce that risk?

This case involved a 46-year-old man who had been involved in an altercation during a recreational ice hockey game and went to his primary care physician the next day, reporting stiffness in his neck. The physician referred the man to a PT, who saw the patient 3 days after the accident.

The patient had severe pain in his cervical spine, severe headaches, and pain in his right jaw. His cervical flexion was only 10%, and he had no other cervical motion without severe pain. He reported occasional tingling sensations that he described as minimal in his right arm and was experiencing severe muscle spasms in his neck. The PT scheduled him for three visits a week and put him on a program of slowly progressive physical therapy.

Over the next week and a half, the patient experienced progress, though the tingling in his arm remained the same. His forward flexion and rotation improved by 45%, his side bending improved by 30%, and his back bending improved by 10%. He reported that his muscle spasms were not as severe and that he was sleeping more comfortably at night.

Twelve days after the patient's initial visit to the PT, he cancelled an appointment because he had the flu and was vomiting. He also told the PT over the phone that the tingling in his arm had increased and that he had some numbness in his hand.

The patient resumed his visits to the PT 2 days later and said that he was continuing to have heightened numbness and tingling. At the next visit, $2^1/2$ weeks after the initial examination, the PT, expressing concern about the continued numbness and tingling, suggested that the patient call his primary care physician and seek a referral to an orthopedist. The patient did so, but the physician suggested, instead, that the patient continue physical therapy.

By 3 weeks into his physical therapy treatment, the numbness and tingling in the patient's arm had worsened. At that point, the PT told the patient that she felt uncomfortable continuing to treat him because her

interventions had not decreased the neurological symptoms. She reiterated that he needed to see an orthopedic surgeon. She gave him the name of one and urged him to make an appointment.

The patient followed the PT's suggestion. A month after the patient's initial visit to the PT, he saw the orthopedic surgeon, who ordered an MRI. The MRI revealed two cervical herniations. The patient subsequently underwent surgery but was left with residual neurological impairment.

Investigation showed that the clinic at which the PT was employed had established written policies governing PT communication with other health care providers, but that the PT had failed to follow those policies.

The patient filed a lawsuit in which the PT was named. The complaint against the PT was that she failed to properly assess and report on the patient's condition to the primary care physician, resulting in delays in diagnosing the cervical herniations that left the patient with residual impairment even after surgery.

Now, turn the page for commentary on this scenario from a risk-management perspective, including a table summarizing risky elements and strategies to address them.

The information presented here is not to be interpreted as specific legal advice for any particular provider. Personal advice can only be given by personal legal counsel, based on applicable state and federal law.

Do you have risk-management questions or concerns? Information about what PTs and PTAs need or want to know will help APTA's efforts to educate members about the types of incidents occurring in the workplace and about appropriate risk-management techniques. Contact Jennifer Baker, Director of APTA Insurance and Member Benefit Services, at 800/999-2782, ext 3145 or via e-mail at jenniferbaker@apta.org.

The PT exercised questionable professional judgment in her evaluation of the patient's neurological symptoms over the course of the first 2¹/₂ weeks of treatment and left herself wide open to legal action by failing at any point to report the patient's changing condition to the referring provider, his primary care physician.

The facts that the patient was experiencing tingling from the time of his first visit to the PT and that this condition remained constant for 12 days before he called in sick with the flu should have sent up a red flag. The onset of numbness and the worsening of both neurological symptoms should have sent up warning flags as well. The PT took no action, however, until 2¹/₂ weeks had passed, and her action at that time was passive rather than decisive. Instead of directly contacting the patient's primary care physician herself and outlining the situation through both verbal and written summaries, the PT left it to the patient to seek the referral to a specialist. The primary care physician, lacking any contact with the PT and possessing no documentation of the patient's changing condition, had no compelling evidence of the need to refer the patient to a specialist and suggested instead that the patient continue physical therapy.

On hearing from the patient about the referring physician's response, the PT compounded her risk when she continued treating the patient for another few days rather than actively trying to connect with the primary care doctor. When the PT again made an attempt to get the patient to a specialist, her action once again was passive rather than direct. She gave the patient the name of an orthopedist and urged him to make an appointment himself.

When the patient finally went to see the orthopedic surgeon, that physician knew nothing about the patient's history, because the PT hadn't communicated that information orally or in writing. It was only after the surgeon conducted an MRI that the cervical herniations were revealed. **PT**

Rita Arriaga, PT, MS, *is an Assistant Clinical Professor in the Graduate Program in Physical Therapy and the Director of Rehabilitation Services at the University of California, San Francisco, and chairs APTA's Committee on Risk Management Services and Member Benefits.*

References:

1. Arriaga R. Stories from the front—part one: PTAs and safe practice. *PT—Magazine of Physical Therapy.* 2001;9(1):22-23.
2. Arriaga R. Stories from the front—part two: Recent PT graduates. *PT—Magazine of Physical Therapy.* 2001;9(2):33-34.

The PT showed questionable professional judgment in her evaluation and management of the patient's condition.

Principle 4 of the APTA House of Delegates' *Code of Ethics* for the practice of physical therapy (HOD 06-00-12-23) states that a PT "shall exercise sound professional judgment." While the patient's charge in the lawsuit that the PT failed to properly assess his condition might be a hard sell in that she did urge him to see a specialist, a PT with better professional judgment would have recognized the worsening neurological symptoms as warning signs. Given the mechanism of injury, the unchanged tingling, and the onset of numbness, the PT should have more assertively managed the patient's care. The PT in this scenario shared no concerns with the patient until 2¹/₂ weeks after the initial examination, however, and then only passively participated in getting the patient appropriately referred to a specialist.

The PT failed to follow written policies governing PTs' interaction with other health care providers.

The "Policies and Procedures" section of the APTA Board of Directors' *Standards of Practice for Physical Therapy* (HOD 06-00-11-22) states that the physical therapy service must have written policies and procedures that apply to "criteria for referral to other appropriate health care providers." Such guidelines were in place at the PT's clinic. If the PT had followed them, she would have contacted the patient's primary care physician directly and shared her concerns at the time she first voiced those concerns to the patient.

The PT failed to properly report on the patient's condition.

A number of positions and standards of the APTA Board of Directors emphasize the importance of PT communication and collaboration with other health care providers to provide the best possible patient care. The policy on *Diagnosis by Physical Therapists* (HOD 06-97-06-19) notes that, "as the diagnostic process continues, physical therapists may identify findings that should be shared with other health professionals, including referral sources, to ensure optimal patient care." In the *Position on Professional Relationships* (HOD 06-94-35-46), APTA endorses a "collaborative, collegial practice relationship between physical therapists and all other health care providers." The *Standards of Practice for Physical Therapy* (HOD 06-00-11-22) state both that "the physical therapy service collaborates with all disciplines as appropriate" and that it is the PT's duty, "in consultation with appropriate disciplines," to "plan for discharge of the patient, taking into consideration achievement of anticipated goals and expected outcomes," and to provide for "appropriate follow-up or referral." In this case, the PT's relationship with other health care providers certainly wasn't collaborative, since she shared none of her findings with either the primary care physician or the orthopedic surgeon. Her actions did not meet best-practice standards of "optimal patient care."

liabilityawareness
by Rita Arriaga, PT, MS

Stories From the Front, Part II:
Complex Medical History and Communication

A real-life scenario illustrates some basic risk-management principles.

T's Stories From the Front series, featuring cases adapted from the claim files of the APTA-endorsed professional liability insurance plan, kicked off its fifth year in June with a scenario that centered on a patient with a complex medical history who had undergone rehabilitation following rotator cuff surgery.[1] In this month's column, the second of three, a patient's history of diabetes is a complicating factor in managing the rehabilitation of a torn ligament. As you read the following scenario, consider these questions:

❖ What elements increased the physical therapist's (PT's) liability risk?

❖ What risk-management techniques could have been used to reduce that risk?

This case involved a 75-year-old man who was referred to a sports physical therapist by his physician for rehabilitation of the torn medial collateral ligament of his left knee. This is not an uncommon injury for referral to a PT. In this instance, however, the patient's medical history of diabetes and a left cerebral vascular accident 2 years earlier added complexity to the case.

The written referral from the physician was open-ended because he knew

he could leave it to the PT to determine the appropriate treatment plan based on her evaluative findings and her diagnosis of the patient's impairments and functional limitations. Because the knee problem involved the patient's stronger leg, the physician simply communicated his desire that the PT determine the best plan by which to improve the man's balance, flexibility, and strength.

In accordance with professional standards, the PT took a complete history, noting the patient's medical background and his desire to resume pain-free, independent function because he lived alone. After conducting appropriate tests and measures, the PT outlined a care plan that included electrical stimulation (e-stim) to reduce the pain and mild swelling, and therapeutic exercises and activities to help the patient regain function. He agreed to the plan of care, and visits were initiated at a frequency of two sessions per week. The PT sent a written summary of the plan of care to the referring physician.

The patient seemed to tolerate the first two sessions without problems. During his third visit, however, he showed the PT two small, round open wounds on his knee. The PT asked him whether he had noticed these wounds after his previous e-stim application.

The patient could not recall when the wounds had first appeared. He told the PT he had done nothing to clean or care for the wounds since he had discovered them. The PT placed sterile dressings on the wounds, reminded the patient that his diabetes made attentive wound care a necessity, and urged the patient to see his physician as soon as possible. She also reviewed the patient's home exercise program and warned him not to irritate the wounds while exercising. She scheduled him for another physical therapy visit in a week.

A week later, the patient came to his physical therapy session with Band-Aids on his wounds but said he had not seen his physician. The PT felt that the condition of the wounds was unchanged. She covered them again with sterile dressings and again advised the patient to see his physician as soon as possible. She did not schedule another physical therapy appointment, but she did ask the patient to call her after he had been seen by his doctor. Subsequently, the PT found that the patient had undergone wound debridement 10 days after her last encounter with him, followed by skin grafts almost 3 weeks later. In the ensuing liability claim the PT was found to have contributed to the patient's injuries.

Now, turn the page for a commentary on this scenario from a risk-management perspective and a listing of relevant APTA policies, guidelines, and resources.

liabilityawareness

This PT certainly was practicing within the standard of care at the outset of her interaction with this patient. During the initial session she took a thorough history to augment the information sent by the referring physician, became acquainted with the man's medical history, and performed tests sufficient to determine his specific impairments and the functional limitations he was encountering as a result of his knee injury. Based on her findings, she outlined a plan of care that included appropriate modalities and procedures for addressing these problems. Two decisions she made in this case, however, put her at risk.

First, given the patient's compromised circulation and sensation, was e-stim the most appropriate modality for the PT to have applied? Experts, after reviewing the documentation as part of the liability claim, questioned the parameters exercised by the PT (specific electrode placement, current, and dosage). While these parameters were within the norm for the modality, the experts questioned whether adequate allowance had been made for this patient's compromised sensation.

Although no specific irritation was immediately apparent after the first two treatment sessions, the subsequent appearance of the wounds seemed to indicate underlying irritation from the electrodes. A history of diabetes may not fully contraindicate the use of certain therapeutic modalities that are available to the PT, but sound risk management requires that the PT exercise prudence in their use. In this case, the PT either should have taken greater precaution in determining her treatment parameters with the e-stim or should have chosen a less-risky, easier-to-monitor method of addressing the patient's pain and swelling.

Second, the PT should have been more proactive and assertive in communicating with the patient's physician. Upon first noting the wounds, she immediately should have contacted the referring physician to describe the problem and provide her assessment of its seriousness and the

Relevant APTA Policies, Guidelines, and Resources

❖ **Referral Relationships (HOD 06-90-15-28)** The section on "Referral to Other Health Care Practitioners" states that "the physical therapist must refer patients/clients to the referring practitioner or other health care practitioners if symptoms are present for which physical therapy is contraindicated or are indicative of conditions for which treatment is outside the scope of his/her knowledge."

❖ **Standards of Practice and the Criteria (HOD 06-00-11-22)** Item "J" ("Collaboration") under section II, "Administration of the Physical Therapy Service," states, "The physical therapy service collaborates with all disciplines as appropriate."

❖ **APTA Guide for Professional Conduct** Principle 5.3 ("Professional Development") states, "A physical therapist shall participate in educational activities that enhance his/her basic knowledge and skills." Thus, PTs always should be broadening their knowledge base. That includes staying up-to-date on medical conditions and their impact on the neuro-musculoskeletal, cardiopulmonary, and integumentary systems, and currency on appropriate use of modalities.

❖ **Evidence-Based Practice (HOD 06-99-17-21)** This position states that "The American Physical Therapy Association supports and promotes the development and utilization of evidence-based practices." This bespeaks the importance of PTs using evidence as the basis for making modality choices (the initial decision and appropriate parameters) and the need for PTs to seek evidence from manufacturers and vendors regarding the efficacy of their products and proof of their claims prior to use of those products.

❖ **Interactive Guide to Physical Therapist Practice, with Catalog of Tests and Measures, Version 1.0 (CD-ROM)** This is an excellent source for tests and measures to use to determine the appropriate plan of care, particularly in light of certain medical conditions.

❖ **Risk Management for Physical Therapists: A Quick Reference** This resource includes step-by-step tips on how to mitigate a potential claim.

❖ **APTA core documents, policies, and positions** are available on APTA's Web site (www.apta.org). Click on "About APTA" for the links.

❖ **Hooked on Evidence** The APTA Hooked on Evidence Web site is a grassroots effort to develop a database for members containing current research on physical therapy interventions. It serves as a Web portal for learning about evidence-based practice. On APTA's home page, click on "Research" to get to the Hooked on Evidence link.

❖ **Descriptions and ordering information** for the Interactive Guide to Physical Therapist Practice, with Catalog of Tests and Measures, Version 1.0 (CD-ROM), Risk Management for Physical Therapists: A Quick Reference, and other helpful publications such as A Normative Model of Physical Therapist Professional Education: Version 2000 also are available on APTA's Web site. Click on "Online Shopping," then "Order From Online Catalog."

need for medical attention. It could be argued that the PT fulfilled her duty by warning the patient of the need for careful wound care given his history of diabetes and by advising the patient to see his physician as soon as possible. Good risk management, however, is a proactive process that includes taking action to minimize negative outcomes once an incident has occurred.

During that third session, the PT in this case was fully aware of the medical complication of diabetes and knew that e-stim might have caused the wounds. She was able to assess the wounds' severity and was told that they had not been cleaned. She was in a position, then, to engage in active, timely communication with the physician to ensure immediate medical attention that might have resulted in a better outcome.

Even given her decision simply to advise the patient, the PT still could have checked up on him within a day or two to see if he had followed her advice. Upon learning he had failed to contact his doctor, she then could have called the physician herself. Even this later communication would have resulted in more rapid attention to the wounds than ended up occurring. Good decision-making is a key component of all activities related to the delivery of patient care. In this case, the PT's decision-making ability fell short. **PT**

Rita Arriaga, PT, MS, is an associate clinical professor in the Graduate Program in Physical Therapy and the director of rehabilitation services at the University of California, San Francisco, and is a former chair of APTA's Committee on Risk Management and Member Benefits. She can be reached at 415/476-3453 or arriaga@itsa.ucsf.edu.

Reference

1. Arriaga R. Stories from the front: documentation and complex medical history. *PT—Magazine of Physical Therapy.* 2003;11(6):25-28.

Do you have risk-management questions or concerns? Insights into what PTs need or want to know will help APTA educate members about the types of incidents occurring in the workplace and about appropriate risk-management techniques. Contact Jennifer Baker, Director of APTA Risk Management and Member Benefit Services, at 800/999-2782, ext 3145, or jenniferbaker@apta.org.

reliableresource

by Lisa L Culver, PT, MBA

The Screening Process

Making the "go" or "no go" decision.

As noted in the *Guide to Physical Therapist Practice*,[1] screening is "based on a problem-focused, systematic collection and analysis of data." It is a form of a decision tree intended to provide a "go" or "no go" for further physical therapist (PT) examination or consultation, or for a referral to another provider. Based on the information gathered, the PT makes one of the following determinations:

1. A more comprehensive physical therapist examination and evaluation is needed;
2. A referral to another health professional is needed;
3. Both 1 and 2 are needed; or
4. No problems are identified that require further examination or referral.

In reality, the screening process is identical to the process PTs initially go through with every patient/client referred for physical therapy. The initial and preliminary decisions that the PT makes as he or she performs the history and systems review contain the same elements and decisions. The following are examples of making determinations 1-4 above as part of the patient/client management process. (The number of each example corresponds to the number of the determination above.)

1. The process of performing a history and systems review is used to confirm a need for physical therapy evaluation and to guide the course of further examination—a "go" for further physical therapy examination and evaluation. It should be noted that the "go" decision does not necessarily indicate that the further examination and evaluation is to be performed by the same PT. And as with any patient/client, if the PT performing the screen or initial examination and evaluation determines that the needs of the

patient/client are outside of the PT's own scope of knowledge, experience, or expertise, the PT should refer the patient/client to another PT who has the appropriate knowledge and skills.

> **Screening:** "Determining the need for further examination or consultation by a physical therapist or for referral to another health professional."
>
> **Consultation:** "The rendering of professional or expert opinion or advice by a physical therapist. The consulting physical therapist applies highly specialized knowledge and skills to identify problems, recommend solutions, or produce a specified outcome...on behalf of a patient/client."
>
> —Guide to Physical Therapist Practice. 2nd ed. *Phys Ther.* 2001;81-9-744.

2. While gathering information in the history or systems review, a potential problem is identified that falls outside the scope of physical therapy. This may require immediate assessment by another provider—a "no go" for physical therapy, with a "go" for referral to another provider. For example, if the nature of the pain and the history of a patient/client complaining of muscle strain suggests a problem that may not be neuromuscular in nature, the decision might be to send the patient/client to a physician to rule out, for example, bony involvement of a metastatic nature.

3. The initial information gathered during the history and systems review of a referred patient/client indicates the need for further physical therapy examination and evaluation. However, the mental state of the patient/client indicates that, for the patient/client to effectively participate in physical therapy, referral to a psychologist or other mental health professional may be indicated in addition to further examination and evaluation by a PT.

4. Based on information gathered in the

history and systems review, the PT performs a targeted examination and determines no need for further examination or evaluation.

Although this process is commonly used as part of patient/client management, the term "screen" is more typically used with an individual who neither is receiving physical therapy services nor has been referred for a physical therapy program that would include intervention.

So, what are typical situations in which a PT would perform a screen?

Where Is the Screening Process Used?

Screens may be used for individuals who are apparently "well"—such as those being screened at a health fair—to identify a need for intervention (either for a problem not recognized by the person being screened or to address goals for a higher level of function). Alternatively, screens may be used in an institution such as a hospital or an extended care facility for an individual who has multiple medical problems but for whom the need for physical therapy has not been determined.

Healthy populations. The *Guide to Physical Therapist Practice* provides examples of prevention screening activities that include:

❖ Identification of lifestyle factors (eg, amount of exercise, stress, weight) that might lead to increased risk for serious health problems.

❖ Identification of children who may need an examination of idiopathic scoliosis.

❖ Identification of elderly individuals in a community center or nursing home who are at high risk for falls.

❖ Identification of risk factors for neuro-musculoskeletal injuries in the workplace.

❖ Pre-performance testing of individuals who are active in sports.

Institutional settings. The Joint Commission on Accreditation of Health Care Organizations (JCAHO) has a requirement that "the hospital … identifies patients who require a functional assessment using criteria developed by rehabilitation specialists and other qualified professionals." The PT's involvement in this process could lead to the development of a screening process. The institution might do an initial screen based on medical diagnosis or on intake information. The PT may then further review those identified by the institutional screen to identify those requiring further examination and evaluation. For example, all patients/clients admitted with a new or recent diagnosis of stroke or joint replacement might be flagged for a screen by a PT. Based on a chart review or brief history, the PT makes a determination as to the need for a physical therapy referral for further examination and evaluation.

What Are Different Ways in Which Screens Might Be Performed?

A variety of methods might be employed to gather information used for the screen, including, but not limited to, the following: chart review only, observation only, history only, history and systems review.

It is important to note, however, that the process of gathering the information alone is not a screen. The screen is the process of making a determination about the information gathered.

Let's consider some further examples of screens:

❖ In a long-term care facility, the PT reviews the charts of all new admissions. Based on indications such as recent change in functional status or ongoing physical therapy at the patient's prior setting, the PT requests a referral to physical therapy.

❖ At a community clinic, participants are screened for leg-length discrepancy and postural abnormalities. Based on observation, the PT determines whether to recommend that a participant schedule a complete physical therapy examination and evaluation.

❖ All patients admitted to an inpatient rehabilitation unit are seen by the PT, who takes a brief history and performs a systems review to determine if the patient has physical therapy needs that require intervention.

❖ All students who are starting a gymnastics program are seen by a PT, who performs a screen—examining their general strength, flexibility, posture, and balance—to determine if they require a full examination and evaluation and possible intervention in order to participate successfully.

❖ The PT conducts gross balance tests on residents of an assisted living facility to determine a risk for falls that might require further examination and evaluation.

❖ At a Parent Teacher Association health fair, parents are interviewed by a PT to

reliableresource

assess potential problems with their children's backpack loads, related musculoskeletal problems their children may have, and the need for children to be seen by a PT.

Is Referral Required for a Screen?

First, consider the possible sources that might require a referral. APTA does not believe that a referral should be required in order for a patient/client to be seen by a physical therapist. Some state laws and many payers, however, require a referral from a physician or others.

To determine if a referral is required for the screen you plan to perform, first consider whether a referral would be required by your state licensing agency. To make that determination, review the specifics of the practice act for your state. (Go to www.apta.org, then "Practice," then "Physical Therapy Licensure/State Practice Acts.") If your state has direct access for evaluation, it is unlikely that a referral would be required. If your state does not have direct access, you would need to consider whether the activity you were performing as a screen would require a referral based on language in the state law. For example, if the screen is performed using only information from a review of the chart, the state may not view this activity as requiring a referral. To meet referral requirements, patient/therapist interaction may be required. Requirements may vary significantly from state to state, however, and may not be explicitly stated. As illustrated by previous examples in this column, all screens are not the same. Be sure you have adequately addressed the requirements of your state's law to determine if a referral is legally required for the type of activity you plan to perform as a screen.

Not all screens are performed for payment. For example, posture screens at health fairs are generally done for free. However, PTs may very well charge for screens such as pre-performance screening for athletes. If that charge is submitted to a payer, the insurance coverage policy for the individual or group receiving the screening may require a referral in order for the screen to qualify for payment.

Can Physical Therapist Assistants Perform a Screen?

This is a frequently asked question. To answer it, one need only to review the definition of a screen: "Determining the need for further examination or consultation by a physical therapist or for referral to another health professional." The decision-making process inherent in a screen includes elements of examination and evaluation, which are appropriate only for the PT.

A Valuable Tool

The screen is a valuable tool for determining the care needs of individuals who may not have an identified need for physical therapy. Used wisely, it contributes to a collegial relationship among providers both within and outside of the profession of physical therapy and facilitates appropriate levels of intervention by appropriate providers. **PT**

Lisa L Culver, PT, MBA, is Associate Director of APTA's Department of Practice. She can be reached at 800/999-2782, ext 3172, or via e-mail at lisaculver@apta.org.

Reference

1. Guide to Physical Therapist Practice. 2nd ed. *Phys Ther.* 2001;81:9-744.

Direct Access: Exploring New Opportunities

Screening: A Basic Obligation

One longstanding bar to direct access has been the opposition of other health care practitioner groups concerned about PTs' ability to function as patients' entry point into the health care system. Fears that medical conditions would escape the PT's notice owing to lack of medical qualifications kept direct access restrictions on the books for many years. With the lifting of the laws, those fears have been shown to be unfounded; in fact, PTs' professional liability insurers, a sure bellwether of risk, make no distinction between direct access and non-direct access states when determining insurance rates.

Still, it's an important issue to consider: Are the PT's medical screening responsibilities toward the patient affected by direct access? According to Bill Boissonnault, PT, DPT, DHSc, MS, of the University of Wisconsin-Madison, who has taught courses on medical screening to physical therapy students for many years, the answer is essentially no.

"The responsibility for screening patients is not a new one. It's been with us in varying degrees since the inception of the profession," he says. "But the advent of direct access has definitely brought the issue to the forefront, and the development of professional documents such as the *Guide [to Physical Therapist Practice]* have clarified our responsibilities in this area. As we evolve as practitioners, and move toward the DPT [Doctor of Physical Therapy] and increasingly independent practice, we are broadening the scope of medical screenings we do. For example, it used to be that when a patient came in with low back pain, we would typically ask about bowel or bladder problems or other manifestations that might raise suspicions of cauda equina syndrome or other serious illnesses being present. Our role wasn't—and still isn't—to make a specific diagnosis of these diseases ourselves, but rather to consult with another health care practitioner, expressing our concerns, which may lead to an earlier diagnosis. Today, as the entry point into the health care system, we still do that level of screening, but we also screen for manifestations associated with illnesses that may not be directly related to the patient's pain complaints. Conditions such as depression, abuse, chemical dependency, adverse drug reactions, or skin lesions are very common in the general public, and the vigilant physical therapist may detect manifestations that again lead to consultation with another practitioner for a subsequent diagnosis."

According to Boissonnault, another aspect of direct access that makes the issue of appropriate screening especially central is the increased emphasis on wellness services. "PTs have defined their roles in the health care system as having a strong component of secondary and primary prevention," he says. "With the big push for wellness and working with the 'healthy' client, screening becomes that much more crucial. For example, in a wellness setting, PTs should be screening for signs and symptoms that may fall outside of something for which patients normally would seek physician intervention."

An online course presented by Boissonnault entitled "Diagnosis by Physical Therapists: Screening for Medical Referral" will be available via the APTA Web site in Spring 2002. Boissonnault describes it as "part refresher, part new material" that will give PTs a good understanding of the issues surrounding screening and tips on how to work the process into an initial evaluation.

For more information on this and other online courses, go to the APTA Web site at www.apta.org and use the QuickFind or Education menus, or call Beth Nolte at 800/999-2782, ext 8521.

APTA's Vision Statement for Physical Therapy 2020[1] reads, in part, "Physical therapists will be practitioners of choice in clients' health networks and will hold all privileges of autonomous practice." Webster's[2] definition of "autonomous" is "having the right or power of self-governance, exhibiting independence in mind or judgment, self-directed, and able to carry on without outside control." APTA defines autonomous practice as being characterized by "independent, self-determined, professional judgment and action."[3]

Autonomous practice, then, encompasses both authority over and bottom-line accountability for decisions made on behalf of and with the patient/client. It describes management of the patient/client from admission to the care of the PT through discharge from that same care. PTs always have had bottom-line accountability for the decisions they make; even in a system in which the majority of physical therapy patients/clients gain access to physical therapy services through a physician referral, the ulti-

Autonomous practice:
Issues of Risk

How PTs can ensure that hard-won freedoms don't literally become liabilities.

by Carol Schunk, PT, PsyD, and Cathy Thut, PT, MBA

mate responsibility is always the PT's—as evidenced by malpractice claims in which PTs have attempted unsuccessfully to hide behind physician referral.

Thus, the *Vision Statement* doesn't change the status of PTs as autonomous practitioners. The prominence given autonomous practice in this official document does, however, emphasize the concept's importance. The profession's focus in the past decade on diagnosis and now autonomous practice bespeak expanded parameters of physical therapy practice and a higher profile in the health care-delivery system.

But the promotion of physical therapy's direct, prominent role in health care carries a challenge for all PTs—even, and perhaps especially, for those PTs who erroneously and at their own peril contend that autonomous practice doesn't apply to them. It brings the potential for increased exposure to liability.

What, specifically, are the risk components of autonomous practice, and what can PTs do to successfully manage them? Let's look at each component.

Self-determination

If self-determination means the privilege and responsibility of making one's own decisions, autonomous practice is not congruent with straightforwardly and unquestioningly doing whatever a physician orders. Autonomous practice *does* demand, however, that the PT is skilled in examination, diagnosis, and understanding and recognizing when physical therapy intervention is appropriate.

Potential for increased risk exists, therefore, when a PT does not conduct a thorough evaluation of the patient/client prior to performing an intervention, does not propose a diagnosis or reason for physical therapy intervention, and/or elects to use practice extenders (PTAs and PT aides) in a manner that is not supported by state law or APTA policies and guidelines.

Case example. *Mrs Smith is a 65-year-old woman who has been having problems with balance. She sees her primary care physician, who refers her to a neurologist. While the neurologist is examining Mrs Smith, she experiences a loss of balance. The*

neurologist decides that she would benefit from a referral to physical therapy. The diagnosis that the neurologist forwards to the PT is "spells" with an order for gait training.

Many questions demand answers. The PT first must determine how extensive a patient history is needed in order to decide which specific examinations are necessary. After conducting the history and the examinations—and requesting and obtaining the patient's medical history, physical, and test results—he or she must correlate the findings to determine the diagnosis and develop a plan of care. It also is the responsibility of the PT to determine Mrs Smith's prognosis for recovery and assess her post-treatment needs. A result of all of these well-documented and evidence-based actions is a determination by the PT of what is appropriate for Mrs Smith. After making that determination, the PT must communicate it with the physician and fully document the communication.

Case example. *A 40-year-old former high school athlete is referred to a PT by a physician and reports bilateral knee discomfort. During the initial examination/evaluation, the patient mentions that she also has low back pain. The PT notices that the patient has a pelvic asymmetry and believes this to be the cause of the knee pain. The PT, therefore, initiates muscle energy techniques for the back, along with a knee therapy program. After seven visits, the pelvis is realigned but the patient still has back pain.*

In a lawsuit, the patient states that she was referred to the PT for management of her knee discomfort but instead received physical therapy primarily on her back without medical directive or consent. She further states that the physical therapy performed on her back was excessive, inappropriate, and negligently administered, causing debilitating low back pain. A claim against the PT ultimately is settled for $50,000.

This case offers an interesting look at self-determination and the importance of communication. It was the PT's professional judgment that realigning the pelvis was instrumental to rehabilitating the patient's knees. The PT proceeded with the realignment, however, without first consulting the referring physician. The lack of communication with the physician was a

case of bad judgment by the PT. Had the PT contacted the physician, she would have discovered that prior to being referred for physical therapy, the patient had been seen by numerous health care providers regarding her low back pain, including an orthopedist (an MRI showed a slight disc bulge at L5-S1), a chiropractor (who diagnosed lumbar intervertebral syndrome), a surgical neurologist (who diagnosed lumbar strain with degenerative disk disease), and the referring physician (who found disc bulges). The PT and the physician then would have discussed whether realigning the patient's pelvis was relevant to rehabilitating the patient's knees. Self-determination means the privilege of making one's own decisions, but only after key information has been obtained through examination, history, and consultation. Documentation of the consultation and the subsequent discussion would have significantly decreased the PT's risk, had she proceeded with the realignment.

Responsibility to Refer

As Jules Rothstein, PT, PhD, FAPTA, editor-in-chief of *Physical Therapy*, stated in his August 2002 editorial,[4] it is not in the physical therapy profession's best interest, or descriptive of the way PTs practice, to limit our understanding and application of the term "autonomous practice" to the concept of total independence. The dictionary definition of autonomy that Rothstein quoted describes it as "developing independently of the whole."[5] As he points out, however, given our relationship with the health care system and patients and clients, being "independent of the whole" is not who we are or how we practice. We cannot, therefore, think of autonomous practice as being a state of total independence. For us to best serve the patient or client, the contributions of other practitioners may be essential—and a PT's failure to consider referring a patient may, in some cases, be the basis for a malpractice suit. With the concept of referral, however, also comes potential risk.

In "A Physical Therapist's Road to Referral,"[6] an article that appeared in the summer 2001 issue of the Healthcare

On the Web

For more information on autonomous practice and the risks associated with it, visit the following Web sites:

❖ **www.apta.org** APTA's home page. Look for information on risk management, evidence-based practice and Hooked on Evidence, documentation, supervision, direct access, and referral responsibilities.

❖ **www.hpso.com** The home page of the Healthcare Providers Service Organization, administrator of the APTA-endorsed professional liability insurance plan. Click on the "Newsletters" tab for the latest on health care liability issues, as well as discussions of specific cases involving PTs.

❖ **www.ahcpr.gov** The home page of the Agency for Healthcare Research and Quality offers information about evidence-based practice (including the Cochrane Collaboration's reviews of the literature), outcomes and effectiveness, and clinical practice guidelines.

❖ **www.jcaho.org** The home page of the Joint Commission on Accreditation of Healthcare Organizations. JCAHO sets many standards that affect PT practice, including determination of staff competency; requirements for documentation, evaluation, and management of patients; and general requirements for rehabilitation services. All of these standards, as well as information on sentinel events (unexpected occurrences involving death or serious injury, and their associated risks) and root-cause analysis (a process for looking at the potential risks revealed by "close calls") can be found on this site.

❖ **www.ahima.org** The home page of the American Health Information Management Association. AHIMA sets the standards for documentation and coding of medical records. The site contains important risk-management information in those areas, and offers helpful processes for managing medical records.

❖ **www.aslme.org** The home page of the American Society of Law, Medicine & Ethics. This site offers access to ASLME's *American Journal of Law and Medicine*. Recent articles in that publication have explored such important risk issues as conflicts of interest, decision-making authority and competency, informed consent, and patient rights.

Providers Service Organization's *Risk Advisor* newsletter, Jonathan Cooperman, PT, MS, JD, and D Kathleen Lewis, PT, MA, JD, stated:

"A patient whose condition calls for a type of physical therapy treatment in which you lack the appropriate training, experience, or expertise needs a referral, too—only in this case it will be to another PT. If you work exclusively with sports injuries, for instance, do not agree to treat an elderly stroke patient. If you're aware of the conflict in advance, decline to even do an evaluation. Otherwise, do an examination within the limits of your experience, education, and expertise and make a referral to a colleague in your facility or a qualified PT in another setting. Tell the patient you want her to see a physical therapist who specializes in treating disorders like hers."

Cooperman and Lewis added, "Accepting or continuing to treat a patient whose condition is not amenable to physical therapy violates the standards of physical therapy practice, at least in instances where you knew or should have known that to be the case. A referral back to the patient's physician is one option. A direct referral to the appropriate practitioner is another. You also have a duty, spelled out in the APTA's *Guide for Professional Conduct,*[7] to communicate your findings to the provider who referred the patient to you."

The challenge for the profession lies in re-framing the paradigm of practice. Many PTs practice in an autonomous manner but may lack full legal authority in their management of the patient (depending on state laws). What PTs must do, and what APTA seeks to encourage, is to balance authority and accountability in a manner that ensures that the patient/client receives the right care, at the right time, by the right provider.

It is the PT's responsibility not only to identify conditions that are outside the scope of physical therapy practice and refer the patient/client accordingly—as would be the case, for example, with a possible ankle fracture—but also to recognize and

act on instances in which the input of another health care professional might maximize the benefits of a physical therapy plan of care. An example of the latter is the PT's responsibility to a patient with diabetes to consider referring him or her to a nutritionist, whose input can augment the effects on the patient of a PT-supervised exercise program.

Case example. *An elderly woman is referred to a PT with a diagnosis of a torn medial collateral ligament and with co-morbidity of diabetes. The PT's plan of care includes electrical stimulation. The intervention results in some reddening of the patient's skin, but nothing more than that. During the course of a subsequent physical therapy session, however, the patient shows the PT two wounds that have developed on her knee. The PT dresses the wounds and instructs the patient to see her physician.*

One week later, the patient still has the wounds and has not gone to her physician. The PT again dresses the wounds and again advises the patient to see her physician. Several weeks later, the patient finally sees the physician, who says that the patient must have surgical debridement, followed by skin grafts.

The responsibility to refer was a main point in a liability suit brought successfully against the PT. Although the PT urged the patient to see her physician, the PT should have picked up the phone and contacted the physician immediately upon seeing the wounds (which presumably resulted from the electrical stimulation). Because diabetes compromises healing, it was imperative that the physician examine the wounds as soon as possible in order to facilitate a plan of care that would promote healing.

Documentation

Documentation of the specifics of care and case management is always a factor in the outcome of malpractice cases. In cases in which the PT has documented well, documentation can be the PT's best friend. The PT's defense suffers, however, when the quantity or quality of his or her documentation is insufficient. APTA's strong statement that autonomous practice is characterized by "independent, self-deter-

Autonomous Practice

mined, professional judgment and action" must be backed up by documentation.

In cases in which the PT is the only health care practitioner involved in the patient's/client's care, with no medical history or assessment from a physician, it stands to reason that the documentation must reflect the PT's enhanced responsibility. The PT's plan of care and course of action always should be backed up in the medical record.

Again, PTs always should consider referral. But just as important as the decision to refer is documentation of the referral. If a referral is made but the communication with the other health care practitioner and the follow-up to the referral are not documented, risk is greatly increased.

In particularly compelling cases—if, for instance, a patient arrives for physical therapy with a wound that wasn't there during the previous physical therapy visit—the PT should call the physician and make an appointment for the patient. In other cases, the PT may advise the patient to schedule the appointment. Should the patient choose not to do so, the PT must decide whether to contact the physician her- or himself, or to discharge the patient from physical therapy because safe continuation of physical therapy requires that the patient first consult with the physician. Whatever the case, everything must be documented. This includes the decision to recommend a consultation with a physician (or another PT, for that matter), the follow-up to that recommendation, and the details of any consultation conducted.

Case example. *The patient is a 70-year-old man who has undergone rotator cuff surgery. Because of another pre-existing condition, he has only one functional arm. The PT has him performing unsupervised and unassisted shoulder exercises, including a "wall ladder" and pulleys. The patient sus-*
tains a shoulder injury while doing the exercises, he claims. As a result, the shoulder is permanently disabled.

An investigation reveals that while the PT had kept notes documenting each visit, there was no written indication that a plan of care had been designed emphasizing the need for only passive interventions—which were what the physician had requested, given the patient's recent surgery and pre-existing condition, and which would not include a wall ladder and pulleys.

Inadequate documentation by the PT and lack of a documented plan of care has greatly increased the PT's risk. The plan of care, including appropriate interventions and their parameters based on the patient's or client's history, always should be documented thoroughly and accurately. This written plan of care then can serve as a guide to the PT and any subsequent PTs who also might participate in the patient's or client's treatment.

Autonomous Practice

Reactions of Referral Sources

Let's look for a moment at a situation involving a group of health care practitioners other than PTs who are moving toward autonomous practice. An article in the October 1998 issue of *Family Practice Management*,[8] a publication of the American Academy of Family Physicians (AAFP), discussed the changing role of nurse practitioners and their potential for competing with family physicians for patients/clients. The piece highlighted a specific nurse practitioner group, Columbia Advanced Practice Nurse Associates (CAPNA). CAPNA is run exclusively by nurse practitioners who have hospital admitting privileges. These nurse practitioners are listed on the provider panels of managed care organizations and are reimbursed at the same rate as physicians.

The response by family physicians has been mixed, the article notes. One physician says, "With very well-trained people, who understand what they can and can't do, there's tremendous synergy" among physicians, nurse practitioners, and other members of the health care team.

Conversely, however, several physicians comment in this vein: "It may make economic sense to bean counters to use nurse practitioners—they're very good at handling single-system disorders, but when you get into multi-system disorders, you need a physician." AAFP, the article notes, takes the position that the "interests of patients are best served when their care is provided by a physician or through an integrated practice supervised directly by a physician."

What can our profession garner from this article? It's instructive to note that the family practitioners' description of nurse practitioners as "focused on health promotion" and "willing to spend the time to get to know patients' needs and concerns" could just as easily be applied to PTs (although that's a very limited and partial description of all the things PTs do). Many physicians, however, may view our profession's move toward autonomous practice as a growing competitive threat.

One possible manifestation of any threat that referral sources may feel from

PTs is that referral sources will increasingly write out specific orders for physical therapy—ultrasound, hot packs, massage, etc—and that PTs who diverge from those specific orders in any way will do so at their own peril in terms of liability. As in the case example presented earlier, in which the PT realigned the woman's pelvis, consultation and thorough documentation will greatly decrease PTs' risk.

Case example. *A 29-year-old man is seen by a PT three times a week following a job-related accident that has resulted in his experiencing severe pain in his cervical spine, severe headaches, and pain in the left jaw. He also has soft tissue restrictions and muscle spasms. Records indicate that the patient stated several times during the third and fourth week of physical therapy that he was having increased numbness, tingling, and flu-like symptoms. The PT encourages him to make an appointment with an orthopedic surgeon on his own, because his general practitioner will not approve it. The patient does make an appointment and the MRI shows a cervical herniation. The patient has surgery and now has neurological impairments.*

The patient brings suit against both the PT and the physician, stating in the PT's case that he failed to assess and report the patient's condition to the treating physician. The delay in treatment is alleged to be the cause of the permanent dysfunction. The judgement against the PT is for about $450,000.

This case is not a simple referral issue because the original physician refused to refer the patient to the specialist. As PTs become more autonomous there may be a negative reaction by physicians who resent PTs' increased independence, as illustrated by this PT's recommendation that the patient seek another opinion. Again, the PT's responsibility is to the patient, however, and he or she can minimize risk by carefully documenting all referrals and communicating subsequent referrals to the original referral source.

Supervision

PTs are legally and ethically responsible for all patient and client care provided by their support personnel. In an

autonomous practice environment in which the PT oversees the totality of patient/client care and management, utilization of support personnel demands competent and consistent supervision. While the majority of the supervisory risk situations that involve a claim settlement involve the PT aide, there are incidents in which the defendant is a physical therapist assistant (PTA). In both cases, the supervising PT will be named in the lawsuit.

The APTA Board of Directors' position on "Levels of Supervision,"[9] which recognizes that even general supervision requires the supervisory PT's availability "at least by telecommunications," clearly implies that accountability always rests with the supervising physical therapist. For that reason it is important that PTs not take their supervisory duties lightly. Actions such as co-signing but not reading notes or logs, underestimating the clinical problem-solving or clinical decision-making required of assigned tasks, or assuming a level of training without verification all show a lack of responsibility. The bottom line is that direction and supervision carry not only obligations, but also risk potential.

If legal action is sought in an incident involving a PT aide or PTA, the supervising PT should be able to defend his or her position on three levels: supervision, assignment of tasks, and training. If there are state regulations addressing these areas, they most likely will be referred to as the standards. In the absence of state guidance, it is quite possible that APTA positions will be referenced by the plaintiff's attorneys.

Case example. *A PT is working as an independent contractor at a hospital, supervising the physical therapy department. One of the patients whose care is being managed is a 71-year-old man who had been injured when his sister dragged him from a burning trailer. The patient had had a prior cerebrovascular accident. The supervising PT asks a PTA to administer hot packs to the patient. The PTA places the hot packs on the patient's lumbar spine and knee. When the packs are removed about an hour later, the patient is found to have sustained second-degree burns in both locations.*

continued on page 40 ▶▶▶

Autonomous Practice

continued from page 38

The PT's documentation and her notes in the medical record are unclear regarding the specifics of the task delegated to the PTA, how long the packs should have been and were kept on, and who removed the packs. The hospital settles with the patient. Suits are brought against the hospital and the PT; the PT settles with the patient for $50,000.

In this scenario, it was the PT's duty to ascertain the competencies of the PTA. In any facility accredited by the Joint Commission on Accreditation of Healthcare Organizations, the clinical competencies of support staff must be current. The PT should have viewed that documentation prior to assigning the PTA the task of administering a hot pack. Further, the PT should have documented the specifics of the hot pack application—where it was applied, for how long, and the skin's condition after removal.

The term "autonomous practice" covers a range of concepts within physical therapy. On one end of the spectrum are principles that should be common practice for all PTs, such as self-determination and independent decision-making. On the other end are burgeoning issues such as direct access and financial ownership. Changes in the profession bring increased exposure to risks that could result in malpractice suits. Increased awareness of these risks, proper attention to the issues underlying them, and smart practice in navigating them can minimize your potential liability as the profession continues to move forward. **PT**

Carol Schunk, PT, PsyD, is a consultant with Northwest Rehab Alliance and TAOS outcomes system. She also works in home health and rehab facilities for PT on Call. Cathy Thut, PT, MBA, is director of physical medicine at Baylor Medical Center at Irving in Texas. Both are members of APTA's Committee on Risk Management Services and Member Benefits. Schunk can be reached at carolschunk@earthlink.net, Thut at cathyt@baylorhealth.edu.

References

1. *APTA's Vision Statement for Physical Therapy 2020.* Available at www.apta.org/About/aptamissiongoals/visionstatement. Accessed September 25, 2002.
2. *Merriam Webster's Collegiate Dictionary.* 9th ed. Springfield, Mass: Merriam Webster Inc; 1988.
3. American Physical Therapy Association. Board of Directors minutes (program 32, competencies of the autonomous physical therapist practitioner). Available at www.apta.org/governance/governance_5/BOD minutes. Accessed September 27, 2002.
4. Rothstein JM. Editor's note: autonomy and dependency. *Phys Ther.* 2002;82:750-751.
5. *Merriam Webster's Collegiate Dictionary.* 10th ed. Springfield, Mass: Merriam Webster Inc; 1996.
6. Cooperman J, Lewis, DK. A physical therapist's road to referral. *HPSO Risk Advisor, Physical Therapist Edition.* Summer 2001. Available at http://www.hpso.com/newsletters/8-2001/pte_risk_advisor.HTM. Accessed September 25, 2002.
7. *APTA's Guide for Professional Conduct.* Available at www.apta.org/pt_practice/ethics_pt/pro_conduct. Accessed September 25, 2002.
8. Flanagan L. Nurse practitioners: growing competition for family physicians? *Family Practice Management.* October 1998. Available at www.aafp.org/fpm/981000fm/nurse.html. Accessed September 25, 2002.
9. "*Levels of Supervision*" (HOD-06-00-15-26). Available at www.apta.org/PT_Practice/For_Clinicians/Use_of_Personnel_/Levels. Accessed September 25, 2002.

liability awareness

by Rita Arriaga, PT, MS

Stories from the Front:
Patient Management

An examination of risk-management principles through the prism of a case scenario.

About this series: With physical therapy moving toward realization of the APTA Vision for Physical Therapy 2020, and in keeping with the goals that represent the 2004 priorities of the Association (see box on page 28), it is imperative that physical therapists (PTs) and physical therapist assistants (PTAs) recognize and appreciate that sound risk management is a hallmark of autonomous practice. APTA's Committee on Risk Management and Member Benefits uses "Stories from the Front," now in its sixth year, as a vehicle for conveying information about emerging and ongoing risk-management trends in clinical practice. Using a case-based format, the three columns in each year's series illustrate risk considerations identified by the committee through its review of claims data, and provide readers with references and documents that can assist them in making risk-reducing decisions.

This, the first "Stories from the Front" column of 2004, looks at an emerging issue of concern, based on claims review: Some PTs either may be inappropriately going beyond the scope of the referral they receive or providing contraindicated treatment. This month's column touches on the need for good communication with referral sources, appropriate decision-making and advocacy when the PT feels the treatment plan in the initial referral is insufficient to the patient's needs, and alertness to contraindications.

The Case

A 69-year-old woman slipped at home and fell onto her left leg. She was able to get up on her own and walk without problems. Although she felt no immedi-

ate pain and saw no bruising or swelling, as a preventive measure she applied ice to her left thigh, laterally from hip to knee. By the next day, she began to note increasing pain, discoloration, and swelling along her left leg. Because the symptoms persisted, she went to a physician 6 days after the fall. The PT involved in this case worked part-time in rented space within the physician's office suite.

On the day of the patient's appointment with the physician, the PT was on site and present when the physician took the patient's history and conducted his physical exam. The physician documented his medical exam, diagnosis, and treatment plan; the treatment plan included instructions to get X-rays to rule out hip fracture, and referral to the PT. The physician's written diagnosis was "status post left hip/thigh injury with large hematoma at mid-lateral thigh, rule out left hip femoral fracture." The physical therapy referral was for diathermy, electrical stimulation, massage, and range-of-motion (ROM) exercises.

The physician advised the patient to go to a nearby radiology clinic for her X-ray. First, because the PT was on site and available that day, the physician asked the PT to initiate treatment. The PT agreed, and administered heat and massage to the thigh (including the bruised area). The patient left, but apparently did not get the X-ray that day, as had been suggested by the physician, opting instead to go home. That evening the patient's leg continued to swell and the pain became severe, so

she went to the physician's office the next day, where she was examined and treated by the physician. The PT was not on site that day and did not see the patient. The physician documented that he performed diathermy, electrical stimulation, and superficial massage to the patient's bruised thigh. He also directed the patient again to get her leg X-rayed, which she did; the results were negative.

The patient went home after the X-ray, but later was taken to the hospital by her family because her leg pain became even more intense. At the hospital, a CAT scan was done and several hours later a fasciotomy of the left lower leg was performed. Subsequently, the woman was diagnosed with compartment syndrome of the left leg and a left foot drop.

A complaint was brought against both the physician and the PT for inappropriate care resulting in the need for emergency surgery and the eventual diagnoses of compartment syndrome and foot drop. The allegations against the PT included negligence due to failure to properly examine and note the severe condition of the left lower extremity, which resulted in the contraindicated application of heat and massage. This negligence, and the PT's failure to refer the patient for emergency care, it was alleged, contributed to the patient's compartment syndrome and foot drop of the left leg.

Although this case eventually was settled prior to trial, the PT was responsible for covering approximately 30% of the six-figure settlement.

The information presented here is not to be interpreted as specific legal advice for any particular provider. Only personal legal counsel, based on applicable state and federal law, can give personal advice.

continued on page 28 ▶▶▶

liability awareness

continued from page 26

The Risks

What risks did the PT in this case incur, and how might they have been avoided? Which APTA documents serve as guides to best practice? Let's take a closer look.

Patient management. Regardless of the venue or referral relationship, PTs are separately licensed health care providers who are responsible for integrating the five elements of patient/client management—examination, evaluation, diagnosis, prognosis, and intervention—in a manner designed to optimize outcomes. Even though this PT's practice setting (in the same office suite as the referral source) allowed her to observe some, if not all, of the physician's history-taking and physical examination of the patient, she still was responsible for conducting and documenting her own examination and evaluation.

Although the PT documented the care she rendered during her initial treatment session with the patient (administration of heat and massage), she made no record of having conducted a physical therapy examination or evaluation. While it is true that patient data, information, and even certain test results from other providers often are available to PTs, PTs nevertheless are independently responsible for assessing patients from their unique perspective, as supported by the profession's specific body of knowledge, and for delineating the movement and functional impairments and limitations that must be addressed. This assessment then must be documented in order for a PT to be able to support the case for care rendered, should the PT's decision-making in that area be called into question.

The APTA Guide for Professional Conduct[1] states, "Regardless of practice setting, a physical therapist has prime responsibility for the physical therapy care of a patient and shall make independent judgments regarding that care consistent with accepted professional standards." It further states that, "Upon

APTA Vision Statement for Physical Therapy 2020 [HOD 06-00-24-35]

Physical therapy, by 2020, will be provided by physical therapists who are doctors of physical therapy and who may be board-certified specialists. Consumers will have direct access to physical therapists in all environments for patient/client management, prevention, and wellness services. Physical therapists will be practitioners of choice in clients' health networks and will hold all privileges of autonomous practice. Physical therapists may be assisted by physical therapist assistants who are educated and licensed to provide physical therapist-directed and -supervised components of interventions.

Guided by integrity, life-long learning, and a commitment to comprehensive and accessible health programs for all people, physical therapists and physical therapist assistants will render evidence-based service throughout the continuum of care and improve quality of life for society. They will provide culturally sensitive care distinguished by trust, respect, and an appreciation for individual differences.

While fully availing themselves of new technologies, as well as basic and clinical research, physical therapists will continue to provide direct care. They will maintain active responsibility for the growth of the physical therapy profession and the health of the people it serves.

Goals That Represent the 2004 Priorities of the Association

[HOD 06-03-07-09]

Goal I: Physical therapists are universally recognized and promoted as the practitioners of choice for persons with conditions that affect movement, function, health, and wellness.

Goal II: Academic and clinical education prepares doctors of physical therapy who are autonomous practitioners.

Goal III: Physical therapists are autonomous practitioners to whom patients/clients have unrestricted direct access as an entry point into the health care delivery system and who are paid for all elements of patient/client management in all practice environments.

Goal IV: Research advances the science of physical therapy and furthers the evidence-based practice of the physical therapist.

Goal V: Physical therapists and physical therapist assistants are committed to meeting the health needs of patients/clients and society through ethical behavior, continued competence, and advocacy for the profession.

Goal VI: Communication throughout the Association enhances participation of and responsiveness to members and promotes and instills the value of belonging to the American Physical Therapy Association.

Goal VII: American Physical Therapy Association standards, policies, positions, guidelines and the *Guide to Physical Therapist Practice*; *Normative Model of Physical Therapist Education and Evaluative Criteria*; and the *Normative Model of Physical Therapist Assistant Education and Evaluative Criteria* are recognized and used as the foundation for physical therapist practice, research, and education environments.

accepting a patient/client for physical therapy services, a physical therapist shall be responsible for: the examination, evaluation, and diagnosis of that individual; the prognosis and intervention; re-examination and modification of the plan of care; and the maintenance of adequate records, including progress reports."

Also, the section of the Standards of Practice for Physical Therapy and the Criteria[2] pertaining to patient/client management states that "the physical therapist performs an initial examination and evaluation to establish a diagnosis and prognosis prior to intervention," and that the examination "is documented, dated, and appropriately authenticated by the physical therapist who performed it." Facility regulations (such as Title XXII of the Public Health Service Act or standards of the Joint Commission on Accreditation of Healthcare Organizations) and state practice acts (such as California's) also may mandate documentation of the PT's evaluation of the patient.

Plan of care. Despite the specificity of the physician referral for physical therapy, PTs are responsible for developing a plan of care that addresses the findings of their own examination and evaluation of the patient. In this case, given the extent of the pain, bruising, and swelling in the patient's thigh, and the absence of X-ray results, heat and/or massage may *not* have constituted the most appropriate physical therapy intervention. PTs are responsible—regardless of the specificity of the referral or physi-cal proximity to the referring provider— for voicing any concerns they might have about ordered physical therapy interventions that are contraindicated or seem inappropriate. At a minimum, in this case the PT should have insisted that X-rays be taken and read prior to initiating heat-related or manual (massage or exercise) therapeutic procedures.

The portions of the same APTA documents as those listed previously apply here. In addition, PTs are well advised to check their practice act for laws and regulations specific to their state. (For a complete list, go to www.apta.org and click on "Practice," "Physical Therapy Licensure/State Practice Acts," then "Directory of State Practice Acts.") PTs also would do well to reference the

liability awareness

Hooked on Evidence database on APTA's Web site to ensure evidence-based practice.)

Referral. The PT has a professional duty to refer the patient to more urgent care if that is warranted by the acuity or severity of the patient's symptoms on presentation to the PT and/or the patient's response to physical therapy intervention. In this case, it is unclear if the patient experienced immediate worsening of symptoms upon application of heat and/or massage by the PT. Given the nature of the injury, at the least, however, the PT should have (1) strongly advised the patient to monitor her symptoms and told her what to do if they worsened (eg, seek immediate care, call the PT, or call the physician's office), and (2) document-

ed all the advice she gave. PTs cannot be held liable for treatment rendered by physicians in their absence. In this case, however, the PT bears responsibility for the reaction to her own treatment (increased pain and swelling), and for her failure to advise the patient (and to so document).

Principles pertaining to patient autonomy and consent in the APTA Guide for Professional Conduct dictate that "A physical therapist shall communicate to the patient/client the findings of his/her examination, evaluation, diagnosis, and prognosis," and that "A physical therapist shall collaborate with the patient/client to establish the goals of treatment and the plan of care." Regarding professional practice, the same document states, "A

physical therapist shall provide examination, evaluation, diagnosis, prognosis, and intervention."

In terms of professional responsibility, the Guide for Professional Conduct states that:

❖ "Regardless of practice setting, a physical therapist has primary responsibility for the physical therapy care of a patient and shall make independent judgments regarding that care consistent with accepted professional standards."

❖ "Upon accepting a patient/client for physical therapy services, a physical therapist shall be responsible for: the examination, evaluation, and diagnosis of that individual; the prognosis and intervention; re-examination and modification of the plan of care; and the maintenance of adequate records, including progress reports. A physical therapist shall establish the plan of care and shall provide and/or supervise and direct the appropriate interventions."

❖ "When the patient has been referred from another practitioner, the physical therapist shall communicate the findings of the examination and evaluation, the diagnosis, the proposed intervention, and re-examination findings (as indicated) to the referring practitioner."

The Standards of Practice and the Criteria state that the PT responsible for the direction of the physical therapy "Ensures compliance with current APTA documents, including Standards of Practice for Physical Therapy and the Criteria, *Guide to Physical Therapist Practice*, Code of Ethics, Guide for Professional Conduct, and Standards of Ethical Conduct for the Physical Therapist Assistant."

Several patient/client management standards in the Standards of Practice and the Criteria also speak to risk management in this case, including those governing initial examination, evaluation, diagnosis, prognosis, plan of care, intervention, and reexamination.

Relationship with referral source. Finally, it is important to consider the risky elements in the referral arrangement the PT in this case has with the physician. Despite the fact that the PT in this case had an independent practice, her practice behavior (as outlined previously) did not reflect her status as an autonomous, licensed professional.

PTs who have a close business tie to a referring provider and/or are located in space that is contiguous with a referring provider may feel they are "safe" in not adhering to clinical practice standards as diligently as they would otherwise, and in following with little or no question referral instructions from such sources. As we see in this case, however, a PT's state license prohibits him or her from abdicating any professional responsibilities.

In terms of APTA documents, the previously cited passages regarding professional responsibility and practice arrangements again apply. **PT**

Rita Arriaga, PT, MS, is an associate clinical professor in the Graduate Program in Physical Therapy and the director of rehabilitation services at the University of California, San Francisco, and is a former chair of APTA's Committee on Risk Management and Member Benefits. She can be reached at 415/476-3453 or arriaga@itsa.ucsf.edu.

Do you have risk-management questions or concerns? Insights into what PTs need or want to know will help APTA educate members about the types of incidents occurring in the workplace and about appropriate risk-management techniques. Contact Jennifer Baker, Director of APTA Risk Management and Member Benefit Services, at 800/999-2782, ext 3145, or jenniferbaker@apta.org.

References

1. American Physical Therapy Association. APTA Guide for Professional Conduct. Available at www.apta.org/pt_practice/ethics_pt/pro_conduct. Accessed February 19, 2004.
2. American Physical Therapy Association. Standards of Practice and the Criteria. Available at www.apta.org/About/core_documents/standardsofpractice. Accessed February 19, 2004.

APTA core documents, policies, and positions are available on the Association's Web site (www.apta.org). Click on "About APTA" for the links.

Also, consult these publications: *A Normative Model of Physical Therapist Professional Education: Version 2000*, Guide to Physical Therapist Practice, Revised 2nd ed, and *Risk Management for Physical Therapists: A Quick Reference*. Descriptions and ordering information are available on APTA's Web site. Click on "Online Shopping," then "Order From Online Catalog."

liabilityawareness

by Carol Schunk, PT, PsyD, Cathy Thut, PT, MBA, and Carol Davis, PT, EdD, MS, FAPTA

Producing Singular Results

Here's how to achieve optimal outcomes and decrease liability risks when two or more providers of physical therapy serve the same patient within an episode of care.

While the norm is for a patient to receive physical therapy services from a single physical therapist (PT) throughout an episode of care, there are several scenarios in which a patient likely may see two or more different providers of physical therapy. For example:

❖ A patient sees more than one staff PT during a multi-day stay at an acute care hospital.

❖ A patient visiting an outpatient facility sees a PT who is available within that time slot—who may not be the same PT the patient saw on his or her previous visit.

❖ At a rehabilitation center in a rapidly growing skilled nursing facility, staffing shortages, vacations, and illnesses necessitate the use of "on call" or contract PTs. Thus, patients may receive care from different PTs on different days.

What are the some of the potential liability issues and risks when more than one PT is involved in patient care?

Issues and Answers

Let's look at some of key issues identified by the APTA Committee on Risk Management and Member Benefits that providers of physical therapy must keep in mind when working together to deliver optimal patient care, and how they might best be addressed.

Patient perceptions regarding <u>continuity</u> of care. A study described in the *Archives of Internal Medicine*[1] asked 45 plaintiffs in medical liability cases why they were suing. Researchers found that litigation often was associated with perceived lack of caring, and that a specific charge was "deserting

the patient." Such desertion needn't be literal—in fact, it seldom if ever is. Rather, it's a matter of patient perception. When a PT examines a patient a professional relationship is established. The patient may feel a sense of abandonment if a different provider of physical therapy conducts follow-up visits. If there is an adverse incident, the patient may file a claim in part because he or she feels abandoned. In some cases, the patient may feel that more direct involvement by the original PT might have prevented the incident.

Emphasizing to the patient the high level of ongoing communication among all members of the care team will help negate any perception of feelings of desertion/abandonment and assures the patient of the continuity of his or her care. Along those lines, such statements as, "As Mary Jones, the physical therapist who initially evaluated you, said Tuesday … ," can go a long way toward building patient confidence that his or her care has been passed along to a PT who is appropriately apprised of and prepared to address that patient's specific therapy issues.

Patient perceptions regarding <u>consistency</u> of care. The patient may perceive that his or her treatment plan is being altered every time someone new enters the scene. While this should not be the case, given the foundation of a written plan of care, there may be slight differences from physical therapy provider to physical therapy provider in the way a patient is positioned, or minor differences in pressure during manual therapy or massage, or, perhaps, an order for home exercise or in-room treatment rather than exercise in the gym. Even these sorts of

changes can provoke patient frustration and comments such as, "John never does it this way."

PTs can reassure most patients relatively easily with statements such as, "I want to do something a little different with you today because X," or "I think home exercise is advisable at this point because Y." The consistent messages should be that slight variations in touch, pressure, and position are to be expected during the course of care, and that the efficacy of treatment may require modifications of the plan of care, regardless of which PT is seeing the patient at any given time.

Communication—and documentation of communication—among providers. If multiple practitioners are involved with one patient and an incident occurs, one of the first things that will be examined is communication among the practitioners. Documentation can be a friend or foe in the event of a lawsuit. Where there is only one health care provider, documentation must support the intervention with details about the patient's reaction to physical therapy. When multiple providers are involved, documentation also must convey the intricacies of those interactions among members of the health care team. For example, communication between providers about a shared patient should be in writing; such written notes can be of benefit if an incident results in a lawsuit. Poor or incomplete documentation can lead to a team member's misinterpretation of the plan of care.

Communication is essential in health care. Although it's a basic principle of effective patient management, it's surprising, in malpractice cases throughout the health care professions, how often the defendant's case is undermined, and large settlements paid, because of insufficient evidence of an appropriate level of communication among providers. State practice acts may dictate specific communication and supervision rules and parameters between PTs and other members of a care team. Every consultation about a patient is an essential part of the medical record. This is especially true should the patient experience any adverse reaction to treatment.

Regarding communication with patients, most patients don't like surprises when it comes to their care. If a PT is going on vacation or plans to change jobs, he or she should notify the patient and assure that individual that all the details of his or her condition and care have been communicated to the PT who will be covering for the vacationing PT or replacing the departing one. While it may not always be possible, it's better yet for the patient's current PT to introduce the replacement PT to the patient. It also is good practice, when applicable, for the PT to introduce the patient to other members of the care team, such as a PTA who may be assisting with that patient's care.

Liability. Even when delegation to support personnel follows all the correct paths of state practice acts and APTA policy, the PT always is responsible to and for the patient. This means that the PT can be held liable for incidents involving those to whom care is delegated, so the need for close PT oversight of all aspects of patient care cannot be overstated.

PTs practice in many organizational environments and sometimes work with others to provide care to a patient. Recognizing the issues presented when more than one provider of physical therapy is involved in rendering care, and reviewing and heeding the APTA documents highlighted in this column, can help minimize risks for providers and,

most important, help PTs ensure positive outcomes for their patients.

Guidance

The APTA Guide for Professional Conduct (www.apta.org; click on "About APTA") is designed to interpret the APTA Code of Ethics and guide PTs in determining the propriety of their actions. Principles that apply directly to the issues presented in this column include:

❖ 2.1 D. A physical therapist shall encourage an open and collaborative dialogue with the patient/client.

❖ 2.4 B. A physical therapist shall communicate to the patient/client the findings of his/her examination, evaluation, diagnosis, and prognosis.

❖ 2.4 C. A physical therapist shall collaborate with the patient/client to establish the goals of treatment and the plan of care.

❖ 4.1 A. A physical therapist shall make professional judgments that are in the patient/client's best interests.

❖ 4.1 B. Regardless of practice setting, a physical therapist has primary responsibility for the physical therapy care of a patient and shall make independent judgments regarding that care consistent with accepted professional standards.

❖ 4.1.E. Upon accepting a patient/client for physical therapy services, a physical therapist shall be responsible for: the examination, evaluation, and diagnosis of the individual; the prognosis and intervention; re-evaluation and modification of the plan of care; and the maintenance of adequate records including progress reports. A physical therapist shall establish the plan of care and shall provide and / or supervise and direct appropriate interventions.

❖ 4.1 G. When the patient has been referred from another practitioner, the physical therapist shall communicate

pertinent findings and/or information to the referring practitioner.

❖ 4.2 A. The supervising physical therapist has primary responsibility for the physical therapy care rendered to a patient/client.

❖ 4.2 B. A physical therapist shall not delegate to a less qualified person any activity that requires the professional skill, knowledge, and judgment of the physical therapist.

In addition, the following standards in the Guide for Conduct of the Physical Therapist Assistant (also under "About APTA" on the Association's Web site) are important to note in considering the scenarios and issues presented in this column:

❖ 3. A physical therapist assistant shall provide selected physical therapy interventions only under the supervision and direction of a physical therapist.

❖ 3.1 G. A physical therapist assistant shall have regular and ongoing communication with the physical therapist regarding the patient's/client's status.

Taking into consideration the applicable portions of the APTA Guide for Professional Conduct and the Guide for Conduct of the Physical Therapist Assistant, the best ways to promote optimal patient care and avoid risky scenarios come into clear focus. ⓟ

Carol Schunk PT, PsyD, is a PT at Central Oregon Home Health and Hospice, a clinical consultant for TAOS (Therapeutic Associates Outcomes System), and editor of the APTA Geriatrics Section newsletter Gerinotes. *Cathy Thut, PT, MBA,* is director of physical medicine at Baylor Medical Center at Irving in Texas. *Carol Davis, PT, EdD, MS, FAPTA,* is associate director of curriculum and a professor in the Department of Physical Therapy at the University of Miami School of Medicine in Coral Gables, Florida. They can be reached at carolschunk@earthlink. net, cathyt@baylorhealth.edu, and cmdavis@miami.edu. Schunk is a current member and Thut a former member of APTA's Committee on Rick Management and Member Benefits. Davis is current chair of APTA's Ethics and Judicial Committee.

Reference
1. Beckman HB, Markakis KM, Suchman AL, Frankel RM. The doctor-patient relationship and malpractice. Lessons from plaintiff depositions. *Arch Intern Med.* 1994;154:1365-1370.

Employer/Business Issues

Non-Discrimination in the Provision of Physical Therapy Services
HOD P06-03-24-21 (Initial HOD 06-89-39-84)

Physical therapy practitioners shall provide quality, nonjudgmental care in accordance with their knowledge and expertise to all persons who need it, regardless of the nature of the health problem. When providing care to individuals with infectious disease, the American Physical Therapy Association advocates that members be guided in their actions by guidelines developed by the Centers for Disease Control and Prevention (CDC) and regulations set by the Occupational Safety and Health Administration (OSHA).

Physical Therapy Practitioners With Communicable Diseases or Conditions
HOD P06-93-15-20 (Initial HOD 06-91-12-15)

Physical therapists and physical therapist assistants with known communicable diseases or conditions have a right to continue careers in physical therapy in a capacity which poses no identifiable risk to their patients/clients.

Physical therapists and physical therapist assistants with known communicable diseases or conditions shall have an ethical obligation to abstain from those professional activities over which they cannot sustain an acceptable level of risk of transmission to the patient/client. An acceptable level of risk is achieved by exercising precautions recommended by the Centers for Disease Control and Prevention (CDC), the Occupational Health and Safety Administration (OHSA), or other authoritative body.

Physical therapists and physical therapist assistants who are both at risk of acquiring communicable diseases or conditions and who engage in professional activities with identifiable risks of transmission of those communicable diseases or conditions should take appropriate measures to determine their health status.

Guidelines: Recruiting and Hiring Internationally Educated Physical Therapists
HOD G06-94-34-45

1. The employer shall comply with the H-1B visa regulations and the "Labor Condition Application" (LCA) process required by the Immigration and Naturalization Service and the Department of Labor.
2. There should be disclosure by the employer of ownership of the practice and the setting type (contract or specific facility).
3. There should be notification by the employer to the physical therapist if the practice is involved in any situation in which a referring practitioner can profit as a result of referring patients/clients for physical therapy and notification that the American Physical Therapy Association (APTA) is opposed to such situations.
4. There should be a clearly delineated, fair, and reasonable buy-out provision in which the physical therapist understands the legal commitment to pay back the recruitment fees in the event that there is dissatisfaction or reason for release from the contract on the physical therapist's part at any time during the term of the agreement. The exact dollar amount should be clearly stated from the beginning of the agreement.
5. A no-penalty bailout provision should be provided in the event of change of ownership, but the physical therapist may be held to adhere to a reasonable payback schedule.

6. The employer shall notify the physical therapist that if the established relationship is terminated, the sponsorship of the physical therapist is invalidated.

7. Avoidance of noncompete clauses is recommended but if there is reasonable limitation of time and distance, one may be incorporated.

8. The employer should advise the physical therapist that his or her interest may best be served by obtaining appropriate counsel prior to signing the contract.

9. The contract should be written for the territorial jurisdiction(s) in which the physical therapist will practice.

10. The employer should give the physical therapist, before signing the contract, a copy of the "Labor Conditions Application" (LCA) that is filed with the US Department of Labor Office.

11. The employer should give the physical therapist a copy of the prevailing wage survey presented to the US Department of Labor Office with the LCA.

12. All agreements should be presented to the physical therapist in both English and the language native to the internationally educated physical therapist.

13. The employer, when assuming the legal responsibility for the application process for a candidate, should monitor the completion of the educational credentialing process for the physical therapist.

14. The employer should provide services for cultural orientation of the physical therapist.

Guidelines: Student and Employer Contracts
HOD G06-92-14-28

Guidelines for fairness in offering student financial assistance in exchange for a promise of future employment:

1. Notification by the employer if the place of employment may be in an isolated area or as a solo practitioner such that the new graduate will not have ready access to mentoring and regular collegial relationships or any resources for professional growth and development.

2. Disclosure by the employer of ownership of the practice.

3. Notification by the employer to the student if the practice is involved in any situation in which a referring practitioner can profit as a result of referring patients/clients for physical therapy and notification that the American Physical Therapy Association (APTA) is opposed to such situations.

4. Student awareness of any potential future tax obligations that may be incurred upon graduation as the result of deferred income.

5. The agreement must not, in any way, interfere with the process and planning of the student's professional education.

6. It should be understood that the school is not a party to the agreement and is not bound to any conditions of the agreement.

7. There should be a clearly delineated, fair, and reasonable buy-out provision in which the student understands the legal commitment to pay back the stipend with reasonable interest in the event that there is dissatisfaction or reason for release from the contract on the student's part at any time during the term of the agreement.

8. A no-penalty bailout provision should be provided in the event of change of ownership, but the student may be required to adhere to a reasonable payback schedule.

9. Avoidance of noncompete clauses is recommended, but if there is a reasonable limitation of time and distance, one should be incorporated.

10. A student's interests may best be served by obtaining appropriate counsel prior to signing the contract.

liability awareness

by Cathy Thut, PT, MBA

A Risk Consideration for Contract Staffing

Rulings by the Office of Inspector General add an extra dimension of risk to contract staffing arrangements.

In the provision of physical therapy services, the use of contract staff has long been a viable alternative to the traditional employer-employee relationship. Rulings by the Office of Inspector General (OIG), however, add a liability risk to these arrangements that bears scrutiny.

The purpose of the OIG, as established by the Department of Health and Human Services, is to identify fraud and abuse in federally funded programs and to promote efficiency in the Department's operations. The OIG has been given authority to exclude individuals and entities from participation in Medicare, Medicaid, and other federally funded programs. Additionally, the OIG has the authority to impose civil monetary penalties for specific incidences of misconduct.

In 1977, Congress mandated the exclusion of physicians and other practitioners convicted of "program related crimes from participation in Medicare and Medicaid."[1] Congress followed this with the enactment of the Civil Monetary Penalties Law in 1981. This law authorized the OIG to assess penalties against individuals and entities who "submitted false or fraudulent, or otherwise improper claims for Medicare or Medicaid payment."[2] By definition, improper claims are claims submitted for services provided while the individual or entity has been formally excluded from participation in Medicare or Medicaid.

The Health Insurance Portability and Accountability Act[3] (1996) and the Balanced Budget Act[4] (1997) further expanded the scope of the OIG in sanctions against healthcare providers. Specifically, the BBA authorized new civil monetary penalties against health care providers or entities that employ or contract with individuals who have been excluded from participation in the federal health programs.

Exclusion Parameters

Exclusion from federal health care programs means that *no payment* may be made for any items or services furnished by the excluded individual, including direct patient care, administrative or management services, or any other services after the date of exclusion. This payment ban includes fee schedules, cost reports, prospective payment systems, or itemized claims. The ban also encompasses individuals who have changed from one health care profession to another while excluded. Additionally, no federal program payment can cover the excluded individual's salary, expenses, or other benefits regardless of whether the individual provides direct patient care or not.[5]

If an excluded individual provides services for which federal health care program payment is sought by another entity, both the individual and the entity may be subject to a civil monetary penalty of up to $10,000, plus triple damage for *each* item or service furnished during the period of exclusion. The 1997 statute clearly states that, for liability to be imposed, "the provider submitting the claims for healthcare items or services furnished by an excluded individual knows or should know that the person was excluded." Thus, the practical effect is to preclude any employment arrangement of an excluded individual by any health care provider or entity that receives federal health care reimbursement, either directly or indirectly.[5]

Risk Prevention

To date, 17,000 individuals and entities have been excluded from participating in federal health care programs due to misconduct ranging from fraud convictions to patient abuse to defaulting on health education loans. Employers should screen candidates and contract staff for OIG sanctions regularly. OIG maintains a list of individuals who have been sanctioned, which can be found on the OIG web site at www.hhs.gov/oig. The list is updated monthly and includes each individual's name, the legal basis for his or her exclusion, and the state where the exclusion occurred.

If an employer wishes to employ an excluded individual to provide services that are not reimbursed with federal funds, the employer should know the limited circumstances under which that individual may be hired. The OIG provides an advisory opinion process for formal, binding guidance on whether an employment or contractual arrangement is in violation of the OIG exclusion. Information about this process can be accessed on the OIG web site. **PT**

Cathy Thut, PT, MBA, is director of physical medicine and rehabilitation at Baylor Medical Center at Irving, Texas. She can be reached via e-mail at cathyt@baylordallas.edu.

References

1. Medicare-Medicaid Anti-Fraud and Abuse Amendments, Pub L No. 65-142 (1977).
2. Civil Monetary Penalties Law, Pub L No. 97-35 (1981).
3. Health Insurance Portability and Accountability Act, Pub L No. 104-191 (1996).
4. Balanced Budget Act, 42 CFR §1003.102(a)(2), § 1128A(a)(6), (1997).
5. Special Advisory Bulletin: The Effect of Exclusion From Participation in Federal Health Care Programs, 64 *Federal Register* 52791-52794 (1999).

LIABILITY AWARENESS
Staying Informed in Risk Management
by Rita Arriaga, PT, MS

Stories From the Front—Part Two: Modalities

A real-life scenario illustrates some basic risk-management principles.

Last month, *PT* ran the first of a three-part Liability Awareness series that adapts actual cases from the APTA-endorsed professional liability insurance claims history and discusses possible risk-management techniques that could have been used. APTA continues the series with this second case

problems, including diabetes and residual right-sided weakness from a prior stroke. The nursing staff also had characterized the patient as a chronic complainer.

The patient was referred for physical therapy to maximize her lower-extremity flexibility and strength during the period of bed rest in preparation for eventual

ent reason (which seemed to substantiate nursing reports that she was a chronic complainer), the PT did not take her complaint seriously. With no support personnel to assist him, he completed his treatment with the other patient and did not check the hot packs.

Unfortunately, when the PT finally returned to the patient's room about 15 minutes later and removed the hot packs from the patient's legs, he found that the packs were, indeed, too hot and had caused a burn. The burn would eventually require skin grafting.

A claim was filed against the PT for negligence due to inappropriate application of a treatment modality and failure to monitor the patient during treatment.

Now turn the page for commentary on this scenario from a risk-management perspective, including a table summarizing risky elements and strategies to address them.

> **Even the application of a simple modality, such as a moist hot pack, can pose a major risk if not applied and monitored according to written procedures and standards of care.**

study.

The following scenario involves the application of a common modality—the hot pack. It demonstrates the need to consistently attend to the safe utilization of all our interventions, even the most simple. It also reminds us that risk management encompasses the PT's responsibility to manage all aspects of patient care, including the scheduling of patients and assurance of adequate staff to address the therapy needs of our patients.

As you read the scenario, consider the following questions:

❖ What are the elements in this scenario that increase the PT's risk of professional liability?

❖ What risk-management techniques could have been used to reduce that risk?

An elderly woman living in a nursing home was bedridden because of a recent hip fracture. In addition to her broken hip, the woman had a history of medical

mobilization. The PT's plan of care included moist hot packs to the legs to relax the patient's muscles and range-of-motion and strengthening exercises. He planned to treat the patient two to three times per week.

On the day of the incident (a week after therapy had been initiated), the PT began the treatment session as usual, by applying hot packs to the patient's legs before initiating exercises. The patient was wearing a pair of long pants, so the PT wrapped the packs in a couple of towels and then placed them on the patient's legs over her pants. He gave her the emergency call button, left her room, and went to treat a patient in the next room.

After 10 minutes, the patient rang her call button and complained that the applied hot packs were too hot. The PT, who was walking with another patient in the hallway outside the room, heard the patient complain. However, because he had already had an experience with her when she had complained without appar-

The information presented here is not to be interpreted as specific legal advice for any particular provider. Personal advice can only be given by personal legal counsel, based on applicable state and federal law.

Do you have risk management questions or concerns? Information about what PTs need or want to know will help APTA's efforts to educate members about the types of claims occurring in the workplace and about appropriate risk-management techniques. Contact Jennifer Baker, Director, APTA Insurance and Member Benefit Services, at 800/999-2782, ext 3145 or via e-mail at jenniferbaker@apta.org.

The PT did not follow written procedures regarding application of hot packs.

Although the application of hot packs is simple, the modality can be a major risk if not applied appropriately. First, the water in which the packs are kept must be checked regularly to ensure that the packs are at an effective yet safe temperature. The PT also should have adhered to the procedure manual regarding the amount and type of padding needed for the hot packs. Patients' garments do not take the place of adequate padding. Indeed, in the presence of possible sensory loss, additional padding is a risk-reduction strategy.

The PT failed to monitor the hot packs regularly during their application, especially in the presence of possible sensory loss.

The PT should have performed a thorough evaluation of the patient's sensation before applying the hot packs. Then, once he made the decision to utilize the heat therapy, he should have monitored its effects through periodic skin checks. The PT in this case should have exercised increased vigilance with monitoring due to the increased risk factors or the patient's age and other medical problems.

The PT ignored the patient's complaints because of a specific perceived personality trait.

A patient's complaints in response to intervention must be appropriately and immediately assessed. Regardless of a patient's behavioral tendencies, all complaints should be evaluated for validity.

The PT was unable to monitor the modality because he had left the room to treat another patient.

PTs are responsible to ensure that they have adequate staff to address patient volume and treatment needs safely and appropriately. APTA's *Standards of Practice for Physical Therapy and the Criteria* (HOD 06-99-18-22) state that "the physical therapy service...provides for appropriate ratios of personnel to patients" (Standard II.G). In this particular case, a physical therapist assistant could have assisted the PT by monitoring the hot packs once they were applied, and, at the very least, could have responded immediately to the patient's complaint. In the absence of support personnel, the PT should have scheduled his patient activity to allow him to monitor the application of the modality.

These days, PTs continue to feel pressures to maximize productivity and to treat patients as efficiently as possible. In times of increased stress, however, PTs must remain attentive to all details of patient care delivery. Even the application of a simple modality, such as a moist hot pack, can pose a major risk if not applied and monitored according to written procedures and standards of care.

Additional precaution was warranted in this case because of the patient's age and medical history, which indicated that sensation could be affected. This case also highlights the necessity of appropriately managing your patient schedule. PTs must ensure that their daily patient schedules can accommodate both patient volume and case complexity. PTs should consider whether they have adequate time and support to perform all tasks required to treat their patients safely. The PT in this case could have managed his risk by directing a PTA to monitor the hot packs once they had been applied. *PT*

Rita Arriaga, PT, MS, is Assistant Clinical Professor in the Graduate Program of Physical Therapy, University of California at San Francisco, and is a member of APTA's Committee on Risk Management Services and Member Benefits.

Suggested Readings

Arriaga, R. Stories from the front—part one: delegation. *PT—Magazine of Physical Therapy.* 1998; 6(7):27-28.

Arriaga, R. Stories from the front—part two: utilization of support staff. *PT—Magazine of Physical Therapy.* 1998; 6(9):31-32.

Arriaga, R. Stories from the front—part three: practice across state lines. *PT—Magazine of Physical Therapy.* 1998; 6(10):31-32.

Arriaga, R. Stories from the front—part one: supervision. *PT—Magazine of Physical Therapy.* 1999; 7(11):55-56.

liability awareness

by Rita Arriaga, PT, MS

Stories From the Front—
Part Two: Recent PT Graduates

A real-life scenario illustrates some basic risk-management principles.

For the third year in a row, **PT** is featuring a three-part Liability Awareness series presenting cases adapted from the APTA-endorsed professional liability insurance claims history. The series examines techniques that could have been used and actions that might have been taken to reduce risk. This year's series began last month with a look at physical therapist assistants (PTAs) and safe practice.[1] This second case study illustrates the need for recent graduates of physical therapy programs to receive adequate staff development, consult with more-experienced PTs when appropriate, and properly document all aspects of patient management.

As you read the scenario, consider these questions:
❖ What are the elements in this scenario that increase the physical therapist's (PT's) liability risk?
❖ What risk-management techniques could have been used to reduce that risk?

> A review of the patient's physical therapy records showed that the PT had documented the interventions but unfortunately made no mention of the patient's reactions to them.

This case involved a 48-year-old man who had undergone a hemilaminectomy and lumbar discectomy at L5-S1 3 days earlier and was experiencing weakness in his right gluteal area and right calf, and numbness in the fifth digit and plantar surface of his right foot. He was referred for physical therapy to address these impairments. The PT managing his care had been licensed for 2 months and was employed in a private PT clinic. Over the next 2 weeks, the patient's foot problems did not markedly improve. One of the therapeutic exercise interventions the PT initiated to address this persistent problem was placing the patient on a mini-trampoline and doing toe raising. The PT also had the patient assume a single-leg stance and throw a ball back and forth with the PT. At no time during the course of treatment did the PT discuss the patient's program with the PT's employer or other PTs in the clinic.

According to the PT when he was asked later, the patient seemed to benefit from and enjoy the interventions and did not experience any adverse incident or pain during them. However, the patient somehow reinjured his back and required a second surgery 5 months later. He filed suit against the PT, claiming that the reinjury was a direct result of the interventions the PT had initiated. The patient further claimed that he had told the PT that he felt slightly unsteady during the interventions. The patient also stated that, on one occasion, he had lost his balance and fell off the mini-trampoline while throwing the ball, but was helped back onto the mini-trampoline by the PT and continued the intervention.

A review of the patient's physical therapy records showed that the PT had documented the interventions but unfortunately made no mention of the patient's reactions to them. Neither did the documentation note the patient's status during the treatment program, nor his safe completion of the interventions without incident.

The clinic's owner, an experienced PT, stated during mediation that, had the recent PT graduate consulted with her, she would not have recommended the use of the mini-trampoline with a patient less than 3 weeks removed from surgery.

Now, turn the page for commentary on this scenario from a risk-management perspective, including a table summarizing risky elements and strategies to address them.

liability awareness

A PT is a PT—a licensed professional with a tested body of skills and knowledge—regardless of how long he or she has been in the profession. The fact that the PT at the center of this case had only been on the job for 2 months isn't an issue here, but his judgment is. While the mini-trampoline exercises he initiated may have been entirely appropriate for the patient given a sufficient period of recovery from the hemilaminectomy and lumbar discectomy, less than 3 weeks may not have been enough time for the patient to be ready to safely undertake those interventions.

The PT's incomplete documentation compounded his risk. By failing to record the patient's positive reaction to the interventions and his safe completion of them, the PT was left with nothing but his word against the patient's as to what occurred during the patient visit. Written documentation would have strengthened his legal case and may have at least reduced the amount of any liability award.

Even the most-accomplished PT graduate can't learn everything in school. Given the PT's limited experience, he may more appropriately have discussed his planned interventions with his employer or another more-experienced PT on staff to confirm that he was making prudent intervention decisions. The employer PT, on the other hand, is responsible for staff development. Had she carried out a more thorough development plan for new staff—one that perhaps involved regularly scheduled chart reviews and discussions with the new graduate to provide him with opportunities to talk about possible interventions in situations such as this—the mini-trampoline might not have been used and the patient might not have reinjured his back. ⊕

Rita Arriaga, PT, MS, is an Assistant Clinical Professor in the Graduate Program in Physical Therapy and the Director of Rehabilitation Services at the University of California, San Francisco, and chairs APTA's Committee on Risk Management Services and Member Benefits.

Reference:

1. Arriaga R. Stories from the front—part one: PTAs and safe practice. *PT—Magazine of Physical Therapy.* 2001;9(1):22-23.

Suggested Readings

American Physical Therapy Association. Board of Directors policies. Available at www.apta.org/governance/governance_5/BODpolicies.
American Physical Therapy Association. Ethics and legal issues in physical therapy. Available at www.apta.org/PT_Practice/ethics_pt.
American Physical Therapy Association. House of Delegates policies. Available at www.apta.org/governance/HOD/governance_10.
Guide to Physical Therapy Practice. *Phys Ther.* 2001;81:9-752.
Pearls for Physical Therapists. Alexandria, Va: American Physical Therapy Association; 1997.

The recent PT graduate lacked good judgment in failing to consult with a more-experienced PT before implementing interventions.

Principal 4 of the APTA House of Delegates' *Code of Ethics* for the practice of physical therapy (HOD 06-00-12-23) states that a PT "shall exercise sound judgment." The best way for this PT to have demonstrated sound professional judgment, given his limited experience, would have been for him to have self-assessed and realized the benefit of discussing his planned interventions with an experienced PT, who would have advised him that a patient who was less than 3 weeks removed from surgery might have difficulty with these particular interventions.

The PT owner of the outpatient facility hadn't developed an adequate plan for recent PT graduates' growth and development.

The APTA Board of Directors' *Criteria for Standards of Practice for Physical Therapy* (BOD 03-00-22-53) state that the physical therapy service's written plan for "appropriate and ongoing staff development" shall include "self-assessment" and "mechanisms to foster mentorship activities." Had the PT owner more strongly emphasized the need for the new PT to self-assess the scenario and ask himself whether consultation was advisable, and had the PT owner been more closely involved in personally mentoring her PT employee or seeing that someone else on staff did, the outcome of this scenario might have been different. Were the PT owner more engaged in recent graduates' development, she might even have instituted a system involving their thorough orientation to clinic policies and procedures (including documentation standards), followed by opportunities for recent graduates to "get their feet wet" by initially working with patients who already are being treated. Under this system, recent graduates would be expected to consult with the original PT regarding any changes in patient management. Periodic chart reviews and case discussions between veteran and new PTs also would be appropriate components of a development plan. In such an environment, the recent PT graduate in this case study would have followed a treatment plan that was developed by or in conjunction with the PT owner or another more-experienced PT.

The recent graduate PT failed to document the patient's reactions to the interventions performed.

The APTA Board of Directors' *Guidelines for Physical Therapy Documentation* (BOD 03-00-22-54) state that documentation of each patient visit shall include "patient/client self-report" and "adverse reactions to interventions, if any." By failing to document the patient's favorable comments and safe completion of the interventions, the PT had no written support to counter the patient's claims that he had reported unsteadiness and that he fell off the mini-trampoline during the intervention.

L E G A L B R I E F S

Part 1: Physical Therapy Contracts

Editor's note: *Part 1 of this three-part series on physical therapy contracts discusses types of contracts, parties that may be involved in contracting, and some of the clauses most frequently used in physical therapy contracts.*

Physical therapists regularly contract in a number of ways. They make a contract with each patient; they provide services (e.g., treatment and consultations). Their contractual relationships are varied: They can be employees, independent contractors, consultants, sellers of goods, and lessors of equipment. The other parties to the contract include not only patients but third-party payers, manufacturers' representatives, agencies (e.g., schools and home health care agencies) and support service providers (e.g., certified public accountants).

In addition to the many varieties of contracts in physical therapy, the increasing complexity of these contracts parallels the increasing complexity of our health care system. With the increasing complexity—and increasing numbers—of contracts in the health care service delivery system, information about contracts may be important to physical therapists.

What Is a Contract?

A *contract* may be defined as "an agreement between two or more persons that creates an obligation to

By Kathy Lewis, JD, PT

do or not to do a particular thing." Contracts may be actual agreements (*express contracts*) or inferred by the law as a matter of justice (*implied contracts*). Although individuals have the right of freedom to contract, statutes and common law impose limitations on that right. When agreements are related to the sale of goods, for example, statutes impose implied warranties to protect the purchaser.

A survey* was conducted in 1991 with three purposes: 1) to provide a perspective on the types of contracts that are actually being signed by physical therapists, 2) to identify the *frequency of clauses* used in these physical therapy service contracts, and 3) to identify examples of legal concerns. *Because contract law is extremely complex, no attempt was made to evaluate the quality or legality of a contract or the clauses within a contract.*

Sixty contracts were submitted from respondents representing 19 states (Figure 1). Parties to the contracts and the amounts of remuner-

*Supported by PT Bulletin, which announced a request for volunteers, and through a grant from the School of Allied Health of the University of Kansas Medical Center, Kansas City, KS.

ation were not disclosed to the researcher. A list of contract clauses and corresponding definitions were determined before reviewing the contracts. Each contract was coded with a reference number for later verification of recording accuracy. This code was recorded on the contract and on the data sheet.

The contract clauses were reviewed and then categorized according to the type. When a clause could have been classified in more than one category, a decision was made to classify it under only one of the options. The assigned category was recorded on the contract and on a data form. To define the parties to the agreement: The physical therapist is the party who is providing physical therapy services and the contractor is the "other party" to the contract.

The types of service contracts represented in this survey were varied (Table). However, when the contract did not explicitly state the service type, no attempt was made to interpret the contract to make a judgment on service type. Figure 1 contains a list of types of clauses and the definitions corresponding to each clause. The frequencies in which these clauses occurred in the contracts are shown in Figure 2.

Concerns for Independent Contractors

A review of these contracts reveals several concerns for physical therapists who are considering contracting to provide physical therapy services as independent contractors.

Contract terms may be contradictory. For example, the declaration that a party is an independent contractor is not sufficient in itself to establish that the therapist is an independent contractor. "Interpreting a contract" means that the entire agreement is reviewed to identify the intent of the parties. Out of the 25 contracts stating the physical therapist was an independent contractor, four held the therapist to policies and procedures of the contractor, without any evidence that these conditions were bargained over by the parties. When a worker's services are integrated with the regular business operations to make that worker indistinguishable from a regular employee, the worker generally is considered "under the control and supervision" of the contractor ("other party") and is considered an employee and not an independent contractor.

Right of control. Another primary element to defeat the physical therapist's claim of "independent contractor" is the right of the contractor'("other party") to control. Whether the contractor actually exercises control is irrelevant when the contractor has the right to control. Five of the 25 "independent contractor" contracts provided the contractor the right to control. In Azad v. United States (338 F.2d 74 [8th Cir. 1968]), the court emphasized the importance of control when it stated that

> the authorities seem to be in general agreement that an employer's right to control the manner in which the work is performed is an important, if not the master test of an employer-employee relationship.

"Look before you leap." Although no attempt was made in this survey to determine the quality of the contracts, the analysis of data indicates that therapists may need to seek consultation before signing contracts and exercise greater care when reading contracts.

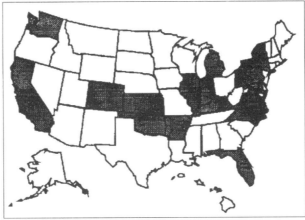

Figure 1. Sixty contracts were sent by respondents from 19 states.

Two contracts were considered to be extremely contrary to the declaration of "independent contractor." Both of these contracts allowed limited freedom for the therapist and required proportionately high liability. These therapists agreed to all or most of the following: 1) accounting of their records, 2) nonassignable agreement, 3) arbitration, 4) providing professional and automobile liability insurance, 5) a hold harmless clause, 6) compliance with policies and procedures, 7) a performance evaluation, and 8) adherence to ethical behavior. In addition, the contractors were given the right to control and supervise.

Legal counsel may be beneficial to identify and explain potential liabilities. Failure to read the contract carefully is not considered a valid defense or excuse when the terms of a signed contract are later questioned. In *Reddy v. Community*

Table. The types of service contracts were varied.

Types	Total
Consulting contracts	1
Educational payment contracts	1
Employee contracts	13
Indepenaent contractor contracts	25
No indication of type	14
Referral contracts	4
Subcontractor contracts	2

Health Foundation of Man (298 S.E. 2d 906,910 [W. Va. 1982]), the court rejected a physician's argument that he failed to read the contract before signing it on the basis that he did so at his own peril and was bound by the terms of the contract.

A written contract is not a guarantee. Physical therapists as service providers may not be adequately protected even when a written contract has been signed by the parties.

The primary advantages of having a written contract are: 1) to avoid later misunderstandings, 2) to allow a court or arbitrator to understand the parties' intentions and enforce their agreement, 3) to encourage the parties to be specific, 4) to refresh memories, 5) to satisfy the U.S. Internal Revenue Service, and 6) to protect the parties. The clauses related to method of payment for services is one example of vague protection of therapists' interests. When remuneration was based on income received for services provided, some contracts specifically identified the responsibilities of the therapist regarding the timeliness of documentation. Some of these contracts were void of statements regarding the responsibilities of the contractor to timely submit the claims for payment and void of statements regarding the therapist's right to review and act on denials of claims. When the contractor is determined to be the provider of services for Medicare beneficiaries, the physical therapist does not have the right ("standing") to challenge the government for denial of claims. In *N.J. Speech-Language-Hearing v. Prudential Ins.* (551 F. Supp. 1024 [D. N.J. 1982], affirmed 724 F. 2d

Accounting of fees and revenues: Provides for rights to obtain and review records for billing.

Agreement not assignable: Limits transfer of rights or duties to another.

Arbitration and mediation: Establishes a mechanism to manage disagreements; may be binding or nonbinding.

Automobile liability insurance: Identifies which party is responsible for liability insurance, amount, type of coverage, etc.

Choice of law: Explicit statement about which law governs in the event of a disagreement or breach of the contract (generally identifies a state).

Compensation and fringe benefits: Remuneration for performing under terms of the contract (including vacation, holidays, and accrual of benefits).

Compliance with policies and procedures: Explicit statement in the contract or by reference (Incorporation of Documents clause in which the content of the policies and procedures become a part of the contract).

Confidentiality: Protects the rights of individual employees and patients and the business interests of the organization.

Contract review: Establishes the process for renewal or changes to the contract terms or both.

Covenant not to compete: Agreement not to compete with the business after termination of an employment contract or upon the sale of an ongoing business; must be reasonable in geographic scope and time.

Delegation/subcontract: Gives the right for one party of the contract to delegate partial or complete duties to a third party.

Disability provisions: Identifies benefits, responsible party for payment, and conditions for disability.

Dismissal (voluntary or involuntary): Establishes the criteria for dismissal.

Exclusive/nonexclusive: Exclusive clause prevents the provider from performing services for one who is not a party to the contract; nonexclusive clause allows the provider to perform services for one who is not a party to the contract.

Fraud and abuse: Explicit methods for managing fraud and abuse (could be covered in dismissal-for-cause clause).

Impaired provider: Methods for managing a provider who is impaired to maintain high quality care and avoid unnecessary loss of practicing clinicians.

Indemnification: One party agrees to reimburse or release the other party for liability of another's actions; also called the "hold harmless" clause.

Independent contractor: Identifies an independent relationship between the parties (the title alone is not sufficient to establish an independent relationship).

Integrated agreement: Delineates the contract as the final and complete agreement of the parties.

Liability: Identifies which party is liable, insurance, type of coverage; a more general clause than specifically identifying automobile and professional liability.

Liquidated damages: Provides compensation to a party of the contract for damages resulting from a specific action.

Medical records: Allows access or submission of medical records for review and identifies ownership of the records.

Notice provisions: Specifies the requirements of notice for changing the terms of the contract and termination of the agreement (when, what, method).

Performance evaluation: Describes the process to evaluate performance (may be a declarative statement or incorporate other documents).

Professional liability insurance: Identifies which party is responsible for liability insurance, amount, type of coverage, proof of insurance, etc.

Retirement: Identifies which party is responsible for retirement benefits and procedures.

Stock purchase options: Delineates options to acquire shares of the benefits and risks of the business (i.e., ownership).

Termination compensation: Describes compensation provided with termination (usually additional to amounts due).

Termination of contract procedures: Delineates terms of severance of the relationship as specified (e.g. as a result of death, disability, or dismissal) and procedures (e.g., giving notice, ensuring fairness, and making appeals).

Termination rights of parties: Identifies who has the right to terminate the agreement and the criteria for termination.

Figure 2. A list of the types of clauses represented in the study and their corresponding definitions.

388 [3d Cir. 1983]), the court determined that the plaintiff's injury (*insufficient payment*) was not the result of Medicare's policies and procedures but was pursuant to contracts freely negotiated with the nursing homes. The court ruled:

> A party which independently contracts with a recipient of governmental funds cannot acquire the right to challenge the method under which those funds are paid to the recipient by the government merely by entering into a contractual provi-

sion under which the amount it is paid by the recipient is governed by the amount that the government provides to that recipient."

Unintended risks. When the writer of the contract uses legal terminology without adequate legal knowledge about the legal implications of those terms, unintended risks may be incurred by one or both of the parties to the contract. In these cases, part or all of the contract may be declared void because of vagueness or contradiction of the

terms, or the contract terms may be interpreted by the court. An example of this is a contract that identified the physical therapist as an independent contractor, listed conditions contrary to criteria for independent contracting, and identified the physical therapist as an agent for the contractor. That same contract held the therapist accountable for supervising and giving directions to others who had a different contract relationship with the contractor. The physical therapist also agreed to indemnification. That is, the therapist may have agreed to be liable for acts performed by these individuals—even though the contractor ("other party") decided on the qualifications of these individuals.

Read Carefully Before Signing!

The figures and tables represent the frequencies of contract clauses in the 60 contracts that were reviewed. The frequencies of clauses do not represent degrees of importance or trends; they only offer a perspective on current physical therapy contracts. Again, the contracts were not reviewed for the quality of the terms. Some of the contracts may have been well written to meet the needs and intentions of the parties, whereas others indicated that precautions should be taken.

When the terms of a contract are vague, contradictory, or incorrectly used, the parties of the contract are assuming unintended risks. Each party to the contract should read the contract carefully before signing. The cost of having an attorney review a contract is minuscule compared with the risks that may be taken *without* such a review. **CM**

Next issue: *Before signing a contract, the physical therapist should be as informed as possible about what that contract means. In "Part 2: Physical Therapy Contracts," the author discusses specific examples from the contracts reviewed, providing case law interpretations.*

Kathy Lewis, JD, PT, is an Associate Professor at the University of Kansas Medical Center, Kansas City, KS.

Legal advice can be given only by your personal legal counsel, based on the law of your state or on federal law, as applicable.

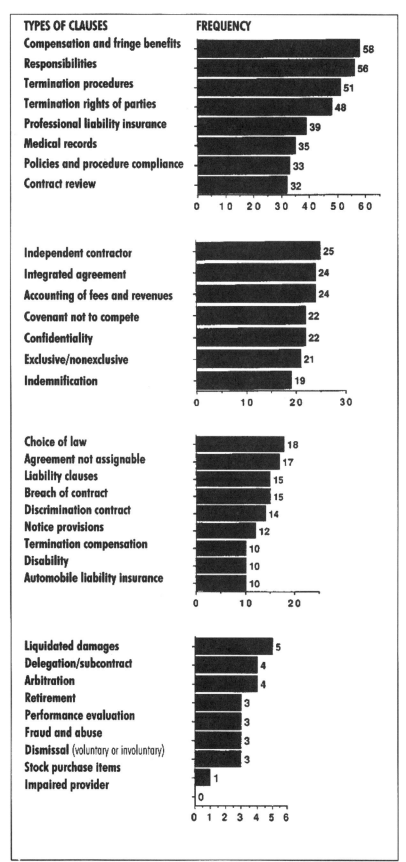

Figure 3. The frequencies in which the 30 clauses occurred in the 60 contracts.

L
E
G
A
L

B
R
I
E
F
S

Part 2: Physical Therapy Contracts

Editor's note: *In Part 1 of this series, a review of physical therapy contracts—types, parties involved, and frequent clauses—indicated that physical therapists may benefit from more information about contract terms. In Part 2, the author compares employer-independent contractor agreements with employer-employee agreements.*

Contracting for health care services is a growing trend. During the past 15 years, for example, there has been a significant increase in the number of contracts established between health maintenance organizations (HMOs) and hospitals. (The HMOs have been more "proactive" in initiating and negotiating these contracts than the hospitals have been.) (Feldman et al. 1990).

Because of the contracting trend, Brody (1986) suggested that contractual principles should be incorporated into personnel policies, giving special attention to the creation of performance incentives rather than to the control of abuses—and using simple, specific language rather than ambiguous terms. A lower rate of staff turnover and a reduced incidence of intent to leave already have been reported among nurses who have contracts that address the need for autonomy, professional development, and communication with management (Dear, Weisman, and O'Keefe 1985).

The Decision to Contract

A knowledgeable decision to contract as an independent contrac-

tor rather than as an employee should be based on the ratio of risks to benefits preferred. As an independent contractor, the physical therapist is directly responsible for paying taxes, acquiring disability insurance (rather than relying on Workers' Compensation), using savings or assets (rather than relying on unemployment compensation), and assuming greater professional liability (which may result in the physical therapist paying higher premiums for liability insurance). When the terms of a contract involve risks and expenses greater than those anticipated by the physical therapist, the professional and financial benefits of being an independent contractor may be negated.

Because of income tax, unemployment compensation, disability insurance, and vicarious liability issues, specific attention and careful drafting are required to accurately describe the correct, intended relationship. When a court defines the relationship, the label "independent contractor" is *not* the determining factor and in fact is minor when compared with other factors (such as those discussed below). Although the bodies of law governing each of these issues (income tax, unemploy-

ment compensation, disability, and vicarious liability) consider the same or similar factors to determine the relationship between the parties, each body of law differs, and the balancing of factors is delicate. The *tax* court may identify a relationship between the parties as an employer-independent contractor relationship; a *Workers' Compensation* judge may identify the same relationship as an employer-employee relationship; and the *trial* court (when deciding tort liability) may identify the relationship as either an employer-independent contractor *or* an employer-employee relationship.

Tax Liability

Bromberg (1991) asserts that "the employee vs. independent contractor is currently one of the hottest issues involved in the tax area."

Through Revenue Ruling 84-71, the U.S. Internal Revenue Service (IRS) has set down 20 common-law factors—gathered from past revenue rulings—to help define an employer-employee relationship (Figure). No one of these 20 factors may be the sole defining factor. The court's application of these factors can be observed in Revenue Ruling 61-178, in which the court ruled that a physician who performed services on a part-time basis for a corporation was an employee of the company for federal income tax purposes. The physician worked a fixed schedule (Factor #7) and was prohibited from responding to emergencies from his own practice. The company supplied the physician's facilities (Factor #9) and equipment (Factor #14), paid the physician a monthly salary (Factor #12), and gave the physician orders in conformity with company policy and procedures (Factor #1).

The judge considered additional factors in this ruling. In situations in which differences of opinion existed,

By Kathy Lewis, JD, PT

for example, the company's head physician made the final decision. The physician was required to submit reports (Factor #11); both parties had the right to terminate employment at will (Factor #20); and, finally, the physician was extended the same benefits extended to the company's employees.

The new IRS audit guidelines for tax-exempt hospitals were publicly announced on April 1, 1992. Steinberg (1992) stated that these guidelines represent "another wave in the ongoing tidal shift of IRS attitudes and policies with respect to tax-exempt hospitals." A primary component of this "wave" is the focus on hospital-based contracts, including physician contracts and employment-related documents (e.g., those related to fellowships and other types of payments to students).

The IRS auditors are instructed to interview hospital-based physicians to clarify and verify contract terms. The following factors are used to determine that a physician is an employee:

1. The physician does not have a private practice.
2. The hospital pays a straight wage to the physician.
3. The hospital provides supplies and professional support staff to the physician.
4. The hospital bills for the physician's services.
5. The hospital and the physician divide the physician fees on a percentage basis.
6. The contract between the physician and the hospital includes the hospital's right to control how the physician delivers services.
7. The hospital requires the physician to be on duty at the hospital during specified hours.
8. The hospital requires the physician to wear uniforms with the hospital name or insignia.
9. Other factors under general

common-law principles indicate an employment relationship.

An Issue of Control

Although control may not actually be exercised, the mere *right to control* (expressed in the contract or by actions between the parties) is a critical factor, as stated in Section 31.3306(i)-1 of the *Tax Regulations*:

> .... An employer-employee relationship exists when the employer has the right to control and direct the individual who performs the services, not only as to the result to be accomplished by the work but also as to details and means by which that result is accomplished.

Some control by an employer *is* permitted in an employer-independent contractor relationship. The amount of control is defined in Reg. 31.3306(i)-1:

> If an individual is subject to the control or direction of another merely as to the result to be accomplished by the work and not as to the means and method for accomplishing the result, he is an independent contractor.

In a recent Private Letter Ruling (LTR 9149001; July 23, 1991), the IRS addressed the issue of whether physicians under contract with a particular corporation should be classified as employees or independent contractors for federal tax purposes. The corporation in question contracted the physicians to work in family health care clinics and consistently characterized the physicians as independent contractors for tax purposes. After evaluating the facts, however, the IRS determined that the physicians were *employees*. Relevant factors included: 1) the supplying of physicians with staff, facilities, equipment, and supplies; 2) the manner in which the physicians were paid; 3) the existence of a termination-at-will agreement; 4) the

liability insurance purchased by the corporation for the physicians.

Vicarious Liability

The employer-employee and employer-independent contractor dichotomy extends to areas other than tax liability. The effect that the classification of a relationship has on a determination of vicarious liability is of particular concern. In recent years, courts in several states—including Texas, Ohio, Washington, New York, and Illinois—have determined that hospitals are vicariously liable for the acts of their independent contractors (Campbell 1989).

Vicarious liability may be defined as a legal principle under which one who is faultless is held accountable for the negligent acts of another. Three different theories can be used in "attaching" liability to an employer: 1) *respondeat superior* (L., "Let the master answer"), 2) *corporate negligence*, and 3) *ostensible* or *apparent agency*. *Respondeat superior* holds the employer liable for negligent acts of employees because the employee is under the control of the employer. *Corporate negligence* holds the employer liable for negligent acts of employees when there has been negligence in hiring and monitoring of those employees. *Ostensible* or *apparent agency* holds the employer liable for negligent acts of employees when the patient has perceived that an employer-employee relationship exists between the employer and the service provider and has relied on that perception (Combs 1987; Scott 1990).

To apply the theories of *respondeat superior* and corporate negligence, the *courts must determine* that an employer-employee relationship exists. The ostensible or apparent agency theory, however, is premised on the *patient's perceptions* that an employer-employee relationship

16

Clinical Management

1. Instructions.
The *right* of the employer to require compliance (e.g., to policies and procedures) by persons performing the service is a "control factor."

2. Training.
Training methods may include requiring a person to attend meetings or work with more experienced workers. Correspondence from the employer to the worker also may be considered "training."

3. Integration.
When the worker's services become integrated with the regular business operations, this generally means that the worker is under the "control and supervision" of the employer.

4. Services Rendered Personally.
The inclusion of this item in a contract indicates that the persons for whom the services are being provided would necessarily be interested in the methods and results of the work.

5. Hiring, Supervising, and Paying Assistants.
These three elements help establish control over workers on the job, not just over the end result.

6. Continuing Relationship.
An ongoing relationship indicates an employer-employee classification. This can be construed when "work is performed at frequently recurring intervals" even though the intervals are "irregular."

7. Set Hours at Work.
Setting hours for the person performing the services indicates control by the employer.

8. Full Time Required.
This requirement explicitly restricts the worker from any other employment. "An independent contractor, on the other hand, is free to work when and for whom he or she chooses."

9. Doing Work on Employer's Premises.
When work is performed on the employer's premises, control by the employer is implied—especially when the work *could* be done elsewhere. The *nature* of the work is important in determining whether the work generally is performed at the employer's facilities.

10. Order or Sequence Set.
The *right* to establish a schedule is sufficient to demonstrate employer control even when this control has not actually been exercised.

11. Oral or Written Reports.
Requiring the submission of reports indicates control by the person or business for whom the work is being performed.

12. Payment by Hour, Week, or Month.
Payment by hour, week, or month indicates an employer-employee relationship; payment by the job or straight commission indicates an employer-independent contractor relationship.

13. Payment of Business and/or Traveling Expenses.
Payment of these expenses demonstrates ability to control expenses, therefore creating an employer-employee relationship.

14. Furnishing Tools and Materials.
Furnishing of tools and materials by the employer indicates an employer-employee relationship.

15. Significant Investment.
When the worker invests in facilities that are used by the worker but typically are not maintained by employees, an employer-independent contractor relationship is indicated.

16. Realization of Profit or Loss.
If the worker can realize either a profit or a loss from providing services, then that worker generally is an independent contractor. The risk of nonpayment for services does *not* help establish whether a relationship involves an independent contractor or an employee.

17. Working For More Than One Firm At a Time.
This generally indicates that the worker is an independent contractor.

18. Making Service Available to General Public.
When the service is available to the general public on a consistent and regular basis, an independent contractor status is implied.

19. Right to Discharge.
The right to discharge is a control mechanism used by employers with employees. Conversely, an independent contractor cannot be dismissed when he or she meets contractual obligations.

20. Right to Terminate.
If the worker can terminate employment at any time without liability, this indicates an employer-employee relationship.

Figure. From Internal Revenue Service's Ruling 84-71: Twenty factors to determine an employer-employee relationship.

exists and on the patient's reliance on that perceived relationship.

A recent Georgia case, *Johns v. Jarrad* (927 F.2d 551 [11 Cir. 1991]), addressed the issue of vicarious liability for an emergency-room physician who had been "supplied" to the hospital by a physician supply company. For the injured party to recover a damages award from the physician supply company, an employer-employee relationship between the physician and the physician supply company had to

be established by the court. A simple "control type test" was applied:

> The true test of whether the relationship is one of employer-employee or employer-independent contractor is whether the employer, under the contract, either oral or written, assumes the right to control the time, manner, and method of executing the work as distinguished from the right merely to require certain definite results in conformity to the contract.

The court ruled that the physician supply company did not satisfy

this test and the physicians were independent contractors, which relieved the company of vicarious liability under the doctrine of *respondeat superior*.

When physical therapists sign contracts that fail to define the intended relationship, their liabilities are unpredictable. This problem is exacerbated when the contract includes a *hold harmless clause* (an agreement to release the other party from liability). If the physical therapist is found to be an independent contractor, the therapist may be vicariously liable for the negligent acts of individuals whom the therapist is *hiring or supervising*. If the physical therapist is found to be an employee, the *employer* may be vicariously liable for the negligent acts of the therapist and those whom the therapist is supervising.

Workers' Compensation and Unemployment

In some of the employer-independent contractor agreements reviewed as a part of a 1991 survey,* physical therapists agreed to a specific waiver of rights to Workers' Compensation and unemployment benefits. The therapists may have believed that this type of a clause supports the intent to establish an employer-independent contractor relationship. Therapists should be cautious and seek legal counsel when considering agreements that include waiver clauses. Four examples illustrate the delicacy of this issue:

1. Some jurisdictions may not allow waivers of rights that are provided by law.
2. Other jurisdictions may disallow Workers' Compensation and unemployment benefits because of the waiver clause, even though benefits would have otherwise accrued.
3. The physical therapist who is injured during employment may decide not to request review for Workers' Compensation because he or she is relying on the waiver clause.
4. The tax court may determine that an employer-independent contractor relationship exists, whereas the Workers' Compen-

*Supported by PT Bulletin, *which announced a request for volunteers, and through a grant from the School of Allied Health of the University of Kansas Medical Center, Kansas City, KS.*

sation law may indicate that an employer-employee relationship exists. Each of these is a different body of law written for different purposes.

Contract Excerpts

Following are specific examples from contracts reviewed as part of the 1991 survey cited above. Given for informational purposes only, these examples are not intended as a judgment of the quality or legality of the contractual clauses reviewed.

Some of the physical therapy contracts reviewed for this study labeled the physical therapist as an independent contractor; however, in these contracts the employer reserved the right to control how the therapist delivered services, requiring compliance with the employer's policies and procedures, dictating the time and place of work, and requiring specific reports.

Some of the contracts for independent contractors made no mention of tax liability or other responsibilities that might be imputed on the independent contractor. Other contracts did mention the tax liability, as follows in this excerpt from one contract:

> If you are an independent contractor, you understand that you are acting on your own behalf and that no employee/employer relationship shall be construed to exist between you and the agency. All taxes and other costs related to the services by you shall be your sole responsibility.

Some clauses in the contracts were more specific and required indemnification, as exemplified by this excerpt:

> Contractor hereby certified that all taxes, tax withholding obligations, or other required contributions that arise out of an employment relationship including, but not necessarily limited to, the obligation to withhold federal and state income taxes, to pay and withhold taxes required under the Federal Insurance

Contributions Act, and to pay required unemployment taxes will be the responsibility of Contractor. Hospital shall not be responsible for employee withholding, social security, unemployment insurance, workers' compensation insurance or other items required or commonly furnished by employers. Contractor will indemnify Hospital as a result of such tax withholding obligation or required contributions in the event the Hospital for any reason is assessed any amount by an appropriate federal or state governmental agency or court with reference to such taxes, tax withholding obligations, or required contributions. Professionals supplied under this agreement are not entitled to any benefits from the hospital.

Weighing the Benefits and the Risks

There are obvious benefits—and perhaps less-obvious risks—with both the employer-independent contractor relationship and employer-employee relationships. Both parties of a contract may prefer the same type of relationship; however, the *reasons* for their shared preference may differ. A physical therapist may prefer to be an independent contractor because of greater professional autonomy, tax benefits, and compensation, whereas the employer may prefer an employer-independent contractor relationship to avoid incurring vicarious liability risks and paying for employee benefits. When the *reasons* behind the parties' preferences differ, the wording in the contract may not equally balance the risks and benefits for both of the parties.

Five major points must be considered when physical therapists negotiate contract terms that identify the relationship of the contracting parties:

1. The relationship of the parties is not determined only by a *declaration* of the relationship. The terms of the entire agreement—

and usually the *actions* of the parties—are reviewed to interpret the intended relationship.

2. A specific waiver of any legal right always is more complex than it appears to be on the face of a document.

3. The relationship of the parties has an impact on various bodies of law (e.g., those covering tax liability, Workers' Compensation, unemployment insurance, and vicarious liability in tort law). Although each of these bodies of law considers similar factors to determine the relationship, the differences among these bodies of law are delicate, and the resulting decisions may differ even when there is an identical set of facts.

4. Physical therapists should clarify liability insurance coverage with their insurance carrier. Liability insurance carriers may request to review the clauses of an independent contractor agreement that relate to professional liability, particularly hold harmless clauses.

5. Consultation with an attorney and careful reading of the entire agreement are recommended. Subsequent actions should be congruent with the express agreement.

Physical therapists must have a firm grasp on the type of relationship they prefer. When they carefully review each of the contract terms and seek legal counsel, they may be less likely to experience unforeseen liabilities. **CM**

Next issue: *In "Part 3: Physical Therapy Contracts," the author discusses contract terms, including "non-compete" and "arbitration," with specific examples from the contracts reviewed and case-law interpretations.*

Kathy Lewis, JD, PT, is an Associate Professor at the University of Kansas Medical Center, Kansas City, KS.

Legal advice can be given only by your personal legal counsel, based on the law of your state or on federal law, as applicable.

REFERENCES

Brody EW. Successful application of contractual principles to hospital personnel policies. *Health Care Manage Rev.* 1986; Winter:15-20.

Bromberg RS. The interrelationship between health contracting and income tax exemption. *Health Contracts Institute.* Philadelphia, PA: National Health Lawyers Association; 1991. Section E, 1-27.

Campbell D. Hospital liability in Texas for acts of independent contractors. *South Texas Law Journal.* 1989;30:333.

Combs G. Hospital vicarious liability for the negligence of independent contractors and staff physicians: criticisms of the ostensible agency doctrine in Ohio. *University of Cincinnati Law Review.* 1987;56:771,772.

Dear MR, Weisman CS, O'Keefe S. Evaluation of a contract model for professional nursing practice. *Health Care Manage Rev.* 1985; Spring:65-77.

Feldman R, Kralewski J, Shapiro J, Chan H-C. Contracts between hospitals and health maintenance organizations. *Health Care Manage Rev.* 1990;Winter: 47-60.

Steinberg RA. IRS issues new audit guidelines for tax-exempt hospitals. *The Health Lawyer.* 1992;6(2):17-19.

SUGGESTED READINGS

Lewis K. Part 1: physical therapy contracts. *Clinical Management.* 1992;12(4):12-15.

Scott RW. *Health Care Malpractice: A Primer on Legal Issues for Health Professionals.* Thorofare, NJ: SLACK, Inc.; 1990.

L E G A L   B R I E F S

Part 3: Physical Therapy Contracts

Editor's note: *Parts 1 and 2 of this series covered general contracting principles, types of contract clauses, and differences between employer-independent contractor relationships and employer-employee relationships. The final installment of the series covers covenants not to compete; compensation related to accounting of fees, revenues, and time; and arbitration and mediation.*

With a basic understanding of contract terms and relationships as expressed in the 60 contracts reviewed in Parts 1 and 2,* the reader now is ready to "critique" specific contract examples. Below are examples of *covenants not to compete, arbitration and mediation,* and *compensation.* For clarity and consistency, the terms "independent contractor" and "employee" are used to identify the physical therapist, and the term "employer" is used to identify the other contracting party; however, these terms were not necessarily used in the actual contracts.

The discussions that accompany these examples were included not to determine degree of legality or level of quality but to serve discussion purposes only.

Covenants Not to Compete

Covenants not to compete, or *restrictive covenants,* are agreements

*These contracts were obtained as part of a survey supported by PT Bulletin, *which announced a request for survey volunteers, and through a grant from the School of Allied Health, University of Kansas Medical Center, Kansas City, KS.*

By Kathy Lewis, JD, PT

Example A:
Covenants Not to Compete
The second party further promises that in pursuit and course of her providing Physical Therapy Services on behalf of the first party, she will not, during the life of this Agreement nor within one year after its termination, solicit, bid for, nor accept contracts/agreements to provide Physical Therapy Services in any agencies or facilities in which Physical Therapy Services are involved and covered through this Agreement.

designed to protect business interests after an employment contract has been terminated or upon the sale of an ongoing business. The specific restrictions must be reasonable in geographic scope and time.

Example A is a clause in a subcontractor agreement that appeared to establish an employer-independent contractor relationship. According to a previous statement in the contract, services would be provided in "designated facilities"; however, no specific facilities were identified in that contract. Example B is excerpted from another contract in which the relationship between the parties was an employer-independent contractor relationship.

Discussion. As a general rule, covenants not to compete are not favored by the law because their validity rests on a common-law or statutory exception to the Sherman Antitrust Act (1890), which prohibits agreements that restrain trade.

Today many states have statutes that govern covenants not to compete. Several states prohibit this type of covenant, including Alabama, Oklahoma, Delaware, and North Dakota.

Alabama, Oklahoma, and North Dakota statutes hold that every contract by which any person or entity is restrained in exercising a lawful profession, trade, or business of any kind is, to that extent, void. These statutes include exceptions that allow restrictive covenants when a person is selling the "good will" (e.g., the referral base) of a business and when partners are dissolving or anticipating dissolution of the partnership. The Oregon Medical Association discourages restrictive covenants; however, the judicial system in Oregon does not prohibit them.

The current view is that covenants not to compete are enforceable only when they are supported by *consideration,* when they are *reasonable,* and when they are consistent with public policy. Courts have stated that there is no hard and fast rule and that each contract with a restrictive covenant must be tested on its own facts (*American Law Reports* 1988).

"Consideration." Within a contract, *consideration* means that there was a bargaining for exchange and that value was given by each contracting party for the other's promise to be legally bound. When covenants not to compete are included in the original and otherwise valid employment contract, the courts generally conclude that the mutual promises provide adequate consideration (Reddy v. Community Health

Example B: Covenants Not to Compete

[Independent contractor] agrees, upon termination of her contractual relationship with [employer], not to establish her own "independent rehabilitation agency" or to work for a "new competitor" of [employer] within a 15-mile radius of [employer's center] for a period of one year following the date of termination. This provision remains valid only so long as [employer] remains in existence. For purposes of this covenant, "independent rehabilitation agency" shall mean a physical facility equipped with supplies and equipment for the provision of physical therapy services, and "new competitor" shall mean any entity coming into existence subsequent to [date] to provide substantially the same services as [employer] within a 15-mile radius of [employer's center]. This provision shall not prohibit [independent contractor] from incorporating to do business as a professional corporation, either as a sole shareholder or in conjunction with other licensed physical therapists, or from doing business as a partnership. Provided further, neither this provision nor this Agreement shall prohibit [independent contractor] in any way, during the term hereof or upon termination from working as an employee or independent contractor for individuals, clinics, or agencies other than "new competitors," as defined herein.

Foundation of Man, 298 S.E. 2d 906 [910] W. Va. 1982). If a contract with a restrictive covenant is a renewal contract—and if the original contract did not contain a restrictive covenant and the restriction was not a condition of employment—the courts typically scrutinize the contract to determine whether it is supported by consideration.

In *Ladd v. Hikes* (639 P.2d 1307-1309 [Or. App. 1982]), an employer inserted a covenant not to compete in a renewal contract with a physician. The employer warned that if the contract was not signed, there could be no further employment. The Oregon appellate court ruled that the covenant was void because there was no "mutual agreement." Even though the employee-physician had received no benefits (including no additional compensation), the employer had gained the employee's promise not to compete. In reviewing the contract, the court found *no consideration* (i.e., exchange of value) *for the employee's promise not to compete*.

"*Reasonability.*" Covenants not to compete must be reasonable regarding the type of activity, the geographic area, and the time period involved. In *Reddy v. Community*

Health Foundation of Man (298 S.E. 2d 906 [910] W. Va. 1982), a physician who had agreed not to practice medicine within a 30-mile radius of the town of Man, West Virginia, for a period of three years disputed his contract. The court upheld the contract and rejected the physician/plaintiff's argument that he was not obliged to fulfill the contract because he had failed to read it before signing.

In *Phoenix Orthopaedic Surgeons v. Peairs* (790 P. 2d 752 [Ariz. App. 1989]), an Arizona appellate court upheld a contract that restricted a surgeon from practicing orthopedic medicine and surgery within a five-mile radius of his employer for three years. The court ruled that the restrictive covenant was *reasonable* and did not contravene *public policy* because the physician was not restricted from practicing his vocation. (There were at least eight other hospitals and surgical facilities outside the five-mile radius.) A restriction of a 30-mile radius during a two-year period was found reasonable in *Gomez v. Chua Medical Corporation* (510 N.E. 2d 191 [Ind. App. 1987]). The Chua Medical Corporation was located within Hammond, Indiana, whose city lim-

its covered approximately 25 miles.

The purpose of the covenant not to compete must be to protect a valid "protectable" interest, that is, a legitimate proprietary interest. Some courts do not uphold a covenant that protects only ordinary competition (that is, the right to market your own business without using "inside" information such as a referral base). Other laws, such as those that prohibit interfering with ongoing contracted relationships (i.e., *tortious interference with a contract*), adequately protect an employer from a former employee who may attempt to "steal" ongoing clients. In these types of cases, the courts generally distinguish between covenants related to employment contracts and covenants related to the sale of a business. The former covenant may be more strictly construed than the latter.

Public policy. Many cases on restrictive covenants as a violation of public policy refer to physicians. *Lowe v. Reynolds* (428 N.Y.S. 2d 358 [N.Y. 1980]), however, involved a speech pathologist who was successful in arguing that patients in her practice were not readily "transferrable" to other therapists—and that such transfer would result in confusion and damage to the patients' well-being. In this case, the argument was that a covenant not to compete would protect patients and thereby uphold public policy.

Consult legal counsel. When physical therapists consider signing contracts that include a covenant not to compete, they should discuss the issue with their personal legal counsel. The discussion should address the following questions:
1. What is the likelihood that your willingness to accept this restriction would change in the future?
2. Does the clause meet requirements of the U.S. Constitution,

Example C: Mediation and Arbitration
The first party and the second party agree to submit any breach of this Agreement to a mutually agreed-upon third party for quick and inexpensive solution of this breach.

Example D: Mediation and Arbitration
Any controversy or claim arising out of or relating to any interpretation, breach, or dispute concerning any of the terms or provisions of this agreement, which disagreement is not settled in writing within 30 days after it arises, shall be settled by arbitration in accordance with the laws of the state of [X] and under the rules then obtaining of the American Arbitration Association (or any successor thereto), and judgment upon the award rendered in said arbitration shall be final and may be entered in any court in the state of [X] having jurisdiction thereof. Arbitrators shall be persons experienced in negotiating, making, and consummating contractor agreements of type contemplated herein. Any party hereto may apply for such arbitration.

statutes, state regulations, case law, and public policy?
3. Are the terms reasonable regarding the type of activity, geographic area, and time period involved?
4. What is a reasonable alternative for dispute negotiations, should a dispute arise?

The Wave of the Future: Arbitration and Mediation

In response to the high costs and long delays involved in the litigation process, alternative approaches to resolving disputes are becoming more popular. Mediation and arbitration may be the wave of the future (Jones 1987; Alhadeff 1991). Several states (such as Michigan) have responded to the need for alternative methods to resolve disputes, enacting statutes that allow arbitration clauses in health care plans. Under these statutes, a patient may agree to arbitrate disputes arising out of health care or treatment by a health care provider (Sokolsky 1987).

Mediation may be defined as a process in which a mediator facilitates agreement between the disputing parties but does not give opinions or render a decision. *Arbitration* may be defined as a process in which a single arbitrator or a panel of arbitrators determines a resolution after hearing evidence. The arbitrator's resolution may be

binding or nonbinding, depending on the parties' previous agreement (as expressed in their contract) to use the arbitration process.

Contract clauses on mediation and arbitration (such as in Examples C and D) should be reviewed by the therapist's personal legal counsel to determine their validity according to statutes, regulations, case law, and the intent of the parties for the particular jurisdiction involved. The parties to the contract should review these clauses to determine whether their intent is clearly expressed. Among the questions to consider during review of these clauses:
1. Is the clause specific, clearly identifying the type of dispute? (Does the dispute involve breach in contract, such as failure to provide services or failure to pay for services provided, or tort, such as malpractice?)
2. Is the clause broad in scope, making it possible to resolve minor matters?
3. *Who pays for the mediation or arbitration costs?* (Does the prevailing party pay? Are the costs equally divided? Does the initiating party pay?)
4. If the qualifications of the mediator or arbitrator are not established, will mediation or arbitration be a satisfactory and cost-effective method?

5. Will discovery of evidence be limited, open, or prohibited? (For example, can documents be reviewed or depositions be taken? Can witnesses testify?)
6. Who selects the arbitrators or mediators, and how many are to be selected?
7. If the clause refers to applying rules of a particular arbitration association, are there critical elements of those rules that should be reviewed?
8. When the agreement reached by the mediator or arbitrator could be interpreted by the courts as a legally binding agreement, do both parties knowingly intend to waive their right to judicial process and their right to have the judgment entered in a court if either party believes the other has not complied with the judgment?

The courts do have a (limited) right to review arbitration decisions; however, they rarely overturn these decisions unless these decisions are deemed to be arbitrary, capricious, discriminatory, or otherwise in violation of public policy.

Mediation and arbitration can be effective, efficient processes. Two organizations that offer mediation and arbitration services are the American Arbitration Association and the National Health Lawyers Association Alternative Dispute Resolution Service, which was specifically created for members of the health care industry.

Compensation: Fees, Revenues, and Time
It is important to realize that the employer's understanding of "compensation for services rendered" may not be in accordance with the physical therapist's subjective understanding of the contract. Following are some of the comments made by respondents to the nationwide contract survey:

1. *"My experience was a nightmare."* This comment was made by the therapist involved in the contract excerpted in Example E. The employer claimed that a significant debt was owed by the therapist because the therapist allegedly worked 25 hours a week rather than 40 hours a week. The employer claimed inadequate profits were generated.

2. *"I don't understand how they can claim that I owe them thousands of dollars."*

3. *"I may go bankrupt if I have to pay back the amount claimed by the employer."*

Compensation disputes can work both ways. On July 26, 1992, a reporter with the *San Antonio Express News* covered a contract dispute between physicians and a hospital. When the physicians ran an extensive audit, they discovered they were not being paid for all the services they had rendered (Finley 1992). They had been given only checks; no accounting mechanism was in place.

Therapists should be aware that litigation over compensation issues is common. To avoid disputes, the terms of a contract must be based on both the type of practice setting and the original source of remuneration.

Type of practice setting. Examples E, F, and G represent three different physical therapy practice settings with significantly different compensation terms. The excerpts in Examples E and F are not clear regarding how much remuneration the therapist should expect because the parameters for payment are not clearly defined. Note that, among the contracts here excerpted, only the contract represented in Example G provided an accounting mechanism to the therapist.

Original source of remuneration. The original source of remunera-

Example E: Physician-Owned Practice

The clauses below appeared in a contract document entitled "Service Agreement for Physical Therapists." There were no statements within this document to specify the percent of charges; however, the therapist included a letter "extending an offer of employment" that specified the percentage (specific percentage was deleted from the copy for the study). Although the terms of this document and the letter were not identical, both documents were signed as though they were separate agreements.

Compensation: For all services to be rendered by the (employee), shall compensate [employee] during the term of this agreement an annual draw of ($___), said sum to be payable at least as often as once a month during the period of this agreement. Said draw is based upon the [employee] receiving a percent of his/her service charges. At any time in which the charges exceed the said draw the [employee] can request a supplemental draw on a quarterly basis. Billings and fees: All billings for services of the [employee] will be made by [employer], and all fees and compensation received by the [employee] as the result of his/her rendition of professional services shall be collected by, paid to, and belong to [employer].

Example F: County School System

In this excerpt, there existed no express statement about the relationship between the parties. Although several clauses indicated specific employer control over the therapist, other clauses obligated the therapist to pay for expenses that typically are paid by the employer as fringe benefits.

Compensation shall be provided solely on a reimbursement basis per unit of service. A unit of service is calculated as one (1) hour of approved therapy service. No other reimbursement or benefits shall be provided. [Another clause in the contract limited the maximum number of units.] The [employee] shall provide monthly billing for services rendered to each program area. Additional billing specificity may be requested by the Board's Superintendent. Each such billing shall be considered for payment by the Board at its next regular scheduled meeting and, if approved, shall be paid within thirty (30) days following the said meeting. Billing for therapy services shall be made only to the Board, and no additional billing shall be sent to parents, guardians, or other funding sources.

tion may have as much of an impact on contract terms as the type of practice setting. The Medicare Act, for example, requires that agreements (between providers and subcontractors and between subcontractors and organizations related to the subcontractor by control or common ownership) include a clause that allows the Secretary of the U.S. Department of Health and Human Services or the Comptroller General of the United States access to certain contracts for services, books, documents, and records necessary to verify costs (§ 952 PL 96-499 [42 U.S.C. § 1395x] v[I]). If this clause is not included in the agreement between the therapist and the employer/provider, the employer/provider

may not be reimbursed for the services that the therapist renders.

When Medicare payments are denied—with subsequent effects on the therapist's compensation—the therapist generally does not have the right to challenge the denial. In *N.J. Speech-Language-Hearing v. Prudential Ins.* (551 F. Supp. 1024 [D. N.J. 1882], affirmed 724 F. 2d 383 [3d Cir. 1983]), the court ruled that the amount of compensation given by the nursing home employers to the therapist was not the result of Medicare's policies and procedures but was pursuant to contracts freely negotiated with the nursing homes—and therefore the amount of compensation would need to be settled between the parties to those contracts.

Therapists may acquire greater

Example G: Home Health

That, in order to verify the cost of contract services, the [independent contractor] agrees to provide access to the necessary books and records. . .pursuant to § 952 of the Omnibus Reconciliation Act of 1980, which provides for access to the books and records of subcontractors of Medicare providers by the Secretary of the U.S. Department of Health and Human Services and the Comptroller General of the United States. The [independent contractor] shall make available . . .such items as are necessary to certify the nature and extent of costs of services provided by the [independent contractor]. Such records shall be available until the expiration of four (4) years. . . . That, when the [independent contractor's] visits are denied and not paid under Medicare waiver of liability because a diagnosis does not qualify a patient for such service, the (employer) will accept liability for the denial and reimburse the [independent contractor]. That, when payment for services is denied and not paid under Medicare waiver of liability for the following reasons: (a) more visits than are medically necessary, (b) inadequate documentation, and (c) failure to document a visit, the [employer] will not reimburse the [independent contractor] for the denied service. . .[independent contractor] will receive a prompt notification by telephone. . .copy of the denial will be mailed. An invoice designating the patient's name, address, number of visits, and the cost of the service denied will be furnished. . .[with] retroactive adjustment. . . .

protection through contract clauses that ensure:

1. An accounting of payment from the employer to the therapist.
2. Timely notice so that there is an opportunity to review the third-party payer's decision.
3. A subsequent opportunity to provide additional information or clarification for denials of payment.

When a therapist's billings are subject to approval by the employer prior to review by a third-party payer (see Example F), the therapist has greater protection when the standards for approval are clarified in the contract.

Covenants not to compete are valid in most jurisdictions when specific elements are met. Unnecessary litigation costs can be avoided if the probable legality of the covenant can be ensured before an agreement is signed. When a contractual dispute does arise, however, mediation or arbitration can be effective means for resolution. Mediation or arbitration may be a viable alternative to lawsuits even when such an alternative is not required by the original contractual agreement. When payment for services provided by a physical therapist is contingent on decisions of an employer, legal counsel can provide advice on how to establish terms to ensure good-faith payment and accountability of the compensation paid.

Cautions and Reminders

Numerous contract issues have *not* been addressed in this three-part series, including liability issues (indemnity and exculpatory clauses); how to determine which state (or federal) law is the governing law in a particular situation, such as for the traveling therapist (i.e., a conflict of laws may exist when a contract is drawn up in one state but the traveling therapist is practicing in another state); exclusive agreements; confidentiality; and antitrust laws.

Part 2 of this series covered indemnification and hold harmless clauses, a subject that requires special attention. Weidner (1991) confirms that—prior to signing a contract with hold harmless or indemnification clauses—the therapist's malpractice insurance carrier should review the contract and send a written statement regarding approval. The reason for this is that malpractice insurance does not cover debts assumed by contract.

Establishing a "Win-Win" Contract

Therapists are signing contracts with greater frequency, the business of contracting for services continues to increase in complexity, and the laws of contracting for services continue to evolve. How can therapists ensure the establishment of a "win-win" contractual agreement?

1. Continue to keep informed about contract issues.
2. Read contract terms with a critical eye.
3. Always seek legal counsel before signing agreements. **CM**

Kathy Lewis, JD, PT, is an Associate Professor at the University of Kansas Medical Center, Kansas City, KS.

Legal advice can be given only by your personal legal counsel, based on the law of your state or on federal law, as applicable.

REFERENCES

Alhadeff A. A preparation guide for mediation. *The Brief.* 1991; (Summer):53-57.

American Law Reports. 1988;61(4th series):1019-1059.

Jones G. Win punitive damages in arbitration. *ABA Journal.* 1987; (May):85-88.

Finley D. Humana targeted in fraud probe. *San Antonio Express News.* 1992; Metro Section.

Sokolsky A. Bad faith expanded to health care—a national perspective. *Journal of the Health Lawyer.* 1987;3(2):6-8.

Weidner DW. *Hospital-Based Physician Contracts.* Philadelphia, PA: National Health Lawyers Association Health Contracts Institute; 1991.

Letters of Recommendation: To Write or Not to Write?

Ronald W Scott, JD, LLM, PT, has some cautionary words for physical therapists who are called upon to write letters of recommendation.

Employers, professors, clinic directors, clinical educators, and other professionals often are called upon to write letters of recommendation for former employees, students, and volunteers. These professionals may be torn between the conflicting duties of helping someone whom they like personally and conveying accurate information about a candidate. Because of a perception that letters of recommendation are inherently biased, some human resources management scholars regard them as "useless," holding the view that "employers usually disregard such letters unless they contain negative information."[1]

Writers of letters of recommendation often are restrained from making candid comments about a candidate by their fear of liability exposure. The legal morass surrounding letters of recommendation indeed is complex. Potential litigation over recommendations may include:

- **Defamation: Communication of information that is injurious to a candidate's reputation in the community.** "Slander" is oral communication of defamatory comments, whereas "libel" encompasses all other forms of defamation, including letters of recommendation.
- **Invasion of privacy: Public disclosure of private facts about a candidate,** such as previous arrests, drug use, or sexual orientation. Courts have imposed liability and punitive damages against employers who unlawfully release confidential employee information, such as credit history, human immunodeficiency virus (HIV) status, and drug test results.
- **Intentional infliction of emotional distress:** "Unreasonable" statements or conduct that result in severe physical and psychological injury to a candidate.

At the opposite end of the legal spectrum, individuals may face litigation for *failure to provide a reference* when they have agreed to do so under an employment contract or pursuant to an employee policy handbook. Litigation also may result when a candidate learns that an employer or other official has written a favorable reference for another candidate but has declined to issue one for him or her.[2]

The growing concern that litigation may result from writing or not writing letters of recommendation has prompted many employers and others to change their policy on references to limit the information they convey to confirmation of basic employment and salary data. This restrictive policy is widely used by employers—even though in many states writers of references have "qualified immunity" from liability for the information they communicate to others. *The burden of litigation over whether this immunity was exceeded is sufficient, in many businesses, to warrant a restrictive policy.*

Physical therapists basically are altruistic, "helping" professionals; it runs counter to their nature to refuse to provide a reference to a prospective student or employee. Following are some useful tips for therapists who want to write letters of recommendation:

- Require a *written request for information from a prospective employer or physical therapy education program* and a *written release from the candidate* (especially when you know the recommendation will be less than sterling) before releasing any information.
- Respond to requests for information *only in writing,* and maintain file copies of correspondence for at least the length of time of the state statute of limitations for legal actions. (This period of time is often 2 to 3 years; however, the length of time varies from state to state and according to type of legal action, so you should check with your personal legal counsel for specific advice.)
- *Centralize formal responses* to reference requests. Have your human resources manager review and send out any responses to requests for information about current or former employees, volunteers, or others. *PT*

Ronald W Scott, JD, LLM, PT, is a major in the US Army Medical Specialist Corps and is a physical therapist and legal consultant at Brooke Army Medical Center, San Antonio, Tex.

References

1 Cherrington DJ. *The Management of Human Resources, ed 3.* Needham Heights, Mass: Allyn & Bacon Publishers; 1991:221.
2 Fishman RH. "Where silence is golden." *Nation's Business.* July 1991:48-49.

OSHA *Ergonomics Guidelines* & the PT C

by Lauren Andrew Hebert, PT

Many employers are seeking PTs' expertise to develop ergonomics programs consistent with the evolving OSHA guidelines. Are you ready to meet industry's needs?

Cumulative trauma disorders (CTDs) such as tendinitis, carpal tunnel syndrome, and back pain can be characterized as "epidemic" in today's workplace. At the landmark Project Focus '93: Conference on Work Related Injury, Marie Haring Sweeney, PhD, of the National Institute of Safety and Health (NIOSH), emphasized that 61% of all occupational illnesses reported to the US Department of Labor (DOL) in the early 1980s were due to repeated trauma and that "the problem continues to increase." She also said that from 20% to 30% of people "are reporting symptoms not only in the hand, wrist, and back area; but in the neck, shoulder, and lower extremities."[1] Unlike single-incident accidents, CTDs are the result of a complex constellation of subtle risk factors, which is one reason why they often lead to controversial Workers' Compensation claims.

The DOL's Occupational Safety and Health Administration (OSHA) has responded to the CTD epidemic with aggressive enforcement efforts that may result in large fines and in court orders for expensive workplace retooling. To help employers avoid these penalties and to reduce the inci-

nsultant

dence, severity, and cost of musculoskeletal disorders in the workplace, OSHA has promulgated *OSHA Ergonomics Program Guidelines 3123*[2] (available from most local DOL offices). As this article goes to press, the *Guidelines* are being elaborated, and they eventually will be promulgated as more strictly applied regulations in a rapidly evolving regulatory process known as the OSHA Ergonomics Standard. The Standard is in the financial-impact-study stage of rule making; the Standard document was

released for public comment in May. There has been resistance to the *Guidelines* and the Standard, both from business and from some members of the US Congress.

In the Workplace: Hostility and Suspicion Giving Way

Historically, many injury prevention efforts have been frustrated by workplace politics and hostility. Because CTDs often are "invisible" both to managers and to healthy workers, the honesty of those who claim to have such disorders may be questioned, leading to conflict, litigation, exaggerated injury costs—and failed rehabilitation. This hostile climate naturally can dampen industry motivation to establish prevention programs. But a growing track record of successful ergonomics programs is beginning to move employers to assign greater value to prevention. Some companies have reported reductions of 60% to 80% in lost-time injuries following the implementation of structured prevention programs.[3,9]

With hostility and suspicion in the workplace giving way to emerging data, financial realities, and regulatory pressures, it is becoming easier to market prevention to corporate managers. Employers are aware that OSHA is moving toward more aggressive enforcement, and they realize that utilizing in-house staff to develop a complex ergonomics program would be a frustrating and possibly insurmountable task. In addition, the Standard document includes a statement that OSHA will *not* require an employer to "reinvent the wheel": If an employer already has established a prevention program that shows a decline in workplace injury, that program will not be subject to the requirements put forth in the OSHA *Guidelines*. This means that employers may be motivated to create programs *before* the new OSHA regulations are finalized and enforced.

These developments present a golden opportunity for physical therapists seeking to expand their career into the prevention market. Using the draft *Guidelines*, they can 1) modify traditional "back schools" to address workplace attitudes and politics in addition to injury prevention training and 2) create "CTD schools" to address upper-quarter musculoskeletal conditions.

What Do the Draft *OSHA Guidelines* Say?

The draft *OSHA Ergonomics Program Guidelines 3123*—which often uses the terms "ergonomics" and "prevention" interchangeably—presents a number of major points around which injury prevention programs can be structured. Below is a summary of these points.

Establish accountability through a written plan. The employer's ergonomics program should be in writing to help make the program accountable for what it achieves and doesn't achieve and to keep it on track. The document should be dynamic, that is, it should be continually modified as the program is implemented. It also should culminate in a complete set of ergonomics policies and procedures.

Demonstrate management commitment to workplace safety. Management should demonstrate both in writing and in actions its commitment to the ergonomics program, showing that it places workplace safety at a level of priority at least as high as that of production. This demonstration can take the form of 1) a statement of commitment in the written plan, 2) participation in training, and 3) support of any and all preventive actions. Without active and visible commitment on the part of management, the program is doomed to fail from lack of valid leadership.

Ensure employee buy-in. Employees should be actively involved at all developmental stages of the company's ergonomics program, from design to implementation to long-term follow-up, including work risk analysis, training, and ergonomics team meetings. (The "ErgoTeam" concept is discussed later in this article.) After all, it is the employee's body that is at risk, and it is the employee who (usually) best knows the job and how its design could be improved. Early and active involvement helps overcome conflict and resistance on safety issues.

Conduct a work risk analysis and an ergonomics survey. The employer should survey its records and jobs to identify potential ergonomics hazards. Again, it is these varied and often subtle hazards that work together to create CTD risks. "At-risk" jobs should be analyzed in detail by a *qualified professional* (this could be a physical therapist experienced in work injury management) to fully document ergonomics hazards and to propose corrective actions.

Develop and implement hazard controls. The employer and its consultant(s) should develop and implement ergonomics hazard-control measures directed toward reduction or elimination of risks that may lead to CTDs. Initially proposed in the work risk analysis and monitored by the ergonomics team to ensure implementation, these controls should be put in place in a timely manner.

Provide management and employee training. The management team should be thoroughly educated about CTDs, ergonomics, hazard identification and controls, and injury case management, whereas employees should be trained in personal ergonomics, self-protection, and self-care of the working body. Training should take the form of "back schools" and "neck-arm CTD schools" both for the management team and for the employees. Because ignorance is what perpetuates the epidemic of injuries, claims, and costs, all parties in the workplace should be informed and committed to prevention.

Provide case management policies. The employer should develop and implement effective, accountable policies for early response to CTD symptoms; encourage effective "conservative treatment"; and ensure rapid and safe return to work. To ensure "maximal recovery at minimal cost," the company should provide for proper medical care and establish an effective restricted-duty program for early return to work.

Allow for ongoing feedback and implementation. The employer should establish

an ergonomics team that is charged with the responsibility of evaluating the ergonomics program and ensuring the program's maximal long-term effective implementation.

The PT Consultant and the "Ergonomics Plan"

Based on *OSHA Ergonomics Program Guidelines 3123*, the physical therapist can initiate the prevention program using a work risk analysis to identify the nature and the scope of ergonomics and worker-behavior hazards. The therapist must visit the workplace to analyze each job category, documenting the physical demands of the job and the body mechanics and work habits of the worker, listing and explaining the risk

> A traditional engineering-based quantitative analysis of mechanical job demands and workplace design can be difficult for the corporate manager to understand. The manager needs to know just as much—if not more—about worker habits and behaviors.

factors observed, and offering a list of corrective actions that the company can consider to correct the risks.

The therapist can help the employer meet *Guidelines* objectives by following a series of steps such as those described below:

Step 1: Conduct both quantitative and qualitative work risk analysis. A traditional engineering-based quantitative analysis of mechanical job demands and workplace design can be difficult for the corporate manager to understand. The manager needs to know just as much—if not more—about worker habits and behaviors. The work risk analysis therefore should include a *qualita-*

tive observation of habits and behaviors—which may be more serious and more common than are job-design and work-station deficits. For one example of a completed work risk analysis form, see Figure 1.

The therapist's analysis also should include a subjective discussion of the sociopolitical issues that may be contributing to excessive claims and costs and that could sabotage prevention efforts, such as negative attitudes toward workers with injuries (see opposite), the presence and level of effectiveness of a restricted-duty program, production demands, the general tenor of employer-employee relations, worker turnover, and issues related to demographics (eg, age and sex).

Step 2: Make initial suggestions for corrective actions. The work risk analysis report to the employer should provide information both on workplace design and biomechanics and on worker habits, behaviors, and attitudes. The report also should offer a variety of suggestions for corrective actions, including job-design modifications, job-task rotation, proper seating, modifications in work assignments, preventive stretching exercises, prevention training, and injury management. The report becomes the company's first draft of a written ergonomics plan; suggests, as called for in the *Guidelines*, the initial set of hazard identification and controls; and provides a baseline from which customized management and employee training may be built. Figure 2 contains a sample report to management.

Step 3: Train the managers. Management training can take the form of a management-level back school or a neck-arm CTD school or both, with the purpose of improving knowledge, raising awareness, and bringing into alignment the attitudes of the entire management team, including union leadership. One essential objective of management training is to correct counterproductive attitudes that result from ignorance about CTDs, building the essential cooperation and commitment of all those in a leadership role. As the *Guidelines* emphasize, management education is the prerequisite to effective employee training.

Step 4: Train the employees. Employees can be taught to view themselves as professional workplace athletes who have only one

Juggling Corporate Politics: An Epidemic of CTDs—and Bad Attitudes

The aspiring PT prevention consultant already has an extensive knowledge of musculoskeletal dysfunction and its management," says author Lauren Hebert. "Insight into the unique political environment of the workplace may be the more critical need for the PT. Lack of this insight can both impair the effectiveness of a work injury prevention training program and impede the success of the PT's marketing efforts." In this *PT* interview, Hebert discusses the role of workplace politics.

PT: You've said that the industrial workplace bears little similarity to the clinical environment to which PTs have grown accustomed. What do you mean by that?

Hebert: In the clinic, the PT is used to being in control and—usually—to being *sought out* by the patient. At the work site, however, the PT is a foreigner—and the patient is not the person, it's the job and the company. And this "patient" may not even think that he needs you! Many employers fear that you're going to change the way they work. The most important thing for the PT to remember is that there is a caste system in corporate culture, a very defined pecking order, which is unlike most physical therapy practices and unlike American society at large.

PT: What effect does that pecking order have on the PT's strategies?

Hebert: First, the PT needs to be aware that there usually is a power struggle going on between employer and employee and that there may be varying degrees of mutual loyalty. In my experience, management and supervisors generally assume that employees with CTDs [cumulative trauma disorders] are faking and that PTs are only going to help employees fake *better*. This is why management typically responds to employee injury with hostility rather than with a rehabilitation mind-set. The PT's challenge is to help management accept that, yes, CTDs are real, and, yes, there is

something that can be done to treat and prevent them. Some companies believe that CTDs are the inevitable cost of doing business, and that's just not true.

PT: What's the biggest challenge with employees?

Hebert: To get them to accept responsibility for their own personal fitness. Just as the employer may assume that the employee is faking, the employee may assume that an injury is the employer's fault. And that's not necessarily the case, either.

PT: What's different about motivating employees in the workplace from motivating patients in the clinic?

Hebert: In both settings, PTs need to teach patients how to take care of themselves. There often is an extra dimension to treating workers, however: their low self-esteem. Especially in industrial settings that employ large numbers of workers, management may have a "workers-are-losers" attitude. After 20 years of hearing that message, many workers start to believe it: "Why *should* I take care of myself? I'm not worth anything."

PT: On one hand, employees may blame employers for their injuries; on the other hand, they also may have low self-esteem and may not choose to take care of themselves. Sounds like a recipe for the failure of rehabilitation.

Hebert: But the PT ergonomist is in a position to change that. I'll give you an example. A manufacturer had an epidemic of tendinitis, carpal tunnel syndrome, and back problems. The workers sent a complaint to OSHA [Occupational Safety and Health Administration], and OSHA visited the plant, declared it unsafe, and levied a big fine. The company went to court over it. In an out-of-court settlement, the company agreed to have our practice do a work risk analysis and set up an ergonomics program. Now, management allowed us into the workplace only grudgingly; after all, it was a court mandate. As it turns out, we

found more safety and ergonomics problems than OSHA did! But after just 2 days of management training, management turned around. We showed them that a light-duty program was critical, that it was more cost-effective to encourage rather than discourage early claims, and that job rotation and simple strategies such as stretching exercises could help prevent injuries. They realized that hostility was what had generated the OSHA complaint to begin with—and that the hostility contributed greatly to their seven-figure Workers' Compensation costs. The workers, on the other hand, needed 2 weeks of training.... I've seen this scenario play out dozens of times, though not necessarily with OSHA involvement.

PT: In this article you emphasize OSHA's new aggressive regulatory stance. Is this the biggest issue for industry today?

Hebert: No. A corporation exists to make a profit, and Workers' Comp costs are an enormous impediment to corporate profits. That's the big issue. If Workers' Comp claims for CTD problems make up the majority of Workers' Comp claims and costs, it makes good business sense for an employer to implement an effective CTD prevention program. The OSHA regs are important, obviously, but the profit motive is what's really driving companies toward expert consultant help in developing an effective prevention program.

PT: Do you find that the work you do has a long-lasting effect?

Hebert: For some companies, it may be necessary to provide a brief annual retraining process, but prevention consultation generally has a lasting effect.... Work injury epidemics often start with a breakdown in loyalty between employers and employees. When PTs go into a company, they are catalysts for sweeping, enduring change—not just in worker safety but in the corporate culture itself. And *that's* what makes ergonomics and the field of work injury management so fascinating.

Figure 1. Sample Work Risk Analysis Checklist.

JOB TITLE ___*Widget Cutting*___ DEPT ___*Widgets*___

- ✔ Sustained standing
- ✔ Standing on cement, metal, vibrating surface
- ___ Standing predominantly on one leg (eg, foot-switch operation)
- ✔ Holding spine sustained in "bent" or "twisted" posture
- ✔ Limited variety of work postures
- ___ Prolonged sitting, required or selected
- ___ Poor chair design and/or ___ Improper chair adjustment
- ✔ Forward-head posture
- ✔ Lack of upper-extremity weight bearing on work surface
- ✔ "Shoulder reach": sustained, repeated, or loaded (forward or to side)
- ___ Elbow flexed more than 90 degrees: sustained, repeated, or loaded
- ___ Forearm supinated: sustained, repeated, or loaded
- ✔ Sustained, repeated, or loaded lifting or pulling across wrist
- ✔ Wrist flexion or deviation: sustained, repeated, extreme, or loaded
- ✔ Grip: sustained, repeated, forceful; holding time significantly exceeds recovery
- ___ Pinch: sustained, repeated, or forceful
- ✔ Grip or pinch that is slippery, vibrating, cold; large or small in diameter
- ___ Holding thumb pinch during wrist deviation
- ___ Improper tool selection and/or ___ Improper tool use
- ✔ Materials difficult to manipulate with hands
- ___ Inadequate training on work procedures
- ___ Inadequate enforcement of proper work procedures

Materials-handling loads (lift-push-pull-carry) that are:
- ✔ Heavy: weight = _*10 lb*_ average   and _____ maximum lb or kg
- ✔ Frequent: frequency = __*8*__ per (min/hr); _____ day
- ___ High or low height: low = _*30"*_   high = _*55"*_
- ✔ Long arc twisted: degree of twist = _*180°*_
- ___ Lifting/carrying across obstructions
- ___ With difficult grip
- ___ With cumbersome shape
- ___ Challenging the capacity of individual workers
- ___ Workers using unsafe lifting techniques

- ___ Attitudes that do not encourage safest work conditions and behaviors
- ✔ Stressful production demands (piecework, overtime, production standards)
- ✔ Lack of work task variety
- ___ Worker demographics risks
- ___ Stressful human relations

OTHER ___*He has been working at this job 20 yrs.*___
_____
_____

Note: This is a checklist of risks from which a narrative is written describing work activities, explaining observed risks, and listing corrective actions that the company may consider to abate the risks.

body on which they can rely to support their family for a lifetime. Extensive discussion about specific disease pathology and symptoms is not necessary. Emphasis instead can be placed on fatigue avoidance, which is a more immediate concern to workers—and which usually is a more readily accepted prevention concept. Emphasizing this aspect may make employees more willing to try the physical therapist's suggestions—and may assure management that the therapist is not spending "too much time" giving employees "too much information" about diseases and symptoms. The validity of emphasizing fatigue avoidance depends on the level of conflict and confrontation between employer and employees. This strategy may be more readily embraced by a hesitant and cautious company that has been plagued by hostile employer-employee relations.

Management team training and employee "work-smart" training can be used to initiate cooperative implementation of hazard controls such as work-design modification, job-task rotation, stretching programs, proper case management, and more effective production policies.

Step 5: Train an "ErgoTeam." Using an advanced seminar format—which might include an ergonomics lecture presented by the therapist, an analysis of in-house case examples, a videotape analysis of jobs, problem-solving examples, and role-playing to overcome resistance to change—the therapist can help the employer train a select team of employees, supervisors, safety-and- health staff, and engineering and maintenance staff. Training also could include a review of CTD injury "pathomechanics" and prevention strategies in addition to instruction in how to gather employee fatigue profiles and perform an ergonomics risk analysis. The objective: to assemble and empower a knowledgeable in-house team to take over the prevention effort from the physical therapist consultant. Ideally, this team should meet every few weeks to analyze and improve at-risk jobs and to ensure effective long-term implementation of the ergonomics program.

At this stage, the physical therapist can provide the employer with the employer's own copy of an "ErgoPlan," a policy and

Figure 2. Sample Work Risk Analysis Report to Management.

JOB TASK: WIDGET CUTTING

Biomechanical description

The worker is in sustained standing on a cement floor. He demonstrates a forward-head posture habit. He reaches forward with his upper extremities, bringing the shoulders to 90 degrees of flexion, to place a metal strip on a cutter. The strip weighs approximately 10 lb. The worker holds the strip to the cutter for 5 seconds. His hand maintains a narrow, slippery, forceful grip, with the wrist in ulnar deviation.

The worker places the cut portions in the box next to him. He is repetitively reaching to the bin on his left to grasp the uncut metal strips. The left shoulder is in abduction (to 50 degrees) and is laterally rotated. The right shoulder is in repetitive abduction (to 40 degrees) and is laterally rotated as he places the cut strips in the box. The worker must rotate his spine from 90 degrees to the left to 90 degrees to the right during this 7-second process.

Observed risks

1. Sustained standing poses the risk of posture fatigue at the lower extremities, lower back, neck, and shoulders. Standing on a cement or steel floor can magnify the posture fatigue of standing.

2. The observed worker has a forward-head posture habit, a common work posture habit that contributes to the risk of cumulative trauma disorders (CTDs). It can stress the neck, shoulder, upper back, and lower back. There also is a change in the muscle tension of various jaw muscles, which may lead to temporomandibular joint problems. The lateral neck muscles may be stressed, which could lead to compression of nerves and blood vessels passing through these muscles on their way to the upper extremity.

3. Reaching with the shoulder can strain various tendons of the shoulder joint. The weight of the metal strip magnifies these risks. The relatively prolonged period of "long shoulder reaching" with a brief period of recovery further increases this stress.

4. Hand grip creates tension within the flexor tendons in the forearm that pass through the carpal tunnel. Excessive work demand on these muscles and tendons creates the risk of tendinitis and carpal tunnel syndrome. The factors affecting this risk include force of grip, large grip diameter, small grip diameter, and excessive holding time. Excessive time spent in gripping—however light the grip may be—is an important risk factor. The small grip diameter, slippery surface, ulnar deviation during grip, and presence of high-frequency vibration during the cutting process greatly magnify the described risks.

5. Ulnar deviation of the wrist is observed. Tipping the wrist in the direction of the little finger results in compression at the carpal tunnel, increasing the risk of carpal tunnel syndrome and tendinitis at the wrist. The range of movement in this direction, the frequency of this movement, and the time spent in this position determine the extent of the risk. Adding grip or pinch greatly magnifies the risk.

6. The repetitive abduction and lateral rotation of each shoulder to move the product from the starting point to the finishing point represents a further loading of the shoulder joint, as previously described. Abduction and lateral rotation are stressful movement patterns for the shoulder joint.

7. Turning the body repetitively over a 180-degree arc is a torsion stress to the cervical and lumbar spine. Twisting the neck and the lower back repetitively and over a wide range of motion can irritate facet joints and disks of the spine (including the disks of the neck and the lower back).

8. The worker does not rotate off this job, which means that there is a highly focused and intense exposure of the spine and upper extremities to the CTD stresses described above.

Corrective recommendations

1. A tall stool should be placed in this work area to allow the worker some brief periods of sitting throughout the day, providing variety in posture and relief from sustained standing.

2. The worker should rotate to another job often, providing for a variety in posture and movement patterns. Rotating to another job also would provide for more mobility, which could greatly diminish the effects of fatigue. To maximize the worker's cooperation, employee CTD training should explain the advantages of job rotation.

3. The worker should stand on an anti-fatigue floor mat or place a viscoelastic material in his shoes. These materials are specifically engineered to help reduce posture fatigue and the fatigue that results from sustained standing on a cement floor. Use of these materials may result in reduced CTD risks and improved worker performance and job satisfaction. This strategy may be particularly valuable for this job because the worker stands near vibrating equipment.

4. Employees, managers, and engineers should discuss modifying equipment to bring the cutting portion of the machinery lower or closer to the worker or both. Reducing the amount of reaching with the shoulder and lowering the level of shoulder elevation (even if only by 1 or 2 inches) could reduce the load placed on the shoulder joint.

5. Employees, managers, and engineers should discuss how the equipment may be modified so that the metal strip is clamped efficiently and securely during the cutting process. This strategy would reduce the need to maintain a position in which there is long, loaded reaching with the shoulder that involves grip.

6. The worker should try wearing open-finger gloves that have viscoelastic material in the palm. This may reduce the mechanical compression and the vibration transmitted to the hand, particularly in the carpal tunnel region. Dampening the vibration could reduce CTD risk and fatigue in the upper extremity. This is particularly important for preventing carpal tunnel syndrome and vibration white-finger syndrome.

7. Employees should be trained to carry out the preventive stretching procedures specific to this job. These exercises require about 60 seconds in total; should be carried out at least once per hour; and include chin tuck, lateral neck stretch, shrug-relax, shoulder pendulum, extensor carpi radialis longus muscle stretch, and wrist flexor stretch exercises. The format of employee training that we are proposing is designed to motivate employees to comply with these recommendations. Management training will discuss how to enforce and encourage maximum compliance.

procedures manual developed around *OSHA Ergonomics Program Guidelines 3123*. Chapters in this manual might contain the work risk analysis report, the attendance lists from management and employee training sessions, customized case management procedures, and the minutes of "ErgoTeam" meetings. The manual should comprehensively and accurately document the employer's ongoing ergonomics program and serves as the final draft of its ergonomics plan.

In real life. For the past 2 years, the state of Maine has implemented a mandatory, experimental OSHA compliance program to encourage employers to develop ergonomics programs consistent with the *Guidelines*. The OSHA compliance program may be extended to other states.

The high level of enforcement of the *Guidelines* in Maine has led many employers to use the program format described above in developing an ergonomics program proposal to submit to the state and federal officials managing the experimental compli-

ance program. Several employers already have negotiated with OSHA to use this type of program in response to OSHA sanctions against them for allowing a CTD epidemic to develop among their workers.

··

The objective is to assemble and empower an in-house resource of knowledgeable employees, supervisors, safety-and-health staff, and engineering and maintenance staff to take over the prevention effort from the physical therapist consultant.

Marketing to Industry

There are two challenges for physical therapists seeking to become work injury prevention consultants. The first challenge is to develop a set of effective prevention services to deliver to the workplace. As this article describes, the *OSHA Ergonomics Guidelines 3123* suggests a structure for these services. The second challenge is to effectively market these services to industry, particularly to those corporate clients who still may be hesitant about prevention programs.

Marketing used to be a distasteful concept among physical therapists. But as recent articles in *PT* (eg, "Lessons in Marketing, Reimbursement, and Real Life," Cirullo and Yuisko, December 1994) have shown, changes in the health care environment have elevated marketing to its proper place in health care.

Physical therapists interested in marketing their work injury prevention services should examine available off-the-shelf back school and CTD school prevention training programs and attend specialized seminars on these topics. Don't be afraid to seek contact with potential mentors who are experienced in the prevention business. Look for examples of "packaged" prevention programs that provide detailed protocols; professional-appearing training materials; strong educational support; high-quality marketing materials; and, most importantly, an extensive track record of success in industry. Indeed, for any therapist who wants to market prevention services, a successful track record will be his or her most critical asset. Specific marketing strategies include announcements mailed to corporate safety managers, presentations to various industry groups, and seminars to industry representatives. Videotapes also can be made to describe the work injury crisis and how physical therapists can help.

Prevention: A Safe Haven from Managed Care

For physical therapists, providing prevention services to industry can be a safe haven from a changing, uncertain health care environment. Work injury prevention is a business arrangement between the therapist and the employer—an arrangement that is completely separate from managed care issues. The employer pays directly for this consulting service on a per-day rate, and the uncertainties of third-party payment are avoided. Client billings generally can be collected at a rate of 100% within 30 to 45 days from billing.

Ergonomics typically has been the forte of design engineers; however, their strategies are limited primarily to job design, neglecting worker habits and non-design prevention tactics such as stretching and worker self-care training. Physical therapists therefore offer employers a distinct advantage, with the option of collaboration with engineers.

Workers often are at high risk for CTDs and usually have little knowledge on how to avoid them. Business and industry are now actively seeking help on these issues. The timing is perfect. You may be able to prevent far more pain and disability in the workplace than you could ever hope to treat in the clinic. Why confine your knowledge to the treatment room?

What are you waiting for? *PT*

....

*Lauren Andrew Hebert, PT, is President, IMPACC, South Portland, Me. He is the author of **The Neck-Arm-Hand Book** (1989), published by IMPACC.*

References

1 *Proceedings of Project Focus '93: Work Injury.* Alexandria, Va: Foundation for Physical Therapy; 1994.
2 *OSHA Ergonomics Program Guidelines 3123.* Washington, DC: US Department of Labor; 1994.
3 Lutz G. Cumulative trauma disorders control: Ethicon ergonomics program. *J Hand Surg.* 1987;12A:863-866.
4 Bullock M, ed. *Ergonomics: The Physiotherapist in the Workplace.* Edinburgh, Scotland, Great Britain: Churchill Livingstone; 1991.
5 Melnik M. Enlisting participation in an injury prevention program. *Work.* 1990;Fall:39-48.
6 Armstrong T. Ergonomics and cumulative trauma disorders. *Hand Clinics.* 1986;12(3):533-565.
7 Isernhagen S. *Work Injury.* Rockville, Md: Aspen Publishers Inc; 1988.
8 Hebert L. Cumulative trauma school for industry. *Industrial Rehabilitation Quarterly.* 1992;Fall:47.
9 Hebert L. Analytic focus reducing CTD claims. *J Occup Health and Safety.* 1993;62(4):56-62.

Managed Care, ERISA, PT

by John J Bennett, Esq

Which providers are eligible to participate in a plan? Which treatments are covered? Who is liable for improper denial of treatment or for premature discharge? APTA's General Counsel guides you through a maze of legal decisions that may have implications for physical therapy.

o reduce their administrative costs and to obtain discounted fees, managed care health plans increasingly seek to limit the panel of providers—including physical therapists—to whom patients have access. To discourage overutilization of services, these plans use strategies such as conditioning patient access to specialists on a referral by the primary care physician and making precertification and concurrent review by utilization management entities a condition of hospital admission or continued stay. These types of strategies shift much of the control over patient care from health care providers and patients to managed care organizations (MCOs).

In addition to raising various professional and ethical questions (see "Protecting the 'Care' in Managed Care," page 69), this shift raises a number of questions that have a legal component. Which providers are eligible to participate in a plan? Which treatments are covered? Who is liable for improper denial of treatment or for premature discharge—the provider, the plan, the plan administrator, or the utilization review entity? These questions are not easy to answer. One complicating factor is the Employment Retirement Income Security Act of 1974 (ERISA) (Pub L No. 93-406, 88 Stat 829, 29 USC §§1001-1461).

ERISA and the Preemption Clause

Although ERISA's name suggests that it applies only to employee pension plans, the statute in fact extends to *all employee benefit plans that provide medical care or benefits to employees*, whether the plans provide the care or benefits through the purchase of insurance or through "self-insurance." (ERISA does not purport, however, to regulate benefit plans created by a state or by a political subdivision of a state for its own employees.) ERISA establishes certain uniform procedural standards governing reporting, disclosure, and fiduciary responsibility, and it authorizes plan participants to sue to recover benefits due and attorneys' fees and court costs (not including punitive damages or compensation for pain and suffering).

From a regulatory point of view, ERISA is important less for what it gives than for what it takes away from state authority. It contains a preemption clause that explicitly provides that ERISA supersedes most (but not all) state laws—including both legislation and case law—"relating to" employee benefit plans. This statutory preemption goes even further than does the clause of the US Constitution that makes federal law supreme, because it overrides state law even when the state law does not conflict with any substantive ERISA policy and even when ERISA is silent on the subject that the state law addresses.

What is the basic rationale for preempting state regulation of employee benefit plans? In *Ingersoll-Rand Company v McClendon* [498 US 133, 142, (1990)], the court determined that the purposes of the preemption clause are 1) to ensure that "plans and plan sponsors would be subject to a uniform body of benefits law" and 2) to "minimize the [employer's] administrative and financial burden of complying with conflicting directives among States or between States and the Federal Government." Federal preemption enables an employer who has employees in more than one state to operate under a unified plan rather than having to tailor multiple plans on a state-by-state basis. ERISA does not *obligate* employers to establish employee benefits plans; however, it can be said that by limiting and simplifying the regulatory burden, ERISA does promote the establishment and continuation of voluntary plans.

How does all of this relate to managed care? ERISA does *not* regulate the substantive content of medical benefit plans or the eligibility of providers to participate in plans, obligate a plan to cover a particular medical condition or type of treatment, or limit a plan's freedom to choose the providers who participate. But even though ERISA is silent on these issues, under ERISA the states may lack the authority to address them because ERISA preempts any state laws that "relate to" benefit plans. This means that there is a regulatory void for certain areas of managed care, which may have an impact on two issues of great importance to physical therapists: provider eligibility and professional liability. To understand the impact of ERISA on managed care, you first must understand more about how ERISA works.

How Do You Know Whether a State Law "Relates to" a Plan?

ERISA preempts any state law that "relates to" benefit plans. The US Supreme Court repeatedly has said that "relate to" should be interpreted broadly, in accordance with its common-sense meaning (ie, a law "relates to" a plan if it has a connection with or reference to the plan). On one hand, a state law may "relate to" benefit plans even when it is not specifically designed to affect such plans and when its effect on them is only indirect. On the other hand, some state laws may affect benefit plans too remotely to be treated as "relating to" them, such as laws that permit garnishment of benefits from a plan regulated by ERISA.

The difficulty of determining whether a state law "relates to" health care plans is illustrated by *New York State Conference of Blue Cross and Blue Shield Plans v Travelers Insurance Company* [1995 US LEXIS 3038 (April 26, 1995), *rev'g* 14 F3d 708 (2d Cir 1993)]. In this case, the US Supreme Court acknowledged the indeterminacy of the phrase "relate to" and looked for guidance to ERISA's goals, especially the goal of permitting the nationally uniform administration of employee benefit plans. At issue: a New York law requiring hospitals to collect surcharges from patients who were covered by a commercial insurer but *not* from patients who were insured by Blue Cross/Blue Shield. Health maintenance organizations (HMOs) also were subject to surcharges, which were linked to the number of Medicaid recipients enrolled with the HMO. The surcharges clearly would have significant effect on commercial insurers

The actual effect of ERISA preemption in any particular case involving physical therapists can be difficult to predict, given the elusiveness of the legal concepts.

Because AWP [any willing provider] laws typically "relate to" benefit plans for the purposes of ERISA, the federal preemption question turns on whether AWP laws are "saved" from preemption through the savings clause.

and HMOs that provided coverage (or could provide coverage) for ERISA plans—and also would be likely to increase plan costs.

The US Court of Appeals held that the law did "relate to" employee benefit plans—and therefore was subject to preemption by ERISA—because the law was intended to increase hospital costs for patients whose health plans were not Blue Cross/Blue Shield, thus affecting the health care benefits of ERISA plans. The US Supreme Court reversed that decision, however, reasoning that although the New York law clearly had an indirect economic impact on the choices available to ERISA plans, it was not "related to" such plans. The court emphasized that the preferential treatment given to Blue Cross/Blue Shield plans did not, as a practical matter, preclude ERISA plans from obtaining coverage from commercial insurers or HMOs or preclude a plan from offering a uniform interstate benefits package or from using uniform administrative practices.

The "Savings" Clause: Insured Plans

Enter the McCarran-Ferguson Act (15 USC § 1011). Enacted in 1945, this act holds that federal laws should *not* be interpreted as

superseding state laws "regulating the business of insurance" (eg, regulating insurer solvency, advertising, and claims practices or regulating the content of the insurance contract—such as a requirement that coverage of infants begin at birth). It is not surprising, then, that the major exception to the ERISA preemption of state regulation of insurance is a "savings" clause that "saves" to the states the power to regulate insurance. This is remarkable because it gives back to the states much, but not all, of the authority taken away by ERISA's preemption clause!

As the US Supreme Court noted wryly in *Metropolitan Life Insurance Company v Massachusetts* [471 US 724, 747 (1985)], although "Congress occasionally decides to return to the States what it has previously taken away, it does not normally do both at the same time." In *Metropolitan*, the court found that a Massachusetts law mandating mental health benefits was "saved" from ERISA preemption to the extent that the state law required health insurance policies to provide a minimum level of such benefits.

ERISA's savings clause raises the question of whether, for ERISA purposes, a particular state law regulates "insurance." In making this determination (essentially defining *insurance*), the courts try to use both common sense and the following criteria developed under the McCarran-Ferguson Act (neither being a foolproof guide):

- The practice [being regulated] has the effect of transferring or spreading a policyholder's risk.
- The practice is an integral part of the policy relationship between the insurer and the insured.
- The practice is limited to entities within the insurance industry.

Even using these criteria, it is not easy to make the determination about what insurance is. For example, in *Nationsbank of North Carolina NA v Variable Annuity Life Insurance Company* [115 SCt 810 (1995)], a case not involving ERISA, the US Supreme Court decided that "insurance" did not clearly cover annuities—even though insurance companies sell annuities and even though annuities are functionally similar to life insurance and are classified as insurance for state regulatory purposes!

The "Deemer" Clause: Uninsured Plans

So far we've seen that ERISA "saves" state regulation of insurance, essentially giving back to the states much of the authority it takes away. The complexity of preemption law is further compounded by ERISA's provision that a self-insured employee benefit plan is *not* deemed an insurance company or considered to be engaged in the business of insurance for purposes of any state law purporting to regulate insurance. This provision is called the "deemer" clause, and it means that the states do not have the power to regulate self-insured or risk-retention plans in which an employer establishes the benefits and pays them using its own funds.

One consequence of the disparity in ERISA regulation between insured plans and self-insured plans is that states may be *tempted* to try to regulate self-insured plans under the guise of regulating "insurance." An employer who sets up a self-insured plan, for example, typically guards against catastrophic cases by purchasing some form of "stop-loss" insurance from a commercial insurer. Although a state cannot regulate the self-insured plan, it *can* regulate the plan's activities as they pertain to the purchase of insurance. In *New York State Conference of Blue Cross and Blue Shield Plans v Travelers Insurance Company*, the New York Department of Insurance ruled that a self-insured plan could not purchase commercial stop-loss insurance unless it provided its members with specified services and afforded them certain conversion rights and protections in case of plan insolvency. The Supreme Court left standing the Court of Appeals' holding that ERISA preempted the New York restrictions, concluding that the restrictions were not the regulation of insurance but rather were a mere pretext to regulate the terms of self-insured ERISA plans.

The actual effect of ERISA preemption in any particular case involving physical therapists can be difficult to predict, given the elusiveness of the legal concepts discussed above. But read on.

ERISA and Any Willing Provider Laws

One of the most contentious issues under managed care involves a health plan's ability to limit the panel of health care providers to whom patients have access. Freedom to restrict the number of providers is advantageous to the plan because it lessens transaction costs (eg, costs of negotiating, credentialing, and reviewing utilization patterns) and because it gives the plan leverage in negotiating with providers for discounted fees (the chosen providers can be assured an increased number of patients *only* if the plan limits the number of other participating providers). On the other hand, freedom to restrict the number of providers may pose a threat to the provider who is excluded from serving the patients in a plan even though he or she is a fully qualified practitioner.

A number of states have enacted or are considering laws, commonly referred to as "any willing provider" (AWP) laws, that are intended to prevent the exclusion of qualified providers who are willing to accept a plan's terms and conditions. (For more on AWP laws, turn to page 35.) Because AWP laws typically "relate to" benefit plans for the purposes of ERISA, the federal preemption question turns on whether AWP laws are "saved" from preemption through the savings clause because they are considered to be state regulation of insurance.

Proponents of AWP legislation could argue that such legislation affects the transferring or spreading of a policyholder's risk (one of the McCarran-Ferguson Act criteria for "insurance") in that it increases the patient's freedom to choose a provider without losing coverage under a given plan. Opponents, however, could point to the fact that an AWP law applies directly to matters that are distinct from the insurer-insured relationship: Because a provider is neither an insured nor an insurer, and because the plans affected by AWP legislation often are not insured plans, ERISA could preempt AWP legislation.

Again, case law illustrates the difficulties in making determinations. In *Stuart Circle Hospital Corporation v Aetna Health Management* [995 F2d 500 (4th Cir 1993), *rev'g* 800 F Supp 328 (ED Va 1992), *cert denied*, 114 SCt 579 (1993)], an appellate court upheld a Virginia law that 1) required an insurance company offering preferred provider organization (PPO) policies to establish the criteria that a provider would need to satisfy to qualify and 2) prohibited the company from excluding anyone willing to meet the terms and conditions. Because the law clearly "related to" benefit plans, its validity depended on the savings clause.

The trial court concluded that the Virginia law did *not* regulate insurance. The court cited the McCarran-Ferguson criteria, reasoning that:

1. The agreements between Aetna and the health care providers did not involve the spreading of risk.

2. Aetna's practice was not an integral part of the insurer-insured relationship—especially when Aetna acted not as an insurer but only as the administrator for a self-insured plan.

3. The regulated practice—the maintenance of PPOs—is not limited to entities within the insurance industry.

The appellate court disagreed with the trial court, emphasizing that the PPO law *did* regulate the insurer-insured relationship by protecting the insured's freedom of choice. The court reasoned that:

1. The Virginia law *did* transfer risk by spreading the cost component of the policyholder's risk. (The policyholder ran the risk of receiving lesser benefits if he or she chose to go to a nonpreferred provider.)
2. The Virginia PPO statute was an integral part of the relationship between insurer and insured.
3. The law *was* limited to entities in the insurance industry *because* ERISA precluded application of the law to self-insured plans.

The decision: The ERISA preemption did not apply. The insurance company had to provide a list of criteria and accept any provider who could meet those criteria.

In *Hollis v CIGNA Healthcare of Connecticut* [Sup Ct of Conn, Nos. 705357 and 705358, 1994 Conn Super LEXIS 3394], however, the court held that ERISA *did* preempt a Connecticut law that required provider networks to file their selection criteria with a state agency and that precluded networks from rejecting or terminating providers on the basis of undisclosed criteria. The court ruled that the savings clause was inapplicable because 1) the law was not limited to practices within the insurance industry (noninsurers also can offer preferred provider networks) and 2) the networks' selection criteria had to be filed with the state's health department rather than with the state's insurance department.

Professional Liability: ERISA and Utilization Review

Under managed care, more and more influence or control over treatment decisions (eg, determining what is "medically necessary") lies with plan administrators and other utilization review personnel who do not actually treat the patient. The exposure of these persons to liability for negligent decisions is a developing area of law that is of growing interest to physical therapists, whether they treat patients or provide utilization review services.

Because malpractice actions are based on state law, ERISA preemption may threaten a patient's ability to recover damages for a negligent utilization review decision. In *Corcoran v United Healthcare* [965 F 2d 1321, 1338 (5th Cir), *cert denied*, 113 SCt 812 (1992)], a case involving a woman with a high-risk pregnancy, the utilization review company hired by the plan administrator refused to approve the hospitalization (for around-the-clock monitoring of the fetus) recommended by the obstetrician and instead authorized 10 hours per day of home health nursing care. The fetus went into distress and died at a time when no nurse was present, and the woman sued the utilization review company.

The court held that state negligence law was preempted by ERISA because although the company had made medical determinations (and had held itself out as having medical expertise), it did so in the context of making a determination about the availability of benefits under an ERISA plan. The court also considered whether the plaintiffs could recover damages, under ERISA's civil enforcement provisions, for their emotional distress. It concluded that the language "other appropriate equitable relief" contained in ERISA did not authorize recovery of such damages.

It should be noted that the court was troubled by its decision—"[plaintiffs] have no remedy, state or federal, for what may have been a serious mistake"—in part because the decision eliminated an important check on the "thousands of medical decisions routinely made in the burgeoning utilization review system."

"For Better or for Worse"

How might ERISA preemption affect a physical therapist's liability in a malpractice suit? Could the therapist be held liable for a treatment decision that was made by an MCO, even if the MCO is not liable because of an ERISA preemption?

It is important for physical therapists to recognize that the preemption of state law by ERISA is a highly technical legal matter that, for better or for worse, has important consequences both for the managed care system and for health care providers. The intrinsic complexity of the preemption, savings, and deemer clauses guarantees that much time, effort, and litigation will be required to sort out the roles of the federal government and the roles of the states under managed care.

Even with the savings clause, the preemption of state law is broad, which means that states may lack power to implement initiatives thought to be desirable (eg, preserving access to provider networks or imposing liability on plan administrators or consultants for negligent utilization decisions—especially negligent failures to issue an advance authorization required by the plan). In addition, ERISA's deemer clause puts the realm of self-insured plans largely off-limits to state intervention, which means, for example, that states cannot require such plans to offer any specific type of medical service or benefit. And, perhaps most important, the scantiness of ERISA's substantive provisions means that many issues will continue to fall within a regulatory void, untouched by the federal law and untouchable by state law. *PT*

John J Bennett, Esq, is APTA's General Counsel. Before joining APTA's staff, he specialized in the regulation of international trade and government contracts at Cahill Gordon & Reindel in Washington, DC.

Point of Interest
Legal cases have been filed regarding denial of necessary care on the basis of physical therapy treatment denials. In one non–ERISA-related case that is pending in Arizona, patients who were receiving Medicare and who were enrolled in an HMO sued the US Department of Health and Human Services, claiming that they received deficient care (eg, 1 week of rehabilitation after a below-the-knee amputation, placement in a nursing home without physical therapy after a spine fracture) and that the government failed to enforce its regulations concerning Medicare.

TAPPING TECHNOLOGY
by Kathy Lewis, JD, MAPT

Legal and Liability Risks on the Internet

It's so easy to be carried away by the ease and allure of the Internet.
Some words of caution: Think before you click on that "send" button.

to many, the Internet has become something of a novel toy. It's in vogue to create a home page on the World Wide Web (a network of online sites containing text and graphics that users "click" through to find information) or to "surf the 'Net." Ease of use, lowered costs, the ability to readily access or transmit a plethora of information, and widespread public awareness of the Internet has created intense gusto for this new transatlantic pipeline to our mailboxes.

Those who are overwhelmed with enthusiasm for the Internet, however, may neglect common sense and professional discretion in its use. As one attorney active in the American Bar Association's (ABA) technology group wrote, "The Internet is really just communications on steroids. We should avoid jumping to the conclusion that the Internet changes everything."[1]

If communication via traditional means such as mail and telephone has raised legal concern about such things as defamation, copyright infringement, unauthorized disclosure of confidential information, or invasion of privacy, then consider the concerns that are stirred when the same messages are transmitted electronically!

Other legal risks related to the Internet may be less predictable. Electronic communication laws are developing at a slow pace compared to the wave of emerging electronic issues. For example, imagine using the Internet from your home or office computer and being haled into court by another jurisdiction for this activity. Cendali and Arbogast cite several recent court decisions that indicate that electronic contacts through the Web may indeed be sufficient to bestow personal jurisdiction.[2]

Herrmann, an attorney and the editor of

The Internet Newsletter: Legal & Business Aspects, has proposed that Internet law is in the budding stage, waiting to develop a root system.[3] For example, state and federal lawmakers are just beginning to discuss issues related to "telemedicine," including professional liability and practicing medicine across state lines. The Physicians Insurers Association of America (PIAA)* suggests that legal issues related to telemedicine—including reimbursement, licensure, access to patient records, abandonment, informed consent, malpractice insurance coverage, and vicarious liability—are just beginning to emerge.

Other concerns related to the ease with which data can be transmitted include the question of who has access to which information. Massachusetts recently passed a law providing public access to a physician database through a toll-free telephone number maintained by the Massachusetts State Board of Registration in Medicine. The information available includes details of physicians' board certification, training, malpractice awards, and disciplinary actions. Currently, there are plans to post this information on the Web. However, although the intent of the law may be favorable for consumers, many physicians are concerned about the potential misinterpretation of information, and they claim that the current methods used to ensure accuracy are insufficient.

How can you be sure that you're using the Internet in a way that maximizes its potential while minimizing exposure to liability for improper use? Consider the following scenarios:

....
* *Telemedicine: An Overview of Applications and Barriers* can be ordered from PIAA (2275 Research Blvd, Suite 250, Rockville, MD 20850; 301/947-9000) for a nominal fee.

List Discussions

A PT is participating in an e-mail list discussion (a forum in which e-mails sent to one Internet address are automatically copied and rerouted to all subscribers on a list). The PT has strong feelings about a particular practice issue, and he wants to provide assistance to the other discussants. These good intentions overpower his professional discretion, and he posts to the general list the name, office address, and telephone number of a colleague whom he considers to be an expert on the subject. Other PTs offer to send copies of their employers' in-house policies on this issue.

Because list participants are limited to an exclusive group made up almost entirely of PTs and PTAs, members of the list have a sense of security. One member is enthusiastic about the valuable information being posted. She also is intrigued with the idea of developing her own home page on the Web. She decides to save copies of the discussions to post on her future Web site.

Had comments similar to the information posted on the list merely been made during personal, professional discussions, *implied consent* might have been a defense; that is, employers' and employees' permission to discuss professional and business matters within the institution may be assumed. Posting such information through a media that is (or could become) accessible worldwide, however, may subject the PT to indefensible legal action by the colleague whose name was posted—and by the colleague's employer, as employers have a vested interest in their business products and have duties to protect the interests of their employees.

The ease with which data can be transmitted also may raise concerns regarding patient confidentiality. Although some PTs may find electronic communication forums a valuable means of discussing or obtaining consultation about complex cases, detailed descriptions about a patient, coupled with the electronic address of the communicator, may disclose a patient's identity.

Legal risks with electronic communication may be greater than with oral communication because electronic communication leaves a trail of evidence, and the distribution is broader. The PTs who posted examples of their employers' policies may have been sharing information meant for a limited audience—perhaps employees only. Invasion of privacy, unauthorized disclosure of proprietary or confidential information, defamation, and violations of an organization's regulatory or legal restrictions are all legal risks to be aware of when posting information on lists, the Web, or even through e-mail.[4]

Posting on a Web Site

A PT decides to develop a Web page for back exercises. The PT lacks talent to draw descriptive pictures of the exercise routines, so she decides to scan copies of an exercise regimen from physical therapy school handouts and another regimen from the handouts her employer provides for patients. These handouts have been sufficient for clinical use; however, in her enthusiasm about the Web page, this PT is forgetting that in the clinic, use of these handouts has always been supplemented with verbal explanation, demonstration, and precautionary guidelines.

PTs may consider the Internet a means to educate the public about wellness, prevention of injuries, or exercise routines for certain conditions. Like the actions in scenario 1, these ideas are probably well intended; however, the legal issues raised may be less predictable. For example, if an Internet user followed the back exercise directions and subsequently noticed aggravation of a preexisting condition, could the PT be held liable?

In addition, the PT may have violated copyright infringement by scanning and posting those images. Most misappropriations of copyrighted material probably are unintentional—that is, the person responsible may not be aware that he or she is violating copyright laws—but regardless of intent, infringement is still infringement.[1,5,6]

Another concern raised by using electronic communication to provide professional advice is the issue of practicing across state lines (or, for that matter, national boundaries). Might a physical therapy examining committee from a jurisdiction different than that of the PT above consider these communications to be the practice of physical therapy without a license? It could happen. PTs and PTAs should remember that the practice of physical therapy includes more than having personal contact with a patient (see Bennett's January and February Liability Awareness columns). Attorneys Beckman and Hirsch have posed similar questions for lawyers: "What happens when a lawyer in Iowa is queried by a Floridian via an e-mail link on a Web page? If the lawyer responds, is he or she practicing law illegally across state lines?"[7]

"...Agrees to Hold Harmless..."

The PT who had posted the back exercises decides that her Web page needs a disclaimer. She develops a statement that all users will encounter on first accessing her page. The disclaimer includes language stating that the reader "agrees to hold harmless the discussants..." from liability related to use of materials found on the Web site.

Authors of disclaimer statements should not be careless when formulating such language, and they should seek consultation from an attorney. Posting a disclaimer may deter some legal action; however, disclaimers are not a panacea for avoiding all legal actions. For example, the addition of "agrees to hold harmless..." may be adding more legal risks than the PT intends. The very word "agrees" presents contract law issues: Would a court find that an enforceable contract had been formed when a reader proceeded with use of materials or advice found on the Web page after reading the disclaimer? Would this particular agreement require a signature to satisfy the requirements of the Statute of Frauds (a Common Law that requires certain types of agreements to be in writing and signed)? If so, would an electronic signature be considered authentic? (The issue of electronic contracts probably will become more prominent with increasing use of the Web for commercial purposes. In the near future, a variety of contracts may be formed through this media, including employment agreements, sales of goods and services, and electronic advertisements implying warranties.)

Security of Information

A PT is director of a hospital-based physical therapy department. The hospital's risk manager and the director of information services come to the PT with information indicating that someone within the institution is using a computer terminal located in the physical therapy department for unauthorized access to and transmission of hospital records, most likely after the department has closed. A competitor of the hospital has been getting information about management policies, long-range plans, referral lists, and identification of patients who are diagnosed with AIDS. A plan needs to be developed to identify the culprit.

Legal issues related to the Internet are not limited to civil law. Computer crimes are increasing at alarming rates. Results of a recent survey by Computer Security Institute/FBI International Computer Crime Squad indicated that 41% of corporations responding had been victims of electronic intrusion or unauthorized searches of their computer systems by disgruntled employees or competitors in the past year.[8] Other computer crimes, such as theft and destruction of records, also seem to be on the rise. Results of a University of Michigan State University study showed that 94% of businesses responding had been victims of computer crime.[8]

Your organization's internal communications, such as e-mail, may not be as confidential or as secure as you might think. Insiders can "sniff" a company network to read every internal message,[9] and hackers from outside can readily break through unsecured or poorly secured systems. Computer forensic firms now can recoup evidence of this activity and testify if a case goes to trial.

Avoiding Abuse

The following tips can help PTs and PTAs avoid exposure to liability and protect private records and proprietary interests when using electronic communication.

Respect the rights of others, including your colleagues, clients, and employers. Refrain from the unlawful use of others' property. Copyright laws also apply to electronic communication (downloading and uploading).

You also can protect your own property rights by embedding imperceptible serial numbers in your images. These "digital watermarks" can survive image changes and can be traced back to an artist's registration list. (See http://www.teleport.coni/-digimarc or http://www.highwaterfbi.com for additional information.)

Communicate clearly. State your purpose in providing any information, especially if the information will be publicly available, as on a Web page or in a list discussion. If disclaimer statements are necessary, be sure that the language relates to the posted information and to your intent, or seek legal counsel. Remember that disclaimer statements do not eliminate your responsibility to do all you can to ensure that the information you post is not misused or misunderstood.

Foster teamwork in your organization. Unfortunately, each person who has access to a computer terminal is a potential risk to the organization. Among the concerns are inadvertent disclosure of confidential records or destruction of patient records.

Avoid building "techno arrogance." An arrogant atmosphere can be very destructive for staff who may be intimidated by the technology, and the department as a whole will lose potential maximum efficiency and effectiveness. Each person should be encouraged to ask questions, share computer knowledge, and have access to training without intimidation.

When electronic communication is sensi-

REFERENCES ON THE WEB

http://www-techlaw.stanford.edu Stanford Law and Technology Policy Center.

http://www.epic.org Electronic Privacy Information Center (EPIC).

http://www.cyberlaw.com Legal issues on cyberspace, with links to intellectual property sites.

http://www.iss.net/secinfo/sniff. btmi Detailed information on internal trade secret theft, embezzlement, and "sniffing" of e-mail.

http:nfic.inter.net./nfic National Fraud Information Center.

http://www.bbbonline.org Better Business Bureau.

tive and should remain confidential, work closely with technical staff and your organization's legal department or risk manager. Developing policies on security, purchasing hardware and software, educating staff, and assessing effectiveness require expertise and cooperation from all relevant departments.

The most secure way to send information is with encryption software, which scrambles messages with complex mathematical formulae. All of an organization's staff who use computers should be trained in using the established security measures appropriately so that a staff member does not innocently open the security gate or carelessly fail to close the latch.[10]

Develop in-house policies on Internet use. These policies should include clear guidelines on what information may be made available and what information may not be posted. Compliance controls should be regularly implemented. As Halpern wrote, "Setting up shop in cyberspace entails plenty of risks—which could be tamed with the right information technology guidelines."[4]

Work for federal and state laws that protect privacy. Senator Conrad Burns (R-MT) has been supportive of implementing appropriate legislation on the national level. He stated, "Within several years, more than 100 million people will be connected to the Internet. The fields of telemedicine and electronic commerce have enormous potential, but the current legal impediments to ensuring security online will prevent optimum utilization of these critical technologies."[11]

Expedite communication with lawmakers by sending them an e-mail. The US Senate and US House of Representatives home pages have links to the e-mail addresses of members of Congress.

Discourage others from using the Internet in a manner that is a poor reflection of the profession. Initiate discussions with colleagues about ethical concerns related to electronic communication. Volunteer to work with the appropriate groups to update APTA documents such as the *Code of Ethics and Guide to Professional Conduct* to address emerging issues related to electronic communication.

If there is any plausible way that your communication could be viewed by the authorities in another jurisdiction as practicing physical therapy (or any other health pro-

fession) without a license via electronic communication, *don't do it.*

Report false, misleading, or fraudulent marketing of health care products and services on the Internet to professional associations or consumer protection organizations. According to Zgodzinski,[12] Cleo Manuel of the National Fraud Information Center predicts significant increases in unscrupulous marketing schemes by scam artists on the Internet. Beware!

Before sending an e-mail message, participating in discussion groups, or posting information on a home page, ask yourself whether you would mind having the content of your message posted on a lighted billboard alongside a heavily traveled intersection. Use professional discretion before using electronic media for any communication. Slow down and think before you click on that "send" button.

Kathy Lewis, JD, MAPT, is Associate Professor and Regional Chair, Amarillo Campus, Texas Tech University Health Sciences Center. She is a member of the Ethics and Standards of Practice Committee of the Federation of State Boards of PHysical Therapy and of PT's Editorial Advisory Group.

References

1 Beckman D, Hirsch D. Rules of the road: legal ethics may be speed bumps on the Internet superhighway. *ABA Journal.* 1996;82(September):86.
2 Cendali DM, Arbogast JD. Net use raises issues of jurisdiction: 'minimum contacts' rules can subject Internet users to lawsuits in faraway forums. *The National Law Journal.* October 26, 1996:C07.
3 Herrmann RK. From the Editor in Chief. *The Internet Newsletter: Legal & Business Aspects.* 1996;1(6):2.
4 Halpern M. Cutting risks in developing and deploying web sites. *The Internet Newsletter: Legal & Business Aspects.* 1996;1(7):6-7.
5 Roberts P. Legal Ease: Scanning Within the Law. *Adobe Magazine.* 1996;8(November):69.
6 Baer M. Copyright and the visual arts: Staying legal in the digital era—it's trickier than you think. *MacWorld.* October 1996:163-167.
7 Antognini RL. What you need to know about intellectual property coverage. *Tort & Insurance Law Journal.* 1996;31(Summer):895-927.
8 Moher RK. Data recovery foils employee theft. *Law Technology Product News.* 1996;3(11):25-27.
9 Rosender J. Late-night thoughts on electronic commerce. *Law Technology Product News.* 1996;3(10):42-45.
10 Swaine M. Protecting your privacy online: Is the Internet a sophisticated communications tool? Or is it just one big party line? *MacUser.* 1996;12(1):135.
11 Burns SC. Export policies hinder Internet development. *Law Technology Product News.* 1996;3(10):46, 47, 51.
12 Zgodzinski D. Buyer beware. *Internet World.* 1997;8(March):43-46.

LIABILITY AWARENESS
by Joy Sterneck, MHA, PT

Beyond the Borders of Hands-on Care

As PTs' professional activities move into arenas beyond direct patient care, unforeseen liability risks may emerge.

Although PTs are becoming more aware of the liability risks that may be present when they perform traditional activities of hands-on physical therapy, they may overlook potential liabilities for professional activities that fall outside the borders of direct patient care. These activities include, but are not limited to:

- Providing consultation services.
- Performing utilization review and claims review.
- Presenting continuing education courses.
- Participating in wellness activities.

The most recent APTA *Model Definition of Physical Therapy for State Practice Acts*[1] includes consultation and education among the activities that constitute physical therapy. As Bennett[2] stated in last month's Liability Awareness column, although each state practice act defines physical therapy for purposes of licensure in that state, professional liability insurers increasingly may look to national standards such as APTA's definition in determining whether certain activities constitute physical therapy for purposes of professional liability coverage.

Consultation

Examples of consulting activities include providing services to the following groups:

- *Health care organizations.* PTs may help develop strategic plans for appropriate staffing and use of rehabilitation resources.
- *Rehabilitation providers.* PTs may give advice regarding successful positioning

for managed care, including capitation contracting.

- *Employers.* PTs may advise on selection of ergonomically appropriate equipment and activities and may help employers develop work readiness programs.

For liability purposes, developing a marketing plan, work reentry program, or departmental reorganization plan for a client is similar in many ways to developing a plan of care for a patient. The PT must first complete a thorough, objective assessment, which might include a job and worksite analysis, an analysis of potential markets, or a productivity study. Based on the initial assessment, objectives of the project are established, and a work plan is developed.

Throughout the project, it is critical for the PT to establish a rapport and good communication with the client, just as it would be throughout the course of treatment in direct patient care. Initially, it is important to determine and clearly articulate what the expectations of both the client and the consultant are. Based on common expectations, objectives should be set and agreed upon, and deadlines for the completion of key tasks should be laid out.

The contract with the client should clearly delineate the responsibilities—and the limits of responsibility—of both parties. For example, is the consultant responsible only for developing the strategic plan, or is he or she responsible for implementing portions of the plan? Just as a patient must consent to treatment, the client must "consent" to the plan, both verbally and via a written contract.

Upon "discharge," the PT must write a full report, with a summary of the objectives met, the key tasks accomplished, and recommendations for the client to follow.

As with any contract, the PT should consider seeking legal advice on both the terms of the contract and the potential liability risks presented by individual consulting arrangements (eg, liability for outcomes).

Continuing Education Courses/Workshops

Scott,[3] in *Promoting Legal Awareness in Physical and Occupational Therapy*, refers to three "breach of contract" liability issues that can arise from continuing education activities. One issue involves the "treatment" of "patients" (ie, subjects) during the course. When soliciting demonstration subjects prior to the course, the PT should make it clear, both verbally and in writing, that the PT is *not* performing treatment/ongoing care for the subject, but rather is "demonstrating" evaluation or treatment techniques for the purpose of participant learning.

The other two "breach of contract" issues include disputes with sponsors regarding compensation or performance and the perceptions of sponsors and participants of the value of the course itself. As with consulting activities, it is important to establish in writing the expectations of all parties. Documentation, usually in the form of a contract, delineates the responsibilities of each party and the agreed-upon compensation. The contract should clearly state the purpose and objectives of the course, and it should spell out whether the sponsor will have the opportunity to review brochures or announcements sent to participants before the course. In addition, it is helpful to conduct a written course evaluation by the participants. Ongoing, careful communication between presenter, sponsor, and participants throughout all phases of the course can help to reduce liability risks.

PTs also should be aware of potential risks related to the content of their presentations. What might happen if a PT teaching a continuing education course recommended a course of action, and a participant followed this "advice" and had a poor outcome? Again, PTs should consult legal counsel and their professional liability insurance carriers to ascertain both the letter of the law and the extent and limits of their liability coverage.

Wellness/Fitness

There is increasing involvement of PTs in "wellness" activities (see cover story). These might include community exercise programs, walking programs for seniors, back injury prevention programs for a local YMCA, or toddler creative movement classes at a neighborhood preschool. APTA's *Model Definition of Physical Therapy for State Practice Acts* now formally recognizes wellness activities as falling within the definition of physical therapy. Specifically, the document defines physical therapy as, in part, "preventing injury, impairments, functional limitations, and disability, including the promotion and maintenance of fitness, health, and quality of life in all age populations." The professional liability insurance program endorsed by APTA expanded its coverage to incorporate these changes; however, PTs should be aware that not *all* wellness activities are considered physical therapy. For example, a service might be considered physical therapy only if there is a direct relationship between the PT and participants (eg, a physical therapy evaluation) and the scope of the activity is directly related to the content of a physical therapist education.

Therefore, although each state practice act may actually define "physical therapy" differently, from a risk-management perspective, a PT providing wellness services such as fitness programs or exercise classes should proceed as he or she would in providing any other type of physical therapy. The PT should work within his or her state

practice act; for example, if a PT is providing services *as a physical therapist*, and the state in which the services are provided requires a physician's referral for physical therapy, a referral should be obtained for each participant in the activity.

Utilization Review/ Claims Review

Claims review and utilization review (UR) for services related to the provision of physical therapy constitute an area in which PTs provide services to payers. These reviews most frequently are performed retrospectively, via chart reviews, to determine medical appropriateness of services rendered to plan members.

One concern related to these activities is the licensure question: Does this activity constitute the practice of *physical therapy* under the state practice act where the therapist is conducting the review activity? As Bennett[4] wrote, no states appear to have explicitly answered this question regarding physical therapy review; however, Clifton[5,6] has described laws that some states have passed regulating certain UR activities, and PTs who perform these services should become familiar with the applicable laws in their states.

Another concern is whether a reviewer is to be held liable for the outcome of care that he or she reviews. According to Gosfield,[7] "The reviewing physician acting within the scope of his employment, performing in accordance with the rules of the review entity, and applying an appropriate standard of care, is not likely to be seriously impinged by bad outcomes from the review process." Although the ultimate responsibility for care rests with the care provider, this does not absolve the PT of the responsibility to conduct reviews according to current standards of practice. It is clear from the sources mentioned above that, just as the health care provider must be careful in choosing "accepted" assessment and treatment methods, it also is critical when performing review to use appropriate and accepted professional tools. These might include—but certainly are not limited to—APTA documents such as:

- *Standards of Practice for Physical Therapy*
- *Code of Ethics and Guide for Professional Conduct*
- *Guide to Physical Therapist Practice, Volume I: A Description of Patient Management*
- *Direction, Delegation, and Supervision in Physical Therapy Services*
- *Guidelines for Physical Therapy Claims Review*
- *Guidelines for Physical Therapy Documentation*
- *Position on Peer Review and Utilization Review of Physical Therapy Services*
- *Position on Modalities*

Just as the roles and responsibilities of PTs are expanding in patient care activities, they also are expanding in other areas. The same ethical and legal practice standards that apply to traditional, hands-on activities in clinical practice must be adhered to in activities that may not be considered "direct patient care." PTs are still bound by their state practice acts, and members of APTA are bound by Association guidelines (including but not limited to the list above). Maintaining positive relationships with clients and keeping accurate and complete documentation are as critical in controlling risks in these areas as they are in the area of hands-on physical therapy.

....

Joy Sterneck is Director of Rehab for Thera-Pedics, a pediatric home care agency in St Louis, Mo, and President, Sterneck Health Care Consulting, Chesterfield, Mo. She is a member of *PT*'s Editorial Advisory Group.

References

1   APTA BOD 03-95-24-64.
2   Bennett J. Practicing across state lines, part 2. *PT—Magazine of Physical Therapy.* 1997;5(2):22-25.
3   Scott RW. *Promoting Legal Awareness in Physical and Occupational Therapy.* St Louis, Mo: Mosby-Year Book; 1997.
4   Bennett J. Practicing across state lines, part 1. *PT—Magazine of Physical Therapy.* 1997;5(1):32-36.
5   Clifton DW. Who's watching UROs? Part 1. *PT—Magazine of Physical Therapy.* 1996;4(10):25-27.
6   Clifton DW. Who's watching UROs? Part 2. *PT—Magazine of Physical Therapy.* 1996;4(11):26-28.
7   Gosfield A. Value purchasing and effectiveness: legal implications. In: Gosfield, A. *Health Law Handbook.* Deerfield, Ill: Clark Boardman Company | a Division of Thomson Legal Publishing, Inc; 1991.

LIABILITY AWARENESS

by Scott Stephens, MS, PT

Impacts and Implications of Employer Liability in a Physical Therapy Practice

What can an employer in a physical therapy practice do to minimize the risk-management issues associated with hiring a new employee?

Our patients/clients often tell us that they have chosen a particular health care practitioner because he or she is regarded as "one of the best in the area." An employer in a physical therapy practice, however, has a responsibility to look much more closely at the credentials and qualifications of potential employees. The employer should be satisfied that the questions he or she has asked prior to hiring an employee will provide the information needed to make an informed decision on hiring and assure the employer that the new employee can meet the expectations of the practice's patients/clients.

Consider, for example, the kinds of questions that anyone might like to have answered when choosing a health care practitioner for himself or herself or a family member.

❖ Has the practitioner experienced malpractice litigations against his or her practice?

❖ Have claims been made against the practitioner relative to the specific procedures for which a patient is seeing the health care professional?

❖ Does the practitioner have adequate liability insurance, and has he or she ever been denied professional liability insurance?

❖ What about the practitioner's education? Was he or she a valedictorian or a "survivor" graduate of a health care education program?

It's important to ask these same types of questions of any prospective employee, and applicants should expect to be asked these questions when they are seeking employment.

What can an employer do to minimize the risks associated with a new employee? What can physical therapists expect an employer to investigate prior to inviting them to join a practice environment?

Employer Liability

PTs have experienced several decades of employment demand over supply. When the need to staff the practice has been great, an employer's potential liability for the actions of an employee may have received little consideration in the decision to hire. In some instances, the mentality of an employer to "hire the license" without regard for the quality of the practitioner may even have been applied.

However, liability for the acts of their employees does exist for employers. This has been documented through litigation across the United States every year when a plaintiff's attorney has convinced a jury that the practice of a defendant as an employee in a health care facility has been improper.

To date, malpractice actions brought against the physical therapy community have not been of the same frequency or severity as those brought against physicians. Potential explanations for the relatively low number of claims against PTs are numerous, but usually are based on the high degree of personal interaction that PTs enjoy with their patients/clients. Regardless of the explanation, however, it behooves a PT to be aware of the potential for litigation and to make every effort to avoid it.

Successful litigations that have held employers liable for the actions of their employees, and the necessity to provide employee credentials when applying for participation with preferred practice panels within managed care organizations (see In Practice, November 1997[1]), have prompted employers to begin to ask for more information on prospective employees.

State Regulation

In most instances, state regulation is in the form of a license to practice physical therapy, based on how that practice is to be conducted as defined in the state's practice act. State regulation is an effort to assure the public that a PT has met the minimum standards necessary for safe practice. When an employer is considering an employment application, verification of an applicant's educational and state credentials is absolutely essential and must include a formal dialogue with the licensing board that credentialed the individual. Merely seeing copies of a diploma and a license is not adequate proof of state approval. There have been documented examples of individuals using forged credentials.

License history should be verified with the regulatory board in each state where the individual has practiced, or, at the least, the most recent regulatory agency should be contacted to confirm that it had thoroughly explored the applicant's history. In addition, a state's credentialing agency can and should be asked to report any sanctions taken against a specific licensee. Until recently, an applicant's failure to report a previous disciplinary action that had occurred in another jurisdiction could go undetected during an application to practice within a new state. The credentialing body to which the new application to prac-

LIABILITY AWARENESS

tice had been submitted had no means of learning about another state's actions against an applicant. Today, however, information sharing between physical therapy regulatory boards has been enhanced through the Federation of State Boards of Physical Therapy. This communication, coupled with a national database into which disciplinary actions against individuals are entered and to which state boards have access, has improved reporting of sanctions against licensed physical therapy providers.

Although an employer may be satisfied that a prospective employee's credentials are legitimate, the employer also must thoroughly check the prospective employee's employment history and background.

Employment History and Background Checks

Employers would be well advised to seek a complete employment history from PTs whom they are considering for employment. There should be no unexplained lapses during the employment years.

When considering a PT for employment, an employer may think that official transcripts from the applicant's academic institution have limited value. Thus, employers more frequently may inquire about continuing education programs that an applicant has attended. However, the more complete both the academic and continuing education background checks are, the more assured an employer can be that the individual being considered is a legitimate and appropriately qualified applicant.

Depending on the practice setting, a criminal background check may be required on each employee. Whether or not it is a requirement, obtaining this report may be well worth the employer's effort in order to limit his or her liability. In many jurisdictions, the state police are responsible for completing requests for criminal background checks. These requests are neither expensive nor particularly time consuming, and they may prevent future problems.

Once an employer has verified that an applicant indeed is the person that he or she claims to be (perhaps by checking a picture identification like a passport or driver's license) and that the applicant possesses the state authorization required to practice in that jurisdiction, it is not the end of the process. The employer cannot afford to become complacent, especially when his or her liability for an employee's actions could be at issue.

After all of the background and employment checks are complete and an employer is confident to make a decision on hiring a new employee, the employer's thoughts must turn toward orienting the new employee if he or she accepts the position.

Liability Awareness

Orientation of a New Employee

All facilities should have written copies of their policies and procedures for employees to review. Employers may wish to have such documents reviewed by legal counsel prior to including them in the employee's orientation packet. An employee should be given the opportunity to ask questions about the facility's policies and procedures before signing a statement that he or she has reviewed them. Subsequent changes to policies and procedures should likewise be reviewed and acknowledged in writing by each employee.

Another important aspect of an employee's orientation to a practice setting is familiarity with its established clinical protocols. When a specified sequence of events has been defined as a facility's adopted treatment protocol, it is incumbent on the employer to ensure that the employee either adheres to the protocol or documents the rationale for deviating from it. Although guidelines or suggested practice patterns are intended to be nonbinding, an attorney may use them as standards to judge care provided by an employee and also to identify deviations from the standard of care in the event of litigation.

Continued Competency

After an employee has been employed in his or her position for a certain period of time, the employee usually will be required to demonstrate his or her continued competency in the practice of physical therapy. Measurement of continued competency in the practice of physical therapy is an oft-discussed but, as yet, unresolved issue in most states. Although continuing education requirements exist in an increasing number of states, competency and continuing education requirements should not be confused as being equivalent. Continued competency should not be assumed through the mere completion of continuing education units.

Because of numerous variables in the activities performed by individual PTs and variables among the PTs themselves, it is important that both the employee and the employer recognize any practice limitations for a specific employee. These limitations may occur as a result of lack of experience in a particular treatment technique or approach. It may be *legal* for a PT to practice in this area of limited experience according to a state's practice act, but not *advisable* from the standpoint of knowledge, skill, and expertise. For example, electromyography and sharp wound debridement may be permissible under a state's practice act, yet these activities have a high potential for malpractice litigation in the hands of a PT without sufficient experience to complete them in a safe and effective manner.

It has been said, "That which can be expected, must be inspected." Therefore, it is imperative that an employer review the quality of care delivered by each employee. A practice environment must meet the standards of practice established within its professional community. An opportunity to show variance from the professional community's standard of practice is an opportunity for a plaintiff's attorney to prove negligence by a PT. When that PT is an employee, there also may be an effort to demonstrate the responsibility of the employer for the employee's actions. Consequently, an employer must be completely informed about the background of his or her employees prior to hiring and also must monitor employees' quality of practice during their employment.

Even the most thorough efforts of an employer may not protect the facility from shared responsibility for the actions of an employee. The goal, however, is to minimize exposure of the employer to liability.*PT*

Scott Stephens, MS, PT, *is Vice President, Rehabilitation Services of Roanoke Inc, Roanoke, Virginia. He serves as Chairman of APTA's Committee on Risk Management Services and Member Benefits.*

Reference

1. Front J. Criteria for credentialing physical therapists (In Practice). *PT—Magazine of Physical Therapy.* 1997;5(11):28-29.

Referral/Advertising
For Professional Services

Financial Considerations in Practice
HOD P06-99-13-17 [Initial HOD 06-81-07-21]

The American Physical Therapy Association opposes participation in underutilization or overutilization of services for personal or institutional gain, or participation in services that is in any way linked to the financial gain of the referral source.

Opposition to Physician Ownership of Physical Therapy Services
HOD P06-03-27-25

Whereas, The American Physical Therapy Association Vision Statement for Physical Therapy 2020 supports autonomy of physical therapist practice and judgment;

Whereas, Financial relationships and incentives between a patient's/client's physician and physical therapist represent an avoidable conflict of interest, reduce consumer choice, and diminish professional autonomy;

Whereas, There is evidence that such avoidable conflicts of interest affect delivery of care, utilization of services, and aggregate costs of treatment, and that patients/clients and payers would benefit from the elimination of such conflicts;

Whereas, In recent years, ownership of physical therapy services has been marketed to physicians as a means to recover revenues lost as a result of managed care, which has led to an accelerating trend of physician ownership of physical therapy services and referral of patients/clients to these services;

Whereas, The American Physical Therapy Association (APTA) opposes physical therapy services provided in practice settings in which the physician profits as a result of the referral;

Whereas, Numerous professions have successfully regulated ownership of their professional services through state legislative provisions; and

Whereas, APTA, through its Goals and Objectives and other documents, has identified and implemented comprehensive legislative strategies to ensure the public's right to direct access to physical therapy;

Resolved, that the American Physical Therapy Association opposes the ownership of physical therapy services by physicians, and supports federal and state laws and regulations that prohibit physician ownership of physical therapy services.

Referral Relationships
HOD P06-90-15-28 [HOD 06-72-12-25]

Services without Referral

The physical therapist may, where permitted by law, be the entry point into the health care system for screening, examination, evaluation, diagnosis, prognosis, intervention, and prevention programs and consultation within the scope of his or her knowledge, experience, and expertise.

Services with Referral

When patients/clients have been referred, the physical therapist, upon identification of conditions other than those inherent in the information provided by the referring practitioner, shall report to the referring source and consultation shall be sought in accordance with the standards of ethical practice.

When admission to a physical therapy service has been originated via a referral, this relationship places a shared responsibility on the referring source and on the physical therapist to exchange all necessary information.

Where a practitioner extender acts on behalf of the practitioner as the referring source, the physical therapist should verify that the referral is consistent with the legal requirements of the local jurisdiction.

No referring practitioner should bill or be paid for a service which he does not perform; mere referral does not constitute a professional service for which a professional charge should be made or for which a fee may be ethically paid or received.

Referral to Other Health Care Practitioners

The physical therapist must refer patients/clients to the referring practitioner or other health care practitioners if symptoms are present for which physical therapy is contraindicated or are indicative of conditions for which treatment is outside the scope of his or her knowledge.

Physician Ownership
of Physical Therapy Services

by Michele Wojciechowski

The issue of physician ownership of physical therapy services (POPTS) has been debated for more than 25 years. Recently, though, Vision 2020, the evolution of the profession, and legislative and judicial actions have brought about a "perfect storm," placing POPTS in the eye of the hurricane.

Lisa Saladin, PT, PhD, president of the South Carolina Physical Therapy Association, (left) and Francis J Welk, PT, DPT, MEd, APTA treasurer and chairman of the Association's Task Force on POPTS.

photo by Michael Terranova

Physician-owned physical therapy services (POPTS) are what the name suggests—physical therapy practices owned by physicians. Whether they are located in the same building as the physician's office or nearby, the physical therapists (PTs) working there are employees.

This arrangement can generate strong opinions. "Nothing good comes out of POPTS," says Lisa Saladin, PT, PhD, president of the South Carolina Physical Therapy Association (SCAPTA). "It is dangerous to our profession and our consumers."

Saladin explains, "There is financial incentive for physicians to refer individuals who might not otherwise be referred or to refer them for more sessions than are required. And we do not know to what extent that is happening. In South Carolina, we have testimonies to that effect from consumers and from physical therapists working in those settings." [See "South Carolina Prohibits POPTS."]

Fran Welk, PT, DPT, MEd, chairman of the American Physical Therapy Association's Task Force on POPTS and treasurer of APTA, adds, "POPTS are an obstacle to physical therapy becoming completely and fully professionalized."

And Dave Mason, APTA vice president of government affairs, states, "[The proliferation of POPTS] is a serious problem that is certainly growing in magnitude all over the country."

Referral for Profit

One concern of most PTs—those not in a POPTS relationship—is that physicians make referrals exclusively to practices they own. It's in their interests financially to make referrals to their businesses rather than other physical therapy practices.

Mason says that he and others at APTA hear from members who work at POPTS and who defend the arrangement. "They may say, 'The physician I work for is different. I understand APTA's concern about the inherent financial incentives, but that's not the way *we* practice.'" Robert DuVall, PT, DHSc, MMSc, OCS, FAAOMPT, adds, "Every PT in a POPTS setting thinks *their* practice is an exception."

Mason says PTs in POPTS will concede, " 'Yes, the physician I work for does refer some patients here, but we provide better service to treat those patients than anybody else does.' It then becomes a *quality* argument rather than a *financial* one."

Or, Mason continues, POPTS employees may say, "If someone else in town can do a better job with the patient, my doctor will refer to that physical therapist rather than his own POPTS."

Other Physician Ownership Issues to Watch

Physical therapists should pay close attention to some other ongoing debates within Congress, advises Dave Mason, APTA vice president of government affairs. One is the fight over the June 8, 2005, expiration of the 18-month moratorium on physician ownership of specialty hospitals. That moratorium came about from the Medicare Prescription Drug, Improvement, and Modernization Act of 2003.

Another ongoing debate involves a Medicare Payment Advisory Commission (MedPAC) investigation of the influence of physician ownership of imaging services. Because the cost of an MRI unit has dropped, some physicians have been purchasing MRI units and installing them in their offices.

"Up until now, radiologists did most of the work with the screening and reading of results of the MRIs," says Mason. "Now, if a cardiologist thinks you need an MRI and has one in his office, he'll take the pictures [there] and read them. This physician ownership thing is a little sticky."

"Nothing good comes out of POPTS. It is dangerous to our profession and our consumers."

Lisa Saladin, PT, PhD
president of the South Carolina Physical Therapy Association (SCAPTA)

"Well, that may be true," Mason responds. "But we also have heard of many situations in which every patient who needs physical therapy [is referred to the physician's clinic]."

For example, Mason says, suppose that a physical therapist at a POPTS and a physical therapist in private practice across the street are equally proficient in treating shoulder injuries. "Where am I going to refer my patient if I own one of these clinics? And *that* is the point," says Mason. "Inherently, there is an incentive that is not in the patient's interest and really is not in the health care system's interest."

Mason explains that APTA often has attempted to reach out to both regulatory agencies such as the Centers for Medicare and Medicaid Services (CMS) and enforcement offices such as the Office of the Inspector General and the Federal Trade Commission. The dilemma is that they request hard evidence of harm.

In the past, though, it has been difficult to collect evidence that demonstrates the negative impact of these problems. PTs who work in POPTS obviously don't want to risk losing their jobs. In addition, for an individual physical therapist to come out against a POPTS would be a double-edged sword. If the physical therapist is still dependent on physicians in his or her area or town for referrals, other physicians could cut off referrals to that physical therapist or to his or her entire practice. DuVall explains, "You

> *"[Stark I] didn't stop them from owning [businesses], but it did absolutely draw a bright line [so] that physicians could not refer patients to entities in which they have an ownership interest."*
>
> Dave Mason,
> APTA vice president
> of government affairs

The Stark Laws

In the late 1980s, Rep Pete Stark (D-CA), then chairman of the House Ways and Means Health Subcommittee, saw an inherent conflict of interest in physicians owning services to which they could refer patients, recalls Dave Mason, APTA vice president of government affairs. Stark believed that the law should prohibit physicians from referring patients to a health care service in which the physician or a member of the physician's immediate family had an ownership interest.

"It didn't stop them from owning [businesses]," says Mason, "but it did absolutely draw a bright line [so] that physicians could not refer patients to entities in which they have an ownership interest."

Physical therapy initially was not included in this law. Passed in 1989, the Stark I law applied to clinical laboratories. The law also had an "in-office ancillary service exception" which encompassed services defined in Medicare as ancillary services for physicians—items such as in-office laboratory testing that could be performed by physicians in their own practices.

"The serious flaw in the law began to emerge when physicians were able to convince members of Congress that there needed to be exceptions—that you couldn't draw a bright line without denying patients access to services that would only be available if physicians used their income to make sure they were provided," says Mason. For example, physicians argued, a problem could occur in rural areas or small towns in which the physician was likely to be one of the larger wage earners. That would give the physician the means to open another office offering, for instance, physical therapy. The physicians argued that proposed prohibitions would deprive these isolated areas of needed health care services.

"So they convinced Congress early on that there had to be exceptions to the Stark rule," says Mason. "The reason that wound up being such a serious crack in the dam is that Congress, as it usually does, defined exceptions in very loose terms and anticipated that the Department of Health and Human Services or the Department of Justice would define those exceptions to hit the target they intended to hit. Essentially, they gave the agencies the authority to come up with regulations to carry out congressional intent."

But when the regulatory agencies became involved, they realized that health care is practiced in many different ways, and there are

likewise many different kinds of health care organizations and practice setups. If they provided an exception for one practice, what would be the rationale for not giving the same to another type of practice?

"What wound up happening over a period of time is that the exceptions grew larger and larger," says Mason.

Congress, led by Rep Stark, decided that more services needed to be included. As a result, in 1993, Congress enacted Stark II, which expanded the list of services to include additional "designated health services," one of which was physical therapy services.

So once Stark II came into effect, it would seem that physicians could no longer make referrals to physical therapy practices that they or their immediate family members owned.

Well, sort of.

"Technically, under current law, physicians are still prohibited from referring to physical therapy services in which they have an ownership interest," says Mason. "But the in-office ancillary services exception is worded so broadly that it is very easy for physicians to structure their practices so this is the exception. So it *is* prohibited, but the exception is so wide that it prohibits nothing."

A Stark III?

Mason says that a Stark III law—legislation with an effective prohibition against self-referral—is not likely as Rep Stark no longer chairs the Health Subcommittee. And the prevailing attitude on Capitol Hill favors fewer restrictions on how health care practices are organized. He says that APTA has spoken with people on Capitol Hill about the possibility of federal legislation regarding this issue and "has been strongly advised that the environment's not right." Mason continues: "We have commented consistently every time the opportunity presents itself to ask the senators for Medicare and Medicaid services and the Office of the Inspector General to examine this issue again and think about redefining, if not eliminating, the in-office ancillary services exception.

"I don't think there is really much chance that it will be eliminated—not so much because of physical therapy services, but because of some of the other ancillary services," Mason says. One way to resolve this, he says, would be to redefine the exception in a way that would remove physical therapy services from it.

Photo by Michael Terranova

have to be able to advocate without fear of retribution. [Our profession is] probably over 95% referral based, and we have to factor that in. We don't have the true freedom to advocate for our body of knowledge without fear of retribution."

APTA's View of POPTS

Welk says that APTA's view of POPTS is best summed up in RC 30-03. In it, Welk explains, "APTA opposed the ownership of physical therapy services by physicians and supported federal and state laws and regulations that prohibit physician ownership of physical therapy services. That was unanimously passed by the House of Delegates, made up of more than 400 people. A unanimous passage of any resolution in a body that size is pretty remarkable."

Mason says that, in a nutshell, APTA believes that POPTS are just wrong. "There was a law passed that was supposed to prevent [POPTS]. To the extent that it is not preventing the situation, folks are just plain getting it wrong," says Mason. [See "The Stark Laws."] "Combined with the Medicare mandatory referral requirement, this is an unbalanced playing field—even for physician offices that are set up for appropriate purposes and have legitimate concerns about patient access.

"It is impossible for there to be another solution. The [medical] doctor controls the referral, and the doctor has a financial interest in where that patient goes. So it is inherently anti-competitive," Mason says.

Taking a Step Backward

As Welk has noted, POPTS are delaying physical therapy's achievement of full professionalism. He explains, "Physical therapy is a profession that from its onset has been evolving. We have grown from being totally dependent on and part of the medical model. When we started

out, our education was controlled and accredited by medicine. We were formally registered prior to being licensed, and that was controlled by medicine.

"We now accredit ourselves. We now have licensure, and we have recognition under Medicare. To be a truly independent profession and to be totally autonomous in our practice, the past concept isn't timely in our progression."

Although the issue of POPTS has been debated for more than 25 years, Welk believes that not enough physical therapists are embracing the concept of professionalism and autonomous practice. For the field to change, physical therapists need to see themselves as physical therapists 24 hours a day, 365 days a year—and to see this as a career and a profession, not as just a job, Welk suggests.

"To be a truly independent profession and to be totally autonomous in our practice, the past concept isn't timely in our progression."

Fran Welk, PT, DPT, MEd, chairman of the American Physical Therapy Association's Task Force on POPTS and treasurer of APTA

Physician Ownership
of Physical Therapy Services

Besides not advancing physical therapy in terms of professionalism, POPTS also divert dollars that might otherwise support physical therapy. For example, Welk says that when he had a physical therapy practice, some of its profits supported professional associations for physical therapy. He questions where the profits go when a medical practice employs physical therapists. Is anything going back into the profession of physical therapy, or is it all going into the medical profession?

"It seems like we're taking a step backward in our professional evolution," says Welk. "Physical therapists historically have looked at themselves as employees rather than members of a group practice or as independent practitioners."

When physical therapists assume

South Carolina Prohibits POPTS

South Carolina Circuit Court Judge J Ernest Kinard in late February signed an order upholding the state Attorney General's opinion that the state's Physical Therapy Practice Act prohibits physical therapists from working for referring physicians. The judge's ruling also lifted the temporary injunction preventing the South Carolina Board of Physical Therapy Examiners from taking action against physical therapists employed by physicians. APTA's South Carolina Chapter and the Attorney General joined in the defense of the licensure board in litigation brought by a physician and various physician groups and other organizations.

The South Carolina Attorney General in 2004 said that "the obvious purpose of [South Carolina Code] §40-45-110(A)(1) is the protection of the consumer against conflicts of interest. Such prohibitions and protection is designed to guard against excessive health care costs, attempting to insure that referrals are based solely upon the patient's best interest rather than a desire by a professional to increase profits. 79 *Ops Cal Atty Gen* 225 (Op No 96-517, September 16, 1996). In this instance, the Legislature was concerned that the physical therapist not engage in 'fee splitting' or in having a financial relationship with the physician who refers a patient to him/her. The question which must be answered is the precise breadth of §40-45-110(A)(1) and whether this Section proscribes a physical therapist from treating a patient which has been referred to him or her by a physician who is that therapist's employer or who owns or is employed by a professional corporation which employs that physical therapist. We conclude that the statute prohibits this conduct."

Referring to the court's action, South Carolina Chapter President Lisa Saladin, PT, PhD, said, "The decision is a major step forward in the effort to prohibit the existence of POPTS [physician-owned physical therapy services]." Saladin also noted that physicians have secured the introduction of legislation that would negate the impact of the court's order, adding, "The chapter will vigorously oppose this physician-initiated legislative effort."

APTA cooperated extensively with the South Carolina Chapter in seeking the Attorney General's opinion and in defending it in court. The Attorney General's opinion was consistent with a detailed analysis prepared by APTA General Counsel John J Bennett, which was submitted to the Attorney General by the legislators who requested the opinion.

In reaching his decision, Judge Kinard came to the following conclusions of law:

1. The South Carolina Physical Therapy Practice Act authorizes the South Carolina Board of Physical Therapy Examiners to discipline physical therapists who receive referrals from employing physicians.

2. A physician who sends or directs a patient to a physical therapist in his or her employ clearly is "referring" that patient to an employee to whom "wages" are paid, as those terms are ordinarily used and understood. There is no conflict between the Physical Therapy Practice Act prohibition on in-practice referrals and the earlier enacted South Carolina Provider Self-Referral Act.

3. The Board's April 8, 2004, announcement of its intention to investigate and discipline physical therapists who receive referrals from physicians by whom they are employed was not a substantive "regulation" requiring compliance with the rule-making procedures of the South Carolina Administrative Procedure Act.

4. Enforcement of the Physical Therapy Act's prohibition on physical therapists working for pay for a person from whom they receive referrals does not "restrict, inhibit, or limit in any way...the practice of medicine pursuant to Chapter 47 of Title 40," the Medical Practice Act.

5. The Physical Therapy Practice Act does not deprive physical therapists, as a class, of the equal protection of the laws, in violation of the Fourteenth Amendment to the United States Constitution.

6. The Board's announcement of its intention to enforce the fee-splitting provision of the Physical Therapy Act did not deprive Plaintiffs of their due process rights.

The South Carolina law is nearly identical to a Delaware statute, which the Delaware Attorney General in 2002 said prohibited the acceptance by a physical therapist of a referral from a physician who employs that physical therapist.

The South Carolina Chapter was represented in the case by the law firm of Nelson Mullins Riley & Scarborough, LLP, Columbia, South Carolina. APTA provided substantial financial support for the chapter's legal representation.

the role of employees of POPTS, Welk says, "they are really putting themselves in a position of ancillary service to that practice, not as a professional entity of themselves."

Welk says that the Task Force on POPTS sees another problem with physician-owned physical therapy practices. When physicians refer patients to their own physical therapy practices, not only is the physician making the money, he or she also is retaining the patient. So the PTs involved with patients aren't necessarily establishing long-term relationships. One result is the consumers' loss of choice. Many consumers simply listen to their physicians and go where he or she recommends. So rather than choosing and establishing a relationship with a physical therapist, the consumer remains with the physician's physical therapy practice.

"If I asked you today who your physical therapist is, I don't know how you're going to answer that," says Welk. "My guess is you're not going to give me the name of an individual." But that's exactly what he would like to see happen in the future. Just as consumers refer to their doctors and dentists by their names, they will likewise do so with their physical therapists.

Not Only A Private Practice Issue

Some PTs assume that POPTS is primarily a private practice issue. Not so, the PTs interviewed for this article say. It affects physical therapists in other facets of the profession as well. As a result, they need to stay just as informed as their private practice colleagues.

"Many physical therapists are not concerned about POPTS until there is a direct impact on their practice. And when I say practice it could be in any physical therapy field— private practice, hospital based, or home health," says Paul Slocum, PT, MS, Director of Physical Medicine & Rehabilitation at Greater Hazleton Health Alliance and a member of APTA's Task Force on POPTS.

Slocum cites physical therapy performed in hospitals. "Hospital-based outpatient departments are competing for the same pool of patients as everyone else in their community. PTs in the hospital environment often are left providing physical therapy to patients with no or minimal insurance and [with] medically complex [problems]. In many instances, we see 'cherry picking' of patients with POPTS—that is, patients who are less medically complex and have adequate insurance for reimbursement are seen in the POPTS setting.

"POPTS can result in the loss of patient care, loss of revenue, and the loss or inability to keep a patient within that organization's continuum of care. And these are critical measures that affect a hospital's operation. Many

APTA Vision Statement for Physical Therapy 2020 [HOD 06-00-24-35]

Physical therapy, by 2020, will be provided by physical therapists who are doctors of physical therapy and who may be board-certified specialists. Consumers will have direct access to physical therapists in all environments for patient/client management, prevention, and wellness services. Physical therapists will be practitioners of choice in clients' health networks and will hold all privileges of autonomous practice. Physical therapists may be assisted by physical therapist assistants who are educated and licensed to provide physical therapist-directed and -supervised components of interventions.

Guided by integrity, life-long learning, and a commitment to comprehensive and accessible health programs for all people, physical therapists and physical therapist assistants will render evidence-based service throughout the continuum of care and improve quality of life for society. They will provide culturally sensitive care distinguished by trust, respect, and an appreciation for individual differences.

While fully availing themselves of new technologies, as well as basic and clinical research, physical therapists will continue to provide direct care. They will maintain active responsibility for the growth of the physical therapy profession and the health of the people it serves.

Physician Ownership
of Physical Therapy Services

of us choose to practice within an institutional environment. Yet we still face the competition and the effects a POPTS can have on our outpatient services, just like any private practice. The hospital organization could be losing far more than rehab to a POPTS group when one considers lab, x-ray, and diagnostic services.

"Coming from a hospital perspective, it is a difficult situation to face, especially if there is more than one organization that a POPTS group can ally with. Hospital-based outpatient physical therapy needs to look at strategies much like the private practitioner when that PT is faced with a similar situation. Those strategies can include diversification of referral sources, expanding into new services and programs currently unavailable in the community, and providing operations and service hours to meet the wants and needs of the community," Slocum says.

Physical therapists in academia also are affected by POPTS.

Kathleen Luedtke-Hoffmann, PT, MBA, PhD, an assistant visiting professor at Texas Woman's University and a member of APTA's Task Force on POPTS, says, "The role of the physical therapy academic is to clearly define and describe the issue of POPTS to professional and postprofessional students, and to prepare them to respond to POPTS in the health care community. Academicians must present accurate and timely information about the actions of APTA, orthopedic physician groups, the OIG, Medicare, and various state boards of licensure around the country. We must strike a balance between awareness spurring appropriate response and hypervigilance triggering uneducated reactions that alienate powerful referral sources."

Where Do We Go From Here?

"The first thing we need is clinician education and awareness," says Welk. He'd like to see additional education of PTs about POPTS and about practice models in which PTs are the owners. Welk hopes that physical therapists realize that they can be partners in their profession as opposed to simply employees, for them to have more camaraderie in terms of the profession, and to see their positions as long-term careers and not solely jobs.

Welk believes that physical therapists need to make Vision 2020 part of their own personal vision. "And then they should ask themselves if working for a source of referral fits that model of where the profession is going." **PT**

Michele Wojciechowski is a freelance writer.

APTA Actions on POPTS Over the Years

For more than a quarter of a century, APTA has been taking action to stop POPTS. Here's a look back at some actions by the House of Delegates.

1979

Assist chapters in amending PT practice acts to preclude physical therapists from having or entering into employment arrangements that result in unearned income for the referring practitioner or for the physical therapist.

Initiate a program to educate physical therapists about the problems that arise in referral-for-profit situations.

1981

Open a dialogue with appropriate organizations (including the American Hospital Association and the American Medical Association and specialty boards) about the possibly unethical practice of physicians owning physical therapy practices.

Encourage APTA chapters to seek legislative alternatives to resolve the problems inherent in referral for profit arrangements.

1985

Oppose situations in which physical therapists or physical therapist assistants are employed by or under agreement with referring practitioners in which the referring practitioner receives compensation as a result of referring.

Oppose ability of referring practitioner to bill or be paid for a service that he does not perform; mere referral does not constitute a professional service for which a professional charge should be made or for which a fee may be ethically paid or received.

1999

Oppose participation in underutilization or overutilization of services for personal or institutional gain, or participation in services that is in any way linked to the financial gain of the referral source.

2003

Oppose the ownership of physical therapy services by physicians and support federal and state laws and regulations that prohibit physician ownership of physical therapy services.

by Dave Mason

A Plan of Care to Protect Physical Therapy Practices

APTA looks to new strategies to combat the reemergence of physician ownership of physical therapy services.

Make no mistake: Physician ownership of physical therapy services (POPTS) is one of the biggest threats to autonomous practice of physical therapy. And if you don't think it affects you, you'd best think again.

Physical therapists (PTs) in private practice across the country are finding themselves confronted with one of the most serious threats they've ever faced. POPTS steal away their patients and virtually eliminate their ability to attract new clients. In many cases it cripples PTs' ability to carry on autonomously.

The Economics of Patient Referral

Physicians' control of patient/client referrals and access to PTs dates back to the dawn of the physical therapy profession. The traditional model of medical practice in the 20th century revolved around the physician as gatekeeper to physical therapy and other health care services. As PTs grew in education, training, and experience, it probably was inevitable that the resulting development of independent physical therapy care would lead to confrontation.

The medical economics of the 1970s and 1980s gave rise to increasing competition for health care dollars. Doctors began to reconsider the financial wisdom of referring patients to other health care professions when they could provide the care and receive the payment themselves. They had the ability to close the gate because they controlled the referral of the patient—no referral, no lost revenue. It was a small step to expand the office, hire a PT (or a less-trained, less-expensive surrogate, if state law allowed), and provide services themselves.

In the early 1980s, APTA began mounting opposition to the development of POPTS, focusing on the problems created when physicians can derive increased compensation from the delivery of physical therapy or other services to which they refer patients. APTA's early efforts concentrated largely on working with its state chapters to revise state physical therapy acts to make a PT's participation in a physician-owned practice grounds for losing his or her license.

Not surprisingly, these efforts were forcefully opposed by physician associations, and as a result were largely unsuccessful. Laws restricting POPTS were enacted in Delaware and Missouri but relatively little progress was made elsewhere. APTA and its chapters pursued other approaches to discourage the spread of POPTS, mindful of ensuring that none strayed into activities that could raise antitrust questions. Refusing to carry advertising for POPTS arrangements and similar strategies had some limited success in slowing their spread.

Stark Reality

Efforts to stop inappropriate referral arrangements got a significant boost in the mid-1980s when Congress took an interest. Congressman Fortney "Pete" Stark (D-CA) became concerned about the impact on Medicare beneficiaries if physicians were able to benefit financially by referring patients to services in which they had an ownership interest. Interest in Congress was heightened by the release of a study conducted by Jean Mitchell, PhD, of Georgetown University on the impact of physician ownership on charges,

utilization, and profits of physical therapy services. The Mitchell study helped build support in Congress for legislation to outlaw inappropriate physician ownership referral arrangements. Despite strong opposition from physicians, Stark's self-referral prohibition bill was enacted into law in 1989 and was expanded to include physical therapy services in 1993.

Despite its positive intentions, however, the Stark self-referral ban encountered problems from the time of its conception. Physicians were able to keep the referral prohibition from applying to ancillary services provided in the physician's office. Other exceptions that had been intended to prevent referral-for-profit schemes led to new and creative financial arrangements that raised more questions about which practices violated the law. The Health Care Financing Administration (now the Centers for Medicare and Medicaid Services) struggled to develop and enforce regulations that carried out the intent of the Stark law. Efforts over the years to refine both the statute and the regulations have been increasingly frustrating.

Passage of the self-referral law did dramatically chill the spread of POPTS through most of the 1990s. Potential risks and liabilities under the new law generally were sufficient to dampen the enthusiasm of most physicians for setting up their own physical therapy practices. As the 1990s drew to a close, however, the cumulative pressure of managed care cost-containment efforts in the private sector and insufficient Medicare payments pushed physicians to look for ways to make up for lost income. With the creative use of exceptions in the rules and

government affairs

with loose enforcement, the self-referral chill began to thaw—and physician interest in physical therapy services as a revenue source reheated.

The resurgence of POPTS comes as federal and state policymakers have little interest in or will to take on physicians and rein in self-referral arrangements. In fact, the current policy environment appears to be more sympathetic to the development of creative physician practice models and less sensitive to the risks associated with incentives to self-refer. In regulations issued late last year, CMS authorized Medicare carriers to enroll PTs and occupational therapists (OTs) employed by physician groups as PTs or OTs in private practice, and ruled that no on-site supervision by the physician is required if the PT or OT obtains a separate provider number. With

that decision the agency brushed aside concerns APTA had raised about the risk of unlicensed personnel providing services in physician offices, and about potential fraud and abuse that could result when doctors refer Medicare beneficiaries to practices in which they have a financial interest. In CMS's view, established procedures for issuing provider numbers are sufficient to address these issues.

Leveling the Playing Field

There appears to be concern among some federal policy experts about the potential impact on patients of lax regulation and unbridled competition among providers of health care services. Last fall, APTA met with officials from the US Department of Health and Human Services' Office of Inspector General to participate in a study of "incident to" billing of physical therapy services by physicians. The 6-month probe examined physician offices to determine who provides physical therapy, whether those services are skilled, and whether they are properly billed. APTA called the inspector general's attention to potential problem areas with these arrangements. At this writing, the report's release is anticipated by early this fall.

The Federal Trade Commission (FTC) is another agency with traditional interest in health care competition. APTA CEO Francis J Mallon, Esq, testified in June as part of a series of joint hearings by the FTC and the US Department of Justice (DOJ) on health care competition law and policy. In his remarks, Mallon described the requirement of physician referral as "one major obstacle for patients seeking access to physical therapists." He further called it "something of an anachronism that is slowly being removed from, or modified in, state laws."

Mallon also warned the FTC that mandated physician control over access to PTs can distort the traditional professional relationship between physicians and PTs—"especially at times when physician revenues are adversely affected by managed care or government policies." Physicians and medical practice management consultants may see physical therapy as "a readily available means of negating some of the revenue losses," Mallon testified, adding that "the requirement that patients obtain a physician referral to receive services from a physical therapist clearly creates an unfair and unlevel playing field between physician-owned physical therapy practices and practices owned by physical therapists."

What You Can Do to Help

To validate concerns about the impact of POPTS arrangements, it is imperative that PTs and PTAs *identify specific situations* that illustrate anti-competitive activity. The APTA Task Force on Physician Owned Physical Therapy Services needs your help and that of your colleagues in identifying these situations and collecting the facts that will help confirm the threat to patients and to PT practices.

Documented evidence of anti-competitive behavior or intent is very important. If you have any documents that describe potentially anti-competitive behavior associated with a POPTS practice, please provide them to the APTA task force. By the same token, if you know of a colleague who has been or is being confronted with POPTS competition, encourage him or her to contact the task force.

POPTS information should be sent to: APTA Task Force on Physician Owned Physical Therapy Services, c/o APTA, 1111 N Fairfax Street, Alexandria, VA 22314-1488. Phone: 703/706-8533. Fax: 703/838-8919. E-mail: govtaffairs@apta.org.

The FTC/DOJ hearings concluded this summer. APTA is continuing to provide information to FTC staff regarding the POPTS problem.

New Strategies for Meeting New Challenges

At its June meeting, the APTA House of Delegates voiced its concern about the reemergence of POPTS in the strongest terms, unanimously endorsing two resolutions submitted by both the Illinois Chapter and the Private Practice Section. These resolutions charge the APTA Board of Directors to develop and implement strategies to secure enactment of federal and state laws and regulations that would prohibit physician ownership of physical therapy services.

The Board has formed a seven-member task force chaired by APTA Treasurer Francis J Welk, PT, MEd, to undertake research and analysis of federal and state laws and regulations and collect the practice information necessary to develop effective strategies to respond to the spread of POPTS arrangements. A major focus of the task force's work will be to provide both offensive and defensive strategies for use by PTs confronted with a physician-owned practice. APTA's Web site already offers information on federal self-referral rules (go to www.apta.org and click on "Government Affairs," then "Regulatory Affairs," then "Fraud and Abuse"). Strategies developed by the task force to help PTs deal with POPTS are being posted as they become available.

There is no quick solution to the threat posed by POPTS. In order to convince federal and state policy makers that this problem must be dealt with, PTs must be able to demonstrate clearly anti-competitive behavior by physicians that increases health care costs and threatens patient care. Physician control of referrals also is a critical component of leveling the competitive playing field and establishing the autonomy of PTs as the appropriate source of the services they are ideally suited to provide by dint of their education, training, and experience.

The fight against POPTS affects the future of the entire profession. No matter how difficult the fight, it is one that we should not and cannot avoid, and one we ultimately must win. **PT**

Dave Mason is vice president of the Government Affairs Department at APTA. He can be reached at davemason@apta.org.

Advertising Professional PT Services: Legal Implications

By Ronald W Scott, JD, LLM, PT

When it comes to advertising professional physical therapy services, the traditional adage of *caveat emptor* ("Let the buyer beware") is tempered by legal and ethical considerations that favor patient rights. For five decades, the American Physical Therapy Association's (APTA) ethical code proscribed professional advertising. A similar generic ban applied to other health care disciplines and the legal bar.

Advertisement in any form by health care and legal professionals was deemed inappropriate for many reasons, including arguments that advertising had an adverse effect on professionalism, was inherently misleading, and engendered undesirable economic effects (eg, increasing overhead costs that would be passed on to consumers and creating a substantial entry barrier to new professional colleagues attempting to penetrate the market). In 1977, these arguments were systematically addressed by the US Supreme Court in *Bates and Van O'Steen v State Bar of Arizona* (433 US 350), the landmark case involving attorney advertising.

In *Bates*, the Supreme Court held that the advertising of professional services fell under the rubric of First Amendment rights (free speech). Specifically, the court found that truthful advertising about the availability and cost of professional services served an important societal interest: helping to ensure that consumers make informed decisions about professional services—that is, decisions based on reliable, complete, and readily available information.

Because professional advertising is a form of "commercial speech," however, it does not have the broadest constitutional protection otherwise afforded to political or even literary speech. In *Bates*, the court ruled that the states are free to regulate professional advertising to prevent the dissemination of information that is false, deceptive, or misleading or to prevent the advertisement of illegal activities. And as with other constitutionally protected forms of speech, states also may impose reasonable restrictions on the time, place, and manner of professional advertising.

Forms of advertising that might properly be prohibited as false or misleading could include health care provider advertisements that make claims about the quality of available services or that attempt to compare the relative quality of services offered among competitors (*comparative competitor claims*). In addition to being subject to constitutionally permissible regulation, such advertisements might expose the advertising professional to common-law liability for the tort ("civil wrong") of business disparagement or trade libel (ie, advertising that damages the competitors' business reputations in the community).

Examples of advertisements containing illegal subject matter might include a physical therapy advertisement equating a physical therapist assistant with a licensed physical therapist or an advertisement for physical therapy services that fall outside the activities permitted under a particular state practice act.

Subsequent to *Bates*, APTA revised its *Guide for Professional Conduct* to reflect the change in legal status of professional advertising. Principle 6.2 now reads in pertinent part:

B. Physical therapists may advertise their services to the public.

C. Physical therapists shall not use, or participate in the use of, any form of communication containing a false, plagiarized, fraudulent, misleading, deceptive, unfair, or sensational statement or claim.

The advertising of professional services requires a balance between legal and ethical considerations and the professional's constitutional right to free speech. This balance is not always easy to maintain. *PT*

Ronald W Scott, JD, LLM, PT, is a Major in the US Army Medical Specialist Corps and is a physical therapist and legal consultant at Brooke Army Medical Center, Fort Sam Houston, Tex. Legal advice can be given only by your personal legal counsel, based on the laws of your state or on federal law, as applicable.

Suggested Readings

Driskell C. Ethics: advertising your services. *Clinical Management.* 1992;12(2): 16-17.

FEDERAL TRADE COMMISSION ISSUES LANDMARK RULING ON A CALIFORNIA SELF-REFERRAL ARRANGEMENT

In a first-ever ruling, the Federal Trade Commission (FTC) has proposed settlements in the San Francisco area involving pulmonologists with financial interests in two home medical care firms to which they referred patients. The federal regulatory agency voted 4-to-1 on Nov 2, 1993, in favor of the settlements after alleging that the physicians used their market power to exclude competitors.

The action signals that the FTC has moved into a new area of antitrust enforcement. Agency officials are not permitted to disclose whether they are considering similar cases. One FTC attorney said, however, if the FTC "finds that the law is being violated, it would take action." In the current climate of cost containment, the agency wants to get the best mix of quality and price. Arrangements such as the one the agency acted on "make it difficult for other providers to compete," the attorney said.

Under the settlement, the two companies and 28 physicians involved agreed to divest themselves of interests in the ancillary businesses that provide oxygen systems prescribed for home use by patients with lung, heart, or other diseases. The settlement agreement requires divestitures so that only 25% or fewer of the lung specialists in the geographic markets would be associated with the partnerships. Before the FTC acted, 60% of the pulmonologists in the area under scrutiny had invested in the joint-venture home medical equipment businesses.

David Alexander, attorney for one company, said the settlement is not an admission of wrongdoing on the part of any of the physicians. Rather, it was agreed to because they could not afford to fight the FTC's claims.

Erika Wodinsky, Assistant Regional Director of the FTC's San Francisco regional office, said the agency is not permitted to disclose the origin of complaints or details of the investigation. She added that FTC officials can become aware of potential violations through complaints filed by consumers, competitors, other government agencies, and media reports.

SIGNIFICANT STATE LEGISLATIVE ISSUES ANTICIPATED FOR 1994

- ○ Referral for Profit
- ● Direct Access
  Health Care Reform
- ○ PTA Issues
- ● Workers' Comp

- ● Chiropractors
- ● Massage Therapists
- ○ Managed Care
- ● Athletic Trainers
- ○ Occupational Therapists

- ○ PT Aides
- ○ Continuing Ed
- ○ Ownership of Term "PT"
- ○ Licensure Boards
- + Special Session

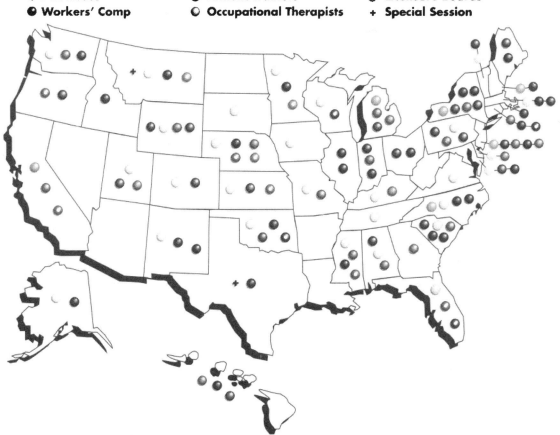

Issues Related to Specific Settings

Physical Therapy for Individuals With Disabilities: Practice in Educational Settings
HOD P06-95-14-03 [Initial HOD 06-79-14-38]

The American Physical Therapy Association (APTA) supports the provision of physical therapy services to children with special needs. Physical therapists have provided services to children with disabilities throughout the history of the profession. Public Law 94-142 (PL 94-142) provided the opportunity for physical therapists and physical therapist assistants to be actively involved in providing services to children with disabilities in educational programs. Public Law 99-457 (PL 99-457) extended this involvement to early intervention services for infants and toddlers with disabilities and their families.

Physical therapists examine and evaluate children having a variety of sensory and motor disabilities. Physical therapists plan and implement programs that will help these children attain their optimal educational potential and benefit from special education. Physical therapists should assume a role in the development of a child's Individual Educational Program (IEP), or Individual Family Service Plan (IFSP), and make recommendations for increasing a child's ability to participate in educational activities. In addition, physical therapists contribute unique administrative, consultative, management, and teaching skills that help modify the educational environment so that children may benefit from their educational placement.

APTA encourages the establishment of working relationships with state education departments, local school districts and other agencies, such as mental health agencies, in order to integrate physical therapy services into school systems and early intervention programs. Such cooperation should be directed toward developing and implementing cost-effective delivery of services to children with disabilities within the framework of federally approved state plans. In all these efforts, the primary goal should be identifying and serving the best interests of children with disabling conditions both within the school setting and in overall quality of life.

I N   P R A C T I C E

By Gloria J Young, EdD, PT

Home Health: Special Risks

Many patients prefer receiving therapy in the home. But for the therapy provider, neighborhood and home settings may pose special risks.

home health care is one of the fastest-growing areas of health care. Many believe home health care is the trend of the future—a trend driven by the gradual aging of the "baby boomer" (post-World War II) generation. Researchers have found that many people prefer to receive health care in their homes when feasible and that home health care may be more cost-effective than extended hospitalization or placement in a rehabilitation facility.[2-4]

Physical therapists providing home health care face many unique risks; managing these risks may require unique strategies. Because these therapists practice in an independent environment, evaluation skills, judgment, and technical skills must be especially well-developed in ways that are very different from those required in more structured health care delivery systems. Creativity is essential.

Head and Horn[1] define risk management as follows:

> The process of making and carrying out decisions that will minimize the adverse effects of accidental losses upon an organization [or individual].

The most important losses to an organization or an individual are those that interfere with the achievement of the organization's or individual's goals and objectives.[1] In physical therapy practice, the overall goal is to promote healing and restoration of the patient to his or her highest level of functioning. Risk management involves either *preventing* losses (risk control) or *paying for* those losses that inevitably occur (risk financing). Potential losses must be identified if risks are to be avoided or minimized.

Because [home health] therapists practice in an independent environment, evaluation skills, judgement, and technical skills must be especially well-developed.

One risk control technique is *exposure avoidance*—in other words, not engaging in home health care at all! Another technique is *loss prevention*, which involves reducing the "frequency" of a particular loss:

A home health care therapist is seeing a new patient who has had a below-the-knee amputation. On arrival to the patient's home, the therapist performs the evaluation and notes a greenish discharge from the stump site and a putrid odor. On examining the patient's medications, she notes that he is not taking any antibiotics. The therapist immediately reports these findings to the rehabilitation coordinator at the home health agency with which she contracts and to the patient's physician. In doing so, she may be sav-ing the patient from further pain. She also may be saving the patient's life.

A thorough physical therapy evaluation gave the therapist the feedback she needed to detect infection in the amputated limb. Thorough evaluation is an example of a loss prevention technique. Checking the patient's medications and constantly monitoring the infection area also are loss prevention techniques (both for the therapist and the patient).

Home health care involves other types of risk—such as driving all day from one patient's home to another. Slowing down to search for addresses, car problems, children playing in the streets—all are potential causes of loss to the therapist and to other people in the environment. Loss prevention techniques include obtaining concise written directions to the patient's home that note landmarks and distinctive physical and environmental characteristics (eg, the front yard has a cactus bed, the house is located on the right hand corner, the front door is hanging off the hinges, a parking lot is located across the street).

In *loss reduction* , the goal is to reduce the severity of a particular loss:

A therapist has a sudden family emergency and leaves town immediately. As a result, her home health patients have no coverage for 5 days. One patient's daughter is convinced that, because of the missed therapy sessions, her mother has had a relapse or a delayed recovery from hip surgery. The home health agency finally finds coverage for the therapist's patients, selecting a therapist they know has excellent patient relations skills. The

patient and her daughter are reassured that the patient has progressed at a normal—if not greater-than-normal—recovery rate. Positive rapport is established, and the patient is given 2 additional weeks of physical therapy (at no charge) to reassure both the patient and the patient's family that the care she is receiving will help her achieve the highest possible level of function.

Segregation of loss exposures involves arranging an organization's (or an individual's) activities and resources in a way that helps ensure no single event will result in simultaneous losses to all of them. Examples of this risk control technique are: keeping copies of clinical notes and periodically assigning different physical therapists and physical therapist assistants when communication problems exist and when patient expectations are unrealistic.

Contractual transfer is a transfer of legal and financial responsibility for a loss. When the physical therapist documents treatments

> Although numerous risks exist for the therapist who provides treatment in the home, risk management techniques can help minimize those risks.

thoroughly and gives the patient a written home program—and when the patient signs that written home program to indicate that he or she understands it and is willing to comply with it—a form of contractual transfer has occurred. *Whether a patient complies with the home program should always be documented.*

Common risks associated with home health care include:

- Entering crime-infested neighborhoods
- Entering homes in which illegal substances are being used (usually by younger relatives of the patient)
- Cluttered homes in which furniture prohibits safe gait training and transfers
- Broken or uneven walkways or a lack of walkways leading into the home
- Loose handrails on steps leading into the home and within the home
- Unattached kitchen sinks that are being used as a base for pulling up from the sitting position to the standing position and for balance training
- Lack of handrails for toilet and bath transfers
- Uneven floors
- Throw rugs
- Unfriendly pets in yards or homes
- Shag carpeting or slippery floors
- Allergies to pets

- Numerous stairs leading into homes or sleeping quarters
- Loose, dangling telephone and television cords
- Lack of compliance on the part of the patient or the patient's significant others
- Lack of the sophisticated equipment that may be available in the clinic
- Lack of financial resources for medications (especially among elderly patients)

Keep in mind that social workers—common providers in the home health care environment—can help you resolve many of the above problems and risks. The durable medical equipment supplier also may be able to provide assistance.

Although numerous risks exist for the therapist who provides treatment in the home, risk management techniques can help minimize those risks. Positive communication with both patient and family, concise documentation, patient and family participation in goal setting, and recognition of loss exposures are essential to ensure high-quality home health care. *PT*

Gloria J Young, EdD, PT, is President, Sunbelt Physical Therapy, PC, Birmingham, Ala, where she specializes in home health care. She is a member of APTA's Committee on Insurance and Member Benefit Services.

References
1 Head G, Horn S II. *Essentials of Risk Management, ed 2.* Malvern, Pa: Insurance Institute of America; 1991.
2 Ginzberg E, Balinsky W, Ostow M. *Home Health Care: Its Role In the Changing Health Services Market.* Lanham, MD: Rowman & Littlefield Publishers Inc; 1984.
3 Spiegel A. *Home Healthcare: Home Birthing to Hospice Care.* New York, NY: National Health Publishing Ltd; 1983.
4 Harris MD. Outcomes of care from the professional's perspective. *Home Healthcare Nurse.* 1992;10(6):48-49.

Suggested Readings
Applebaum RA, McGinnis R. What price quality? Assuring the quality of case-managed in-home care. *Journal of Case Management.* 1992;1(1):9-13.
Feldman C, Olberding L, Shortridge L, et al. Decision making in case management of home healthcare clients. *J Nurs Adm.* 1993;23(1):33-38.
Pray JE. Maximizing the patient's uniqueness and strengths: a challenge for home health care. *Soc Work Health Care.* 1992;17(3):71-79.
Rhoads C, Dean J, Cason C, Blaylock A. Comprehensive discharge planning: a hospital-home health-care partnership. *Home Healthcare Nurse.* 1992;10(6):13-18.

LIABILITY CONSIDERATIONS IN CONTINUING EDUCATION

By Ronald W Scott, JD, PT

n 1992, there were 19,707,374 civil lawsuits filed in the United States (Natalie Davis, Courts Statistics Project; personal communication, March 23, 1994). Some commentators say the nation is in the throes of a litigation crisis. More than 25 physical therapy malpractice cases have been reported since 1972[1]; there may be hundreds or even thousands of additional cases that are not reported (eg, dropped actions, settled or not appealed beyond the trial court level). Although there currently are no reported cases involving liability for continuing physical therapy education, physical therapists who provide continuing education need to be aware of the types of situations that may expose them to civil or criminal liability. There are three common classifications of legal actions relevant to this discussion: tort, contract, and criminal.

Tort Actions

Tort (or civil wrong) actions include under a broad umbrella most civil law cases involving alleged injury to private-party litigants. (It does not include those cases involving alleged breach of contract). Some of the scenarios from which tort actions may arise include automobile and airplane crashes, accidents occurring on business premises, and the delivery of health care services.

Tort subclassifications include negligence, strict liability, and liability for intentional conduct. *Negligence* involves cases in which the party or parties being sued (defendant[s]) allegedly violated a legal duty of due care owed to the party bringing suit (plaintiff), causing physical, mental, or economic injury. Under *strict liability* for injuries sustained by the plaintiff because of dangerously defective commercial products or abnormally dangerous activities, courts impose civil—not criminal—liability regardless of whether the defendant was careless, reckless, or otherwise blameworthy. *Intentional conduct* may involve defamation of character, business disparagement, sexual assault and battery, or fraud, among other actions.

The term "physical therapy malpractice" *may* encompass any or all of the above actions in which a patient is plaintiff and a physical therapist is defendant.

Negligence

Professional negligence. Continuing education presenters may be held liable for professional (treatment-related) negligence when they treat actual patients as part of a "demonstration." In some cases, sponsors of physical therapy continuing education courses may engage patients from the local community who agree to be evaluated and treated, without charge, by nationally prominent physical therapists—in exchange for serving as "demonstration models." In other cases, attendees who have conditions being covered in the presentation may volunteer to become demonstration patients.

In terms of legalities, regardless of whether money is exchanged, *a professional-patient relationship is formed when the presenter and*

PTs who provide continuing education should be aware of the potential for malpractice exposure. A review of principal legal actions and risk-management strategies.

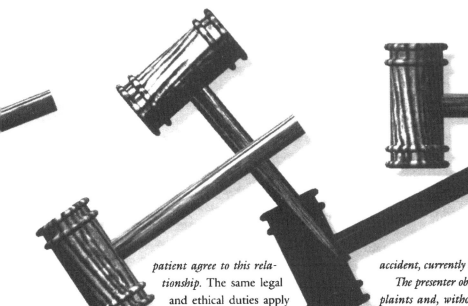

patient agree to this relationship. The same legal and ethical duties apply to the presenter during the demonstration as apply in ordinary clinical practice. These duties include, among others:

1. The duty to obtain *legally sufficient* informed consent* before evaluation and treatment.
2. The duty to obtain a proper physical therapy treatment referral, if required by state law.
3. The duty to conduct the evaluation and carry out the treatment within legal standards and scope of practice.
4. The duty to respect patient privacy and dignity during the evaluation and treatment.
5. The duty not to improperly abandon the patient after the demonstration or course is concluded.

An out-of-state physical therapist is conducting a 3-day course on cervical spine evaluation and mobilization and manipulation. Fifty physical therapists are in attendance. When the presenter's assistant (also a therapist) asks if anyone currently has neck pain, five attendees raise their hands, three of whom agree to be evaluated and treated during the course. One of the three, who was involved in an automobile

That is, to appraise the patient of the nature of the proposed treatment, the material risks (if any), and the expected benefits; to appraise the patient of reasonable alternatives (if any) and the risks and benefits; and to solicit and satisfactorily answer patient questions.

accident, currently is in litigation with the driver of the other car.

The presenter obtains a brief oral history of the latter patient's complaints and, without reviewing any health records or obtaining a physician referral (as required by state law in this jurisdiction), proceeds to examine him, explaining pertinent findings to the audience throughout the evaluation. At the conclusion of the evaluation, the presenter explains to the patient that she would like to mobilize his cervical spine in an attempt to relieve his pain symptoms, and the patient nods his head in agreement. The patient is placed in the supine position on a treatment table, with his head cradled by the presenter.

The presenter carries out manual distraction of the patient's cervical spine. When the patient reports a moderate increase in pain, the presenter halts the demonstration and has her assistant apply an ice pack to the patient's shoulders. She advises the patient to return to his treating physician immediately after the conference for reevaluation, and she carries out no further treatment with him. She inquires daily about his condition, which gradually moderates.

The patient in the above hypothetical case just may have a new party to claim against in his lawsuit—the presenter. The presenter potentially violated several legal and ethical practice standards when she treated this patient, including:

1. Treating a patient when she did not have a license to practice in that state.
2. Failing to obtain a proper referral before commencing treatment.
3. Failing to obtain proper informed patient consent to treatment.
4. Carrying out treatment without the customary health records review.

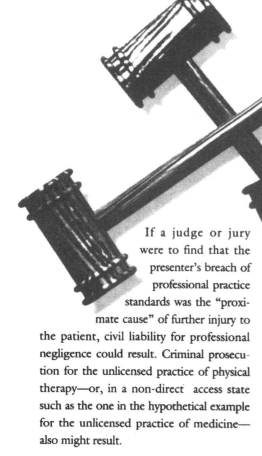

If a judge or jury were to find that the presenter's breach of professional practice standards was the "proximate cause" of further injury to the patient, civil liability for professional negligence could result. Criminal prosecution for the unlicensed practice of physical therapy—or, in a non-direct access state such as the one in the hypothetical example for the unlicensed practice of medicine—also might result.

Ordinary negligence. Liability on the part of a continuing education presenter or course sponsor also may result from ordinary negligence; for example, liability may result when a patient or course participant slips and falls on a wet surface in the dressing area of a pool that is being used for the continuing education program. In legal cases brought against physical therapists,[2] ordinary negligence—even though it does not constitute "health care malpractice"—is alleged by patients as a basis for liability almost as frequently as is professional negligence. Continuing education presenters and sponsors must ensure that lecture, demonstration, and practice areas are reasonably safe (ie, clutter-free and hazard-free) for participants, patients, and any other persons involved in the course.

Although having participants and patients execute waivers or releases from liability is a common practice, continuing education presenters and sponsors normally cannot insulate themselves from liability for professional or ordinary negligence through those waivers and releases.[3] Courts are reluctant to permit exculpatory clauses in health care contracts (which include continuing education course agreements), especially in cases in which 1) participants with pathologies are treated or 2) inexperienced participants are supervised during practical exercises by experienced presenters and their associates.

Strict Liability: Dangerously Defective Products

Strict, or absolute, liability for dangerously defective commercial products involves imposition of liability whenever a "foreseeable user" or other person coming in contact with a product is injured by that product. Any person or entity who is part of the regular commercial chain of distribution for a product may be held accountable for injury.

In the past, courts were reluctant to impose strict product liability on health care clinicians because the law viewed the treatment relationship as a professional service rather than as the sale of a product. Courts today, however, *are* likely to impose such liability when providers market or sell equipment to patients and others. In continuing physical therapy education courses, presenters and sponsors often "pitch" products—from electrotherapy systems and other modalities to exercise equipment to tables and other apparatuses—to course participants.

Intentional Conduct

One potentially devastating consequence of a finding of liability for intentional conduct is that the plaintiff(s) may be awarded punitive damages for "egregious conduct" (eg, reckless disregard for patient safety) on the part of the defendant, in addition to being awarded normal compensatory damages such as medical expenses, lost income, and pain and suffering. Depending on the nature of the intentional wrong, insurers may not be obligated to indemnify (pay for) punitive damages.

Defamation of character. Defamation involves a communication—made by one person about another person to a third party—that results in legal injury to the aggrieved party's good reputation in the community.[4] There are two primary classes of defamation: slander, or oral defamation, and libel, including written and other forms of defamation (eg, through videotape or other media).

During one of her lectures, Dr X, a prominent presenter of a continuing education musculoskeletal course, names a known competitor, Dr Y, who uses a wholly different approach to treatment, describing him as a "lecher" who "routinely gropes and otherwise inappropriately touches patients and course participants of the opposite sex during presentations."

If a judge or jury finds that X's comment is untrue, X may be liable to Y for the intentional tort of slander and may have to pay compensatory damages for injury to Y's reputation in addition to punitive damages designed to punish X and deter others from similar misconduct.

Business disparagement. Business disparagement, or injurious falsehood, is a tort similar to defamation, except that it concerns statements or other communications that injure the reputation of a business (rather than personal reputation in the community).[4]

If Dr X in the case above had told course participants, "Dr Y's approach to evaluation and treatment of patients is fraudulent," the attack would have been against Y's business interests more than against his personal reputation, and the tort involved would be business disparagement rather than defamation.

Sexual assault and battery. Sexual assault and battery is an intentional tort that involves any nonconsensual touching of a patient's sexual or other bodily parts by the defendant for the purpose of arousing or gratifying the sexual desire of either party or for the purpose of sexual abuse.[†] Although an allegation of sexual assault and battery should rarely, if ever, arise in the continuing education setting, presenters are cautioned to ensure that demonstration models and participants in hands-on practical exercises 1) fully understand the nature of treatments carried out or practiced and 2) give unconditional informed consent, particularly when intensive hands-on therapies, such as myofascial mobilization, are involved.

Contracts

Virtually every business relationship involves a contract, express or implied. Contract law is unique in that private parties are privileged to fashion their own rules governing each other's conduct—as long as those rules comply with law and public policy. *A binding contract does not necessarily have to be written to be enforceable.* One exception involving continuing education contracts would be a contract to conduct a course that is to be held more than a year from the date of the agreement. According to the "1-year rule," contracts that cannot be performed within 1 year after the date of their making are required to be made in writing to be enforceable under a legal rule known as the "statute of frauds"[5,6] (a rule that, despite its name, has nothing to do with fraud).

Most business and personal contracts are "bilateral," that is, two parties exchange mutual promises for "consideration" (ie, exchange goods or services for money or

[†] *This definition of "sexual abuse" is adapted from Model Penal Code, Section 213.4, ALI (Proposed Official Draft 1962) and Colorado Statutes, §18-3-401(4).*

other goods or services) and agree to be legally bound to fulfill their promises. *Breach of contract* occurs when one party to a contract fails to perform and has no valid excuse. Breach of contract entitles the aggrieved party to a damages award.

In the continuing education setting, breach-of-contract actions can arise in at least three ways:

1. Between presenters and sponsors, based on compensation or presentation performance. This class of contract actions typically involves straightforward interpretation of an express (preferably written) or implied agreement.
2. Between presenters or sponsors and participants, based on the content or value of a presentation. This class of contract actions is more complex and may require that a court interpret language in a course brochure or letter of acceptance. To avoid these kinds of contractual disputes, presenters and sponsors are urged to carefully review language in their marketing brochures to ensure that what is promised is substantially delivered.
3. Between presenters and patients, based on the scope and duration of treatment.

This class of contract actions concerns the legal issue of patient abandonment, that is, whether termination of care comports with the contractual understanding of the parties and meets legal practice standards.[7] It is advisable that presenters who treat patients or participants in the continuing education course setting 1) define the scope and duration of their treatment in a signed, written agreement with patients to avoid any misunderstanding and 2) determine the legal requirements to continue care after the course is ended.

Criminal Actions

A presenter or sponsor rarely will face criminal liability related to continuing education course presentations. Although legal actions that allege criminal behavior typically are initiated when a complaint is made by a private party, they are *not* private legal disputes (unlike tort and breach-of-contract actions). These actions are brought by public officials on behalf of a city, county, state, or the federal government to redress wrongs against public interests.

Presenters and sponsors who travel out of state for presentations could be charged with a criminal offense—the unlicensed practice of physical therapy—if they treat patients during these presentations but do not hold a valid license in the state in which they are presenting. Similarly, they may face criminal liability for aiding and abetting another person in the unlicensed practice of physical therapy if they encourage or allow unlicensed persons to violate an applicable state physical therapy practice act (*O'Neill v Board of Regents*, 83 NE 2nd 469 [NY 1948]; licensure suspension for aiding and abetting an unlicensed person to practice physical therapy affirmed). They also may face criminal liability for the unlicensed practice of medicine if they evaluate and treat without a valid referral order when such an order is required. In cases of alleged sexual assault or battery, criminal actions may be prosecuted in addition to civil actions.

Recommendations

In today's litigious society, it is recommended that continuing education presenters and their support staff and sponsors formulate risk-management plans to reduce the potential for malpractice. Prudent steps include ensuring that:

1. Course descriptions comport with actual course performance.
2. Legal and ethical physical therapy practice standards are met exactly as they would be met in ordinary clinical practice.
3. Safety hazards on the course premises are eliminated or minimized.
4. Compliance with licensure and referral requirements is complete.

In addition, because courts take a dim view of such instruments, presenters and sponsors should think carefully before requiring the signing of exculpatory waivers that attempt to "release" the presenters and sponsors from liability for malpractice committed against participants and patients.

With careful preparation, due care in presentation, and attention both to quality and to risk management, presenters and sponsors of continuing physical therapy education can continue to provide an invaluable service to the professional community and the public. *PT*

Ronald W Scott, JD, PT, is Assistant Professor, Department of Physical Therapy, School of Allied Health Sciences, The University of Texas Health Science Center, San Antonio, Tex.

The information in this article should not be interpreted as specific advice for any particular practitioner. Personal advice can be given only by personal legal counsel, based on applicable state and federal law. Characters depicted in hypothetical examples in this article are fictional and are not intended to represent any particular physical therapy practitioner, living or dead. Any similarity to an actual person is coincidental and unintended.

References

1 Scott RW. Malpractice update. *PT—Magazine of Physical Therapy.* 1(12):62-64; 1993.
2 Scott RW. *Health Care Malpractice: A Primer on Legal Issues for Professionals.* Thorofare, NJ: SLACK Inc; 1990:27.
3 Furrow BR, Johnson SH, Jost TS, Schwartz RL. *Health Law, ed 2.* St Paul, Minn: West Publishing Co; 1991:292-294.
4 Prosser WL. *Handbook of the Law of Torts, ed 4.* St Paul, Minn: West Publishing Co; 1971:739.
5 Calamari JD, Perillo JM. *The Law of Contracts, ed 2.* St Paul, Minn: West Publishing Co; 1977:704.
6 Lewis K. Part I: Physical therapy contracts. *Clinical Management.* 1992;12(4):12-15.
7 Scott RW. Liability for patient abandonment. *Clinical Management.* 1992;12(2):18-19.

IN PRACTICE

by Ron Scott, JD, LLM, PT, OCS

CIs and Liability

*Who's responsible for student conduct—student,
CI, site, school? What CIs need to know.*

A number of factors are converging to change clinical education, such as the explosion in the number of professional education programs at different degree levels, governmental health care reform efforts, and managed care. With the use of innovative clinical education models such as the 2:1 collaborative model discussed by Zavadak et al (pages 46-55), in which students supervised by one clinical instructor (CI) may be working as a team to treat patients, now is the time for CIs to strengthen their understanding of liability issues.

What are the basics of malpractice law as it relates to physical therapy?

Any physical therapist who has the legal duty to care for a patient is *primarily* liable (responsible) for physical or mental injury incurred by the patient as a result of 1) professional negligence (substandard delivery of care), 2) intentional (mis)conduct, 3) breach of a contractual promise made to the patient, or 4) use of a dangerously defective modality or piece of equipment. (Sources such as Prosser[1] and Scott[2] elaborate on these basics.)

The clinician who supervises the activities of physical therapist assistants, physical therapy aides, students, and others (eg, athletic trainers) may be *vicariously* (indirectly) liable for patient injury resulting from the liability-generating conduct of these persons when it occurs within the scope of their employment or affiliation.[3,4]

When is the school liable, and when is the site liable?

The party vicariously liable for student conduct usually is the party who has accepted such responsibility under a clinical affiliation agreement, or contract. This contract should clearly delineate the scope of vicarious liability for both site and school and should be undertaken only in consultation with both parties' attorneys. As an additional protective measure for both site and school, the contract also can include language that "memorializes" the mutual understanding that the school will send only those students who are prepared to participate in clinical experiences.

In addition to vicarious liability, sites and schools may incur primary liability for their own negligence in supervising or preparing students who injure patients. A school, for example, may incur primary liability for the negligent instruction or preparation of a student or for the negligent or intentional misrepresentation of a student's competency or status.

In the absence of clear language spelling out who (or whose insurer) is liable for student conduct, a court may rely on the common-law "borrowed servant rule" to assign responsibility, based on whose interests (site or school) the student primarily was serving at the time of an adverse patient incident.

What is the CI's supervisory responsibility?

A CI (or site) may incur primary liability for the negligent failure to review a referral order, a patient's treatment records, or a student's evaluation note before allowing the student to treat a patient. CIs (or sites) also may be primarily liable for the negligent failure to provide on-site and, when appropriate, direct supervision of a student during patient intake, evaluation, and treatment. As Smith[5] noted, the supervisory responsibility defined in certain state practice acts "may subject clinical faculty to a potential role of liability." He cited the Georgia State Physical Therapy Practice Act, which states that physical therapist students "in approved education programs can only perform physical therapy if they are supervised by a licensed physical therapist." Whether the supervision should be "direct" also differs from state to state.

Failure-to-supervise liability often is couched in legal terms, such as "patient or student abandonment." A CI who allows a student to evaluate and treat patients without supervision may face criminal legal action for aiding and abetting physical therapy practice by an unlicensed practitioner in addition to adverse licensure and professional association action for practice and ethical violations.

Malpractice exposure also may occur if a CI gives negligent instruction or guidance to a student that results in patient injury or if there is "negligent failure" to include students in systematic quality monitoring and evaluation processes carried out in the clinic.[6]

Center coordinators of clinical education (CCCEs) and managers need to ensure that CIs understand the rules of appropriate supervision of students and that CIs exercise sound professional judgment when assigning patients to students, based on factors such as student competence and special considerations associated with particular patients.

It is essential that CIs review all student evaluations and countersign their notes before students carry out initial treatment of patients. This precaution helps protect all participants in the treatment process: patient, student, CI, and site. Because students are not licensed health care providers, the "student note" is not legally binding. The CI adopts, or is deemed legally to have adopted, all of the student's patient evaluation and treatment notes as the CI's own. If a malpractice monetary settlement is paid or a court judgement is awarded to a patient, it would be the CI's name, and not that of the student, that would be reported to the National Practitioner Data Bank (a data bank that stores malpractice information on health care practitioners[7]).

CIs have not only an ethical responsibility but a legal duty to honestly and accurately evaluate and report a student's clinical performance to academic coordinators of clinical education (ACCEs). Any critical, candid comments should be accurate, fair, and well-documented in prior written counseling statements given to the student, in which the student was afforded clear notice of deficient performance, an opportunity to respond in writing to the allegation(s), and an opportunity (reasonable time) to remedy any deficiencies. A CI who misrepresents a student's level of competence may be held legally accountable for patient injury that results from that student's conduct.

Remember: Both statutory (legislative) law and common (judge-made) law require that clinical site personnel and academicians handle information about students as confidential.[2,8] Everyone who has official knowledge about students and their performance should understand the gravity of this responsibility.

What role does informed consent play?

As is supported by APTA's *Code of Ethics* and *Guide for Professional Conduct*, the basic rule of law is that all health professionals have the ethical and legal duty to gain a patient's informed consent before treatment.[9] Informed consent is based on the patient's inherent right to self-determination or autonomy. The disclosure elements (ie, the information that must be disclosed to the patient) required for legally sufficient patient informed consent to evaluation and treatment when students are involved include:

1. Type of treatment recommended or ordered.
2. Any material (decisional) risks associated with the proposed treatment.
3. The expected benefit(s) of treatment (ie, treatment-related goals).
4. Information about any reasonable alternatives to the proposed treatment.
5. *The role of a student or students in evaluation and treatment.*

CIs should remember that it is their personal legal responsibility—not the student's—to obtain patient informed consent to physical therapy treatment. (Similarly, this responsibility cannot legally be delegated to a PTA.)

What *is* the student's responsibility?

A student may be *singularly* responsible for patient injury when that student was negligent and failed to follow a CI's instructions or when the student's injurious conduct was malicious.

As may licensed PTs, students may engage in intentional liability-generating conduct. A student, for example, may commit or be accused of *battery* (inappropriate or offensive touching of a patient); *defamation* (false assertions about a patient that damage the patient's good reputation); *invasion of (patient) privacy* and, in particular, public dissemination of confidential patient information; or *sexual harassment*.[1,10]

What about liability in clinical education and the ADA?

The Americans with Disabilities Act may require that facilities make reasonable accommodation for students with disabilities. The burden typically is on the student to apprise the school or site of the disability and request accommodation.[11] Although facilities must show flexibility in providing necessary assistance and accommodation so that qualified students can reasonably meet clinical education requirements for graduation, the ADA does not say that quality and safety standards can be lowered to the point of risking injury to patients.

What risk management strategies can sites use?

- Require students to wear name badges, and instruct and compel them to use identifying initials such as "SPT" after their signatures on patient treatment record entries.
- Assign only seasoned clinicians as CCCEs and CIs.
- On their arrival in the clinic, orient all students to the physical facility and its written policies, protocols, treatment guidelines, and other standardized operating

procedures before they begin to evaluate and treat patients.

- Orient students to the equipment they will be using in the treatment of patients.
- Have students sign in an appropriate place that they have read all applicable policies and guidelines.

As Smith[5] wrote in his overview of liability and clinical education, there are "no cases of a physical therapy student being named in a malpractice suit....[and] physical therapists have enjoyed relative freedom from malpractice suits." But CIs (and clinical sites and schools) still should take risk management seriously, both to protect the health interests of the patient and to protect their own professional and legal interests. *PT*

Ron Scott, JD, LLM, PT, OCS, is Assistant Professor, Physical Therapy Department, University of Texas Health Science Center, San Antonio, Tex. He is a member of APTA's Judicial Committee and of APTA's Risk Management—Liability Awareness Program Faculty.

The information in this article should not be interpreted as specific advice for any particular practitioner. Personal advice can be given only by personal legal counsel, based on applicable state and federal law.

References

1 Prosser W. *Prosser on Torts, 4th ed.* St Paul, Minn: West Publishing Co; 1971.
2 Scott R. *Health Care Malpractice.* Thorofare, NJ: SLACK Inc; 1990.
3 Scott R. *Legal Aspects of Documenting Patient Care.* Gaithersburg, Md: Aspen Publishing Co Inc; 1994.
4 Scott R. Vicarious liability. *Clinical Management.* 1991;11(5):14-15.
5 Smith HG. Introduction to legal risks associated with clinical education. *Journal of Physical Therapy Education.* 1994:8(2):67-70.
6 Kearney KA, McCord EL. Hospital management faces new liabilities. *The Health Lawyer.* 1992;6(3):1,3-6.
7 Fraiche D. Peer review and the data bank. *Clinical Management.* 1992;12(3):14-17.
8 Family Educational Rights and Privacy Act of 1974, 20 USC §1232f(a)(b).
9 Rozovsky FA. *Consent to Treatment, 2nd ed.* Boston, Mass: Little Brown & Co; 1990.
10 Finley C. What is sexual harassment? *PT–Magazine of Physical Therapy.* 1994;2(12):17-18.
11 Mirone JA. Cases in higher education. ADA Case Law. *PT—Magazine of Physical Therapy.* 1994;2(6):33.

Liability Concerns in Aquatic Physical Therapy

When physical therapists treat patients in an aquatic environment, they assume risks and potential liabilities. Annie Clement, PhD, JD, describes liability concerns in aquatic physical therapy. Following this feature, look for a new column "Liability Awareness," designed to keep readers informed of current issues related to risk management.

Photography by David M Enck

When physical therapists use a swimming pool, a spa, or any area containing a significant amount of water for rehabilitation, they assume not only the usual risks and potential liabilities associated with physical therapy treatment, but also the risks and potential liabilities of an aquatic professional. Recognized standards of care, certifications, and designated qualifications exist in the aquatic environments just as they do in physical therapy, and when PTs manage an aquatic environment, in addition to being held to the professional and legal standards governing physical therapy, they also will be held to the standards that govern swimming pool operation.

Communities and states have laws relating to swimming pools and spas. These laws typically are found under aquatics, building, and health and sanitation codes. In addition, some states have supervision standards dictating swimmer-to-lifeguard ratios and aquatic personnel requirements. Health codes usually specify water temperature and sanitation.

Numerous federal statutes, including the Americans With Disabilities Act (ADA), the Occupational Health and Safety Act (OSHA), and related business codes also affect the business of aquatics. For example, OSHA requirements in handling swimming pool chemicals and blood-borne pathogens are among the most important federal statutes in aquatics.

Aquatic professionals typically have degrees in such areas as human movement, biomechanics, or physical education. They have a comprehensive knowledge of water safety, first aid, and emergency assistance. Certificates and programs are tailored to guide aquatic professionals and inform consumers of the conditions associated with a safe, supervised aquatic environment. In part as a result of these programs, there have been relatively few court cases related to incidents occurring in supervised aquatic settings; the majority of incidents leading to litigation have occurred in unsupervised environments.

Although swimming frequently is listed as the number one participatory activity in surveys, more than half of the US population cannot swim.[1] In addition, aquatic specialists believe that of the survey respondents who report that they can swim, another 50% would not be able to pass the American Red Cross Advanced Beginner's swimming test, a standard measurement indicating at least a minimum level of water survival skills.

Aquatic environments are considered high-risk environments, meaning that the chance there for injury or death is considered to be far greater than the chance for injury or death in the normal course of daily events. In 1994, unintentional injuries accounted for 92,200 deaths in the United States; 4,186 of these deaths were from drowning. Accidents in aquatic environments are estimated to be responsible for 10% of all head injuries and spinal injuries resulting in quadriplegia.[2]

If an injury sustained in the aquatic environment results in death or requires expensive rehabilitation, the guardians or relatives of the injured party will be likely to litigate for damages to finance that rehabilitation or to compensate the next of kin. In the past, defendants named in lawsuits related to accidents in aquatic environments have typically been lifeguards, swimming instructors, and pool owners and managers. A review of litigation related to aquatic physical therapy shows that few court decisions have been rendered regarding liability in this area; however, increased participation in specific physical activities and provision of services in those areas sometimes has been shown to correlate to increased numbers of lawsuits related to those activities. As the use of the aquatic environment for physical therapy increases, both physicians and PTs may find themselves named in lawsuits.

Anyone can be sued. Both outstanding and very weak professionals have been sued over incidents that have taken place in a variety of physical activity settings. When a patient under a professional's care sustains a serious injury and believes that the professional contributed to the injury, the chance of a lawsuit increases measurably.

Despite the best efforts of the professional to safeguard against exposure to liability, sometimes a lawsuit cannot be prevented. A professional can, however, be prepared to respond confidently to a complaint. PTs who practice in aquatic settings are encouraged to prepare for a lawsuit with the same

diligence used in preparing to meet emergencies. A comprehensive risk management program provides the structure for that preparation, and one key element of risk management is knowledge. An understanding of some of the key legal concepts that have a direct impact on the working environment is a must. Not only does a risk

> **Despite the best efforts of the professional to safeguard against exposure to liability, sometimes a lawsuit cannot be prevented. A professional can, however, be prepared to respond confidently to a complaint.**

management plan help PTs be alert to and avoid potential sources of liability, it also enables them to communicate with insurance representatives and legal advisors should a lawsuit occur. Below are some of the most important legal issues and concepts that have an impact on aquatic physical therapy.

Negligence

Negligence occurs when a person fails to do something that either a "reasonable person" or a professional in the same situation would have been expected to perform. Negligence also occurs when a person does something that the "reasonable person" or professional would not have done. In a case of negligence, the professional's behavior falls below the standards established for the protection

of others by law or by the various professional organizations governing both physical therapy and aquatics. Ultimately, in a lawsuit claiming negligence, the court will determine if the defendant has met or breached either a professional standard or a duty of care.

The minimum standard of care is the behavior to which all members of the profession must adhere. Professional standards for both physical therapy (eg, APTA's *Standards of Practice for Physical Therapy*) and aquatics exist in writing to provide general guidance on the behavior expected of individuals in these professions; however, standards specific to *aquatic physical therapy* are evolving and currently are not in writing. When a standard is not in writing, or if the contents of the written document are challenged in litigation, experts may be called to define an appropriate standard of care for the circumstances in question. If the standard of care required of the professional has been met, and that fact can be documented, the professional should prevail in a court of law.

All of the following elements[3] must exist for the court to find negligence:

1. A legal duty of care,
2. Breach of that legal duty,
3. Breach of that legal duty as the cause of the injury (ie, "proximate cause"),
4. Substantial damage.

The seriousness of negligence is identified in degrees as *negligence, gross negligence,* and *willful and wanton neglect.* An example of negligence might be failure to inspect the pool entry stairway before taking a client into the water. Gross negligence might be failure to fix the stairway into the pool when the professional knew that it was not secure and could cause harm. Willful and wanton neglect is "an intentional act of an unreasonable character in total disregard of human safety."[3] Allowing clients to enter the pool when the water is so cloudy that the bottom cannot be seen would be an example of willful and wanton neglect.

Because professionals are required to adhere to a higher standard of care than the "ordinary person," professional negligence and ordinary negligence are viewed separately by the courts. For health care providers, professional negligence typically is related to treatment (eg, malpractice issues), whereas ordinary negligence might be related to maintaining unsafe premises. However, in cases where maintaining safe premises could be deemed to be within the scope of a person's professional responsibility, a finding of professional negligence is possible.

Negligence findings in lawsuits related to physical activity are found most frequently in cases involving faulty equipment and facilities, failure to supervise, faulty instruction, failure to provide emergency care, and faulty emergency care.

Two defenses frequently used in negligence cases are assumption of risk and contributory or comparative negligence. An *assumption of risk* defense seeks to prove that the patient knew what he or she was doing or was going to do when he or she was injured; that is, that the patient understood and accepted the risk. The legal value of an assumption of risk defense differs from state to state, but most states do have laws allowing adults to waive certain rights to litigation, as long as they "know the risk exists, understand the nature of the risks, and freely choose to incur the risk."[4]

One way to help ensure that patients do understand the risks associated with the aquatic environment is to use a written statement, which might be reviewed by an attorney, educating the client about risks specific to the water environment. However, assumption of risk related to an individual's entering a high-risk environment such as a swimming pool should not be confused with the issue of patient informed consent to treatment, and it should be noted that exculpatory contracts between patients and health care providers that are used as either waivers of liability for malpractice or conditions precedent to treatment generally are unenforceable. In addition, an assumption of risk defense does not apply in cases of intentional torts or in cases where the defendant has broken a law designed to protect a class of persons to which the plaintiff belongs.

Contributory negligence describes actions taken by the plaintiff that put the plaintiff at risk. The patient who fails to follow instructions, the adult who returns to the aquatic environment when it is not super-

vised, or the person who dives into shallow water from the pool stairway are examples of contributory negligence.

Comparative negligence (or *comparative fault*) describes situations in which the plaintiff's contributory negligence in a particular case constitutes a percentage of fault and the defendant's negligence constitutes another percentage of fault. For example, the plaintiff's dive into shallow water might place him or her at 60% fault, and the defendant's failure to secure the stairs, causing the plaintiff to lose balance and sustain a direct

> ## PTs providing aquatic physical therapy in deep water for patients below the Intermediate swimming category should consider a personal flotation plan.

hit as he or she dove from the stairs, might place him or her at 40% fault. In such a case, the percentage of fault of the plaintiff would be used to reduce his or her recovery (money damage) from the defendant.

Vicarious Liability

Under the legal theory of *respondeat superior*, an employer is responsible or vicariously liable for torts committed by employees in the work place. The owner or employer of an aquatic facility or the hospital that houses the aquatic facility may be liable for the torts of lifeguards or PTs (and he or she could be found to be negligent for hiring an incompetent employee).

Volunteers are held to the same vicarious and regular liability determinations as salaried employees, unless a state statute has reduced liability for volunteers.

Damages

Courts award two types of damages in tort cases, compensatory and punitive. Compensatory damages include medical bills, lost wages, and the costs associated with disability. Punitive damages are dollar awards based on the assets of the agency that caused the harm, and they are assessed to deter defendants from continuing the unsafe behavior that caused the injury. Punitive damages usually are awarded only in negligence actions deemed to be willful and wanton neglect.

Risk Management in the Aquatics Environment

Risk management is the identification, evaluation, and control of loss to property, patients, employees, and the public. A risk management system includes an audit or identification of all risks; evaluation of each individual risk in terms of probability, severity, and magnitude; and the establishment of controls that eliminate or reduce risks, provide alternative programs, or retain risks and cover with insurance.

Among the things that should be considered in a risk management program for aquatic physical therapy: local, state, and federal codes, professional guidelines (for both aquatics professionals and physical therapy professionals), facilities, equipment, personnel, supervision, and emergency action plan. Other factors, such as leasing arrangements, may be deemed equally important depending on the setting. Work environments are unique and thus require individual plans.

The following safety considerations are provided as examples to guide PTs in risk management planning. Insurance representatives and legal advisors should always be involved in the development of specific risk management plans for a program or facility.

Fear of the water. It's important for PTs working in aquatic settings to assess their patients' level of fear of the water. Can the patient:

- Put his or her face in the water or tolerate water near his or her face?

- Put his or her face and whole body below the surface of the water when assisted by another person or while holding on to another person?

- Sit on the bottom of the pool and return to the surface without assistance?

- Move three or more body lengths under water and return to a standing position in shallow water (4 feet or less)?

- Move his or her body effectively to the edge of the unit in which therapy is provided?

- Pass a regulation deep water swimming test?

Physical capacity in the water. In addition to the routine physical therapy examination, PTs in aquatic settings must assess their patients' physical capacity in the water. Can the patient:

- Perform all movements in the water without assistance?

- Relax and lie on his or her back in the water without assistance?

- Move from back floating or layout position to standing position without assistance?

- Move from back float to standing position by placing his or her weight on the edge of the pool or on a rope?

- Repeat above sequence for face float?

In addition, any balance problems the patient may have will need to be considered in planning activity and supervising the patient.

PTs providing aquatic physical therapy in deep water (more than 4 feet) for patients below the Intermediate swimming category should consider a personal flotation plan. Equipment selection should be influenced by the patient's confidence in the water and capacity to move his or her body to safety without assistance. Attention to the security of the equipment, ensurance of proper fit, and accuracy in putting on the equipment are vital. When appropriate, patients should be encouraged to learn to swim.

The Emergency Action Plan

Another aquatic safety consideration is a plan for action in case of emergency. This plan should be in writing, and it should be posted where all employees can see it and be included as a part of all new employee orientations.

Again, state and local pool and water safety requirements provide detailed standards for swimming pools. Within the definition of swimming pool are structures slightly larger than a bath tub, 50-meter pools, and areas the size of a small lake. All pools within the limits of the code must follow the code; on occasion, if the number of participants in aquatic physical therapy exceeds seven, these standards also must be in effect. The standards were created for the public in general, and, most of the time, the aquatic PT is faced with smaller numbers of patients and a requirement to be cost effective. However, even if the aquatic therapy pool is smaller than a "swimming pool" as defined by the code, or the PT is working with a small number of patients, the PT should still have an emergency action plan in place.

Ideally, the aquatic PT should be certified in first aid, life saving, and water safety. Emergency plans for facilities should be worked out in conjunction with municipal emergency assistance services (eg, fire and rescue), and facilities, including tubs, spas, and pools, ideally should be equipped with an emergency help button to alert these services. When a PT is providing one-to-one therapy in a tub or spa, the button should be within the reach of the PT at all times.

Consider the following questions:

- Is the PT able to rescue and remove a near-drowning patient from the water?

- Is the PT qualified for rescue breathing?

- Will the patients other than the person being rescued be able to gain safety without assistance?

If the answer to any of these questions is no, a lifeguard is essential (in fact, many aquatics facilities require that a lifeguard be present at all times when the pool is in use).

Another safety consideration is the PT-to-patient ratio under lifeguard supervision in a large pool. Factors to be considered are participants' level of fear of the water and the amount of assistance required in righting the floating patient. Intense fear of water or the need for assistance in righting the patient from a back layout position argue for a one-to-one patient-PT ratio, whereas small-group therapy may be appropriate for patients who are confident in the water and who can recover from the back layout floating position independently. Decisions made in this area should be put in writing and are part of the emergency action plan.

PTs have documented the value of water in rehabilitation, and many use the aquatic environment. This subjects the PTs to the additional liabilities and responsibilities of an aquatic specialist. Fortunately, both physical therapy and aquatics have well-established standards of care. Aquatic PTs may only need to "fine tune" the transitions

> *Aquatic PTs may only need to "fine tune" the transitions between physical therapy standards of care and aquatics standards to be able to develop a comprehensive aquatic physical therapy standard of care.*

between physical therapy standards of care and aquatics standards to be able to develop a comprehensive aquatic physical therapy standard of care. By developing a standard of care for aquatic physical therapy and documenting their adherence to it, PTs may not only prevent injuries in the aquatic environment, they also may have the means to defend themselves against litigation.

Annie Clement, PhD, JD, is Professor, Sports Management, Cleveland State University, Cleveland, Ohio, and Managing Editor, Aquatic Law Reporter.

References

1   National Sporting Goods Association. *Sports Participation in 1993.* Mt Prospect, Ill: National Sporting Goods Association; 1994.
2   National Safety Council. *Accident Facts.* Itasca, Ill: National Safety Council; 1995.
3   Restatement of the law (second) of torts 2d. Vol II. Washington, DC: American Law Institute; 1965:587.
4   Clement A. *Law in Sport and Physical Activity.* Dubuque, Iowa: Brown/Benchmark; 1996:34.

of Dignity *and* Mobility

Helping to restore dignity and functional mobility for residents of nursing homes and long-term-care facilities is the driving factor behind the Health Care Financing Administration's (HCFA) National Restraint Reduction Initiative. As the vest restraints, wrist straps, and bed rails are carefully removed, physical therapists are creating new roles for themselves on resident assessment teams, developing environmental alternatives to restraint use, and rebuilding strength and, often, mobility in those who were once confined.

by Kimberly E Wynn
photography Steve Barret

Dan Ciolek, MS, PT, GCS, and his wife Cathy Ciolek, PT, GCS, have made restraint reduction a mission in their respective facilities.

Restraint Reduction Resources

HCFA's *National Restraint Reduction Newsletter.*
www.hcfa.gov/pubforms/rrnews.html

Untie the Elderly Web page:
www.ute.kendal.org

Untie the Elderly: Resource Manual Fourth Edition. Kennett Square, Pa; The Kendal Corporation: 1997. (A compilation of literature on restraint reduction efforts)

Everyone Wins! Quality Care Without Restraints: Resident Care Library. New York, NY: Independent Production Fund; 1995.

"Clinical Management of Physical Restraints." *Topics in Geriatrics: Home Study Series.* APTA's Section on Geriatrics. Authored by Cathy Haines Ciolek, PT, GCS, and Daniel E Ciolek, MS, PT, GCS.

"**f**our years ago, I took a position in a nursing home," recalls Dan Ciolek, MS, PT, GCS, Legislative Chair for APTA's Section on Geriatrics. "When I walked into the facility that first day I remember looking down a long hallway as I approached the nurses' station to check in. Elderly residents were lined up along the walls, seated in geriatric reclining chairs and staring up at the ceiling. At the other end of the hall, I saw even more residents wearing devices like vest restraints, lap buddies, and wheelchair belts. The scene was incredibly depressing, and my gut reaction was to turn around and walk out."

But Ciolek remained. Fortunately, he and his new administrator saw eye-to-eye on improving the quality of the residents' lives. For Ciolek, who recently co-wrote a section home-study module, entitled "Clinical Management of Physical Restraints"[1] with his wife Cathy Ciolek, PT, GCS, restraint reduction became a personal mission. He not only had passion on his side, but Federal laws were in place that would support him in his endeavor to reduce restraint use at Marriott-Millcroft in Newark, Del, where he is Director of Rehabilitation Services.

of Dignity *and* Mobility

"Physical therapy is the promotion of functional mobility and independence, and restraint use is simply contrary to our practice," says Dan Ciolek. "PTs have always been concerned with identifying measures and alternative devices to enable a person to function at his or her highest level. That is why physical therapy has such an important role to play in an interdisciplinary approach to this initiative."

OBRA

In 1987, the Omnibus Budget Reconciliation Act (OBRA) was passed, which included the Nursing Home Quality Reform Act. According to Jerry Arzt, editor of HCFA's *National Restraint Reduction Newsletter*, "Historically, restraints had been used in nursing homes for medical purposes, but also as a means of discipline and convenience. OBRA regulations aimed to reduce restraint use and stated these devices should only be used to ensure the physical safety of the resident or other residents, and only upon the written order of a physician that specifies the duration and circumstances under which the restraints are to be used."

OBRA was implemented in 1990, and by 1993, restraint use in some states was still as high as 35%, which is the percentage of residents who are reportedly restrained in Medicare-certified nursing homes in those states, says Arzt. "The issue of restraint reduction became problematic because many facilities were not prepared to deal with those residents who were suddenly having their restraints removed. Facilities reported numerous falls, there was concern about wandering residents, and relatives complained," he says.

In 1993, Arzt spearheaded a special project on behalf of HCFA to track statistics related to restraint use. As a result of the findings, education on how to properly reduce restraint use was identified as key, and a regional restraint reduction initiative was initiated. Virginia was selected as the "pilot" state for the program, primarily because it had the highest percentage of restraint use in the country at that time.

A task force with representatives from HCFA, state survey agencies, long-term-care providers, advocacy groups, and medical professional organizations, developed and conducted seminars in nursing homes on restraint reduction strategies and "train the trainer" courses throughout the state. The program evolved into other states over the next 3 years, and, in 1996, HCFA's National Restraint Reduction Initiative was launched.

Today, the national rate for restraint use stands at 15.5%, and is falling. HCFA's National Restraint Reduction Initiative has three goals for the year 2000:

- That every "high-use" state have a restraint reduction initiative in place.
- That there will be a high level of national awareness regarding the need to minimize physical and chemical restraint use.
- That physical restraint use will be below 10% nationally.

PT and Restraint Reduction

"Physical therapy is the promotion of functional mobility and independence, and restraint use is simply contrary to our practice," says Dan Ciolek. "PTs have always been concerned with identifying measures and alternative devices to enable a person to function at his or her highest level. That is why physical therapy has such an important role to play in an interdisciplinary approach to this initiative."

However, he says, it is essential to understand that restraint reduction is a process that must begin incrementally, followed by careful observation of the individual needs of each patient and the development of environmental alternatives to restraint use.

Ciolek offers an example of a daughter who places her mother in a nursing home because her mother has a problem with falling. Because she works, the daughter is unable to fully care for her mother, and feels that her mother would be "safe" in a nursing home. "In the past, bed rails and chair straps would have been applied to this resident immediately. But today, in a facility with a restraint reduction effort like Marriott-Millcroft, that resident will be assessed when she arrives by an interdisciplinary team that includes a physical therapist. With a history of falling, a physician and a nurse will assess risk factors including medications, blood pressure, and nutritional status. A physical therapist and an occupational therapist will evaluate the resident's strength and mobility to determine her physical capabilities and why she may be demonstrating an unsafe behavior like falling. Everyone on the assessment team will confer on whether she is doing anything that will cause immediate jeopardy to herself or others."

If it is determined that the resident is in no immediate jeopardy, the team will make recommendations for restraint alternatives by making her environment safer. "We look at her room to determine if it's arranged appropriately for a person who may fall, like if there should be more space or if the furniture should be arranged in a way that she could use the various pieces as support to move about," says Ciolek. Her bed may be lowered and a mat placed next to her bed to cushion a low fall. The lighting will be checked to ensure that it is adequate, and tripping hazards will be removed.

Ciolek shares a success with a resident whom he describes as a "walker." "This particular woman loved to walk about the facility. However, her blood pressure would drop rather quickly, and, after about 100 feet, she'd fall. Facilities can do one of two things: Apply restraints to keep a resident like her from walking and assign her to a restorative nursing walking schedule, or take a good look at the environment. We chose to arrange the chairs in the hallway closer together so this resident would be able to rest periodically and resume her walking as she was able. This sounds simple, and it is, but it worked. We just changed the environment, and she was no longer in jeopardy of hurting herself."

OBRA regulations state that a restraint should only be used to protect residents from seriously harming themselves or another. "If a resident is trying to stab someone with a knife, immediate jeopardy is apparent, and that is temporary justification for applying a device," says Ciolek. "However, the next step is to assess through clinical processes why that patient demonstrated unsafe behavior and to see how that cause can be removed. Perhaps a resident has been at home with family and not been taking his or her medication properly. A situation like this can often be easily remedied, and restraints can be removed after a short period of time of clinical assessment.

Section on Geriatrics Taking a Lead in Restraint-Free Care

As Dale Avers, MSEd, PT, President of APTA's Section on Geriatrics, travels around the country addressing town meetings for section members, she will begin by asking, "How many of you practice in long-term care?" Nearly 95% of them will raise their hands. She then asks, "How many of you want to live in long-term care some day?" No one makes a move.

"We have a problem here, and we are part of the problem," replies Avers. "We need to do something to fix it—now."

"I believe that physical therapists are the best people in a nursing home to facilitate a major philosophical change such as a move to "restraint-free" care in these settings, because of our education, awareness, and perspective of a patient or resident as a whole being. Restraints are the antithesis of what physical therapy is all about—physical mobility. Who, again, is better to facilitate the idea of a restraint-free environment then physical therapists?" asks Avers.

The Section on Geriatrics has just published a "restraint module" for its home study course, entitled "Clinical Managment of Physical Restraints," which was written by section members Cathy and Dan Ciolek. The module addresses how to do an initial assessment, the clinical management aspects of a restraint reduction effort, the pros and cons of a restraint reduction effort, 50 references of articles that cite statistics on death rates from restraint use, and the psychological effects of restraint use on patients.

Physical therapists can use this information to be proactive in implementing a restraint reduction initiative in their own facility. "Every change effort requires a visionary, and that is where the physical therapist comes into play here. In a nursing home, the physical therapist not only needs the support of the administration, but 'buy in' from colleagues. Just start talking and be enthusiastic about the initiative; you'll find that people will come on board. Recognize that you will need to plan carefully and that restraint reduction doesn't happen overnight," advises Avers.

"Restraint free or alternative environments will provide for physical therapists a nice blend of the traditional hands-on physical therapy and this new, expanded role of looking at the quality of life of the older individual. This refreshing perspective will make us more effective as rehabilitation professionals. When you start taking restraints off and people start walking more, balance and other problems may need to be addressed, but will be addressed more successfully, because residents will not be strapped back down following therapy. Physical therapy will become more authentic in that residents will be up and walking, and we will be able to observe their increased activity level as well as the more subtle problems that a person may be having, which may have gone unnoticed had he or she been made to sit back down," she explains.

"The restraint reduction initiative is a great 'calling' for physical therapists," says Avers.

"Clinical Management of Physical Restraints," which is part of *Topics in Geriatrics: A Home Study Series,* is now available. Contact APTA's Orthopaedic Section at 800/444-3982, ext 213, for ordering information.

"The bottom line is that if devices are used, they should not just be left on. Care providers need to look at the root or the cause of the unsafe behavior—not just the behavior."

What can a physical therapist uniquely bring to this effort? "Physical therapists have an incredible wealth of knowledge that we can offer others about the underlying physiological reasons why some behaviors may be occurring, including muscle strains and atrophy, and limited range of motion and flexibility. Residents who have been restrained in the past have often sustained decubitus ulcers, bone demineralization, incontinence, constipation, and damage to nerves and circulatory system. These conditions can be painful and can contribute to certain patient behaviors that are construed as negative.

"Furthermore, many in the nursing home industry have been trained under the 'one size fits all' mentality. Physical therapists can contribute that individuals are different, not only in their psychological needs, but in their physical mobility needs. No one device is going to solve every problem. We can recommend proper walkers, wheelchairs, and assistive devices to meet a person's functional needs. For residents who rely on wheelchairs for mobility, seating wedges and antislip pads can replace lap belts and vest restraints, which are often used to keep individuals from slipping out of their wheelchairs.

"In yet another scenario, therapy sessions for strength and balance may not be carried over into other shifts. Subsequently, residents may not be receiving consistent functional care. This inconsistency leads to risk for falls because relearning movement patterns requires repetition. Physical therapists can conduct staff training on the need for consistency and for developing assistive approaches. Although different residents may have different movement techniques, the staff will be consistent with treating each individual resident. The treatment will become resident focused vs device focused," explains Ciolek.

Making the Transition

Cathy Ciolek, PT, GCS, shares her husband Dan's fervor for restraint reduction and urges physical therapists nationwide to become resident advocates. "To initiate an effort like this, you need to be armed with supportive literature to get 'buy in' from the top," says Cathy Ciolek. Having done her homework a few years ago on restraint reduction strategies and statistics, Cathy Ciolek, who was then Director of Rehabilitation Services at ManorCare in Wilmington, Del, went straight to the director of Nursing and the administrator at ManorCare with her proposal.

"It often takes a little money up front to replace geriatric reclining chairs with wheelchairs, and purchase adaptive seating devices like wedges and bolster supports and soft mats for use next to the low beds. Administration needs to understand how these changes will benefit them in the long run, especially when state surveyors come in to inspect the facility on compliance with OBRA regulations and restraint use. Staff also need to be educated on how to undertake this type of initiative, which is one of the most challenging aspects of this effort," says Cathy Ciolek.

A shift in staff, patient, and family perception is essential. "Care providers in this setting were taught in school that restraints made people safer, but that is not the case. Studies have shown that the risk of serious injury is much higher with people who are restrained. Residents who are strapped to wheelchairs have been known to get up and drag the wheelchair behind them, only to fall and be trapped underneath.

"People need to accept that there will be some inherent risk with the residents' new mobility. Residents did not live a risk-free life before they were placed in long-term care, and we cannot guarantee that this will be a risk-free environment. We are striving to make it as safe as possible without tying them down. Yes, there may be more falls once the restraints come off, but they won't be any more severe. Especially if physical therapists initiate aggressive strengthening therapy for the resident. Care providers need to approach this gradually and work with the residents who are stronger and are more

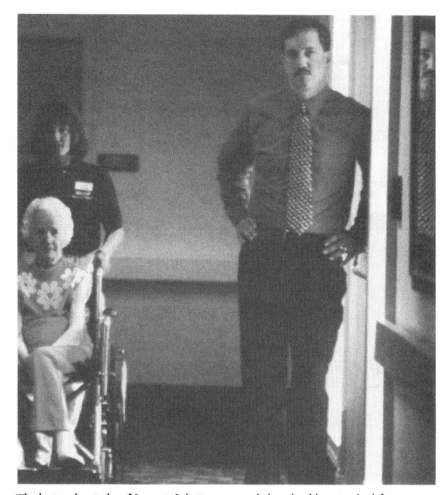

"The bottom line is that if [restraint] devices are used, they should not just be left on. Care providers need to look at the root or the cause of the unsafe behavior—not just the behavior," says Dan Ciolek.

likely to succeed in a restraint-free environment. Successes like these early on will encourage staff, other patients, and their families," says Cathy Ciolek.

Today, the mission of the rehabilitation department at ManorCare is to enable residents to have maximum mobility in a healthy environment. ManorCare provides MerryWalkers™ for people who require assistance to ambulate. "We have people who will walk for hours and hours during the day, and this device enables them to do so. We also use personal alarms for people who are likely to fall. Instead of tying them down, we are alerted to residents who are trying to get out of a chair or bed. We can then help them to do what they need to do," says Cathy Ciolek.

"In the past, residents were rarely questioned about why they were trying to get up. Perhaps residents had to go to the bathroom or were suffering from too much pressure on

their bottoms. Today we need to address the behaviors and respond appropriately. We cannot necessarily change their actions, but we can change how we react to them. It is an ongoing process of reminding ourselves."

Cathy Ciolek emphasizes that physical therapists have a new and expanding role in this type of setting. "We are capable of making a difference here, and we need to get more involved on the front end when patients are initially assessed. Physical therapists are the mobility experts, we are the ones who have the training to decide what type of device may enhance someone's limited mobility, and we have the expertise to enable residents to function at their highest level." *PT*

Kimberly E Wynn is News Editor.

References:

1 Ciolek C, Ciolek D. "Clinical Management of Physical Restraints." *Topics in Geriatrics: A Home Study Series.* APTA's Section on Geriatrics. June 1998.

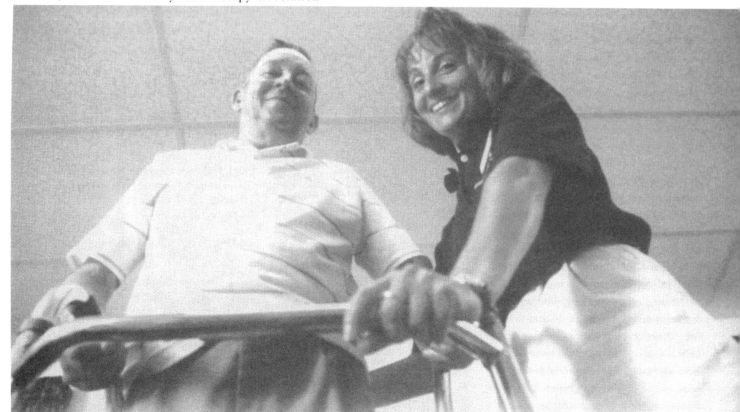

Physical Restraint— Legal and Risk Management Issues

by Jonathan M Cooperman, JD, MS, PT; Ronald W Scott, JD, PT, OCS

Although there is a growing movement toward restraint-free or alternative environments in the nation's long-term-care facilities and nursing homes, physical therapists continue to work with residents who have been or are currently being restrained, and may even be called upon to restrain residents themselves. An awareness is essential of the relevant laws and regulations controlling the use of restraints, as well as applicable risk management strategies.

Physical restraints may be defined as any manual method or physical device, article, garment, material, or equipment attached or adjacent to an individual's body that restricts freedom of movement or normal access to one's body. This includes, but is not limited to, leg and arm straps, hand mitts, soft ties, geriatric reclining chairs, isolation in a room, Posey vests, or side rails. For regulatory purposes, if a resident perceives a device as limiting or prohibiting his or her freedom of movement, it is considered a restraint.[1] Chemical restraints include any drug (usually listed in schedules of controlled substances) having a depressant effect on the central nervous system, such as tranquilizers. Although the Federal and state statutes usually include both chemical and physical restraints, a discussion of chemical restraints is beyond the scope of this article.

Justification for Restraint Use

Today, physical restraints continue to be used in nursing homes and acute care hospitals. The most common pretext for restraint use is to protect the resident from falls or self-inflicted injury, or to protect medical devices. Some rehabilitation professionals may justify restraint use as a means to keep a resident in a bed or chair or to maintain sitting balance.

However, it is paradoxical that restraints work in direct contravention of the goals of rehabilitation, namely—functional independence. Most authors who have studied the use of restraints conclude that these measures seldom eliminate the risk of injury, especially from falls.[1,2] Indeed, there are quite a few studies that show that the risk of injury from falls out of bed actually increases with the use of restraints.[3]

Miles and Irvine[4] undertook a retrospective study of 122 deaths caused by restraints. They found that 78% were women and that the median age was 81. Eighty-three percent were in nursing homes. Victims were found suspended from chairs in 42% of the cases, and from beds in 58%. They postulated that many die from asphyxiation because the restraint wraps around the chest and does not allow the victim to inhale, and less often from the restraint sliding up around the

neck. In a case report on sudden death, Robinson et al described an 83-year-old man who went into sustained ventricular tachycardia after being restrained.[5] The authors believe there is a causal link between the psychological stress of being restrained and the sudden cardiac death. Despite these reports, it appears that the overall use of mechanical restraints is declining. Previously estimated use of restraints was as high as 70% in nursing homes, whereas current estimates show that restraints may be used as infrequently as 4% of the time.[6]

Applicable Laws and Regulations

In 1987, a major government attempt to improve the quality of care in nursing homes took the form of the Nursing Home Quality Reform Act (NHQRA),[7] which was part of the Omnibus Budget Reconciliation Act (OBRA).[8] OBRA changed all the Federal requirements for nursing homes. With regard to the use of restraints, OBRA states, in part:

Restraints may only be imposed to ensure the physical safety of the resident or other residents, and only upon the written order of a physician that specifies the duration and circumstances under which the restraints are to be used (except in emergency situations).

The Code of Federal Regulations[9] states that the resident has a right to be free from any physical or chemical restraints imposed for purposes of discipline or convenience,

Federal Restraint Standards

The US Department of Health and Human Services developed the following standards[1] for restraint use in a nursing home:

- Orders indicate the specific reason for the restraint.

  - Restraint use is temporary, and the patient will not be restrained for an indefinite amount of time.

  - Orders for restraint shall not be enforced for longer that 12 hours, unless the patient's condition warrants.

  - A patient placed in restraints shall be checked at least every 30 minutes by appropriately trained staff, and an account is kept of this surveillance. Reorders are issued only after a review of the patient's condition.

  - Restraint use is not employed as a punishment, for the convenience of the staff, or as a substitute for supervision.

  - Mechanical restraints avoid physical injury to the patient and provide a minimum of discomfort.

- The opportunity for motion and exercise is provided for a period of not less than 10 minutes, during each 2 hours in which restraints are employed, except at night.

- Nursing facilities are also affected by the Food and Drug Administration (FDA), the federal agency charged with controlling the manufacturing of restraints. Under the Safe Medical Devices Act of 1990 (SMDA), health care facilities must report incidents involving medical devices and a patient's death to the FDA within 10 working days.[2]

References:

1 *Use of Restraints—Federal Standards.* Washington, DC: US Dept of Health and Human Services;1984.
2 The Safe Medical Devices Act of 1990, 21 USC, Sections 301note, 321, 360d, 360hh et seq.

Physical Restraint—Legal and Risk Management Issues

and not required to treat the resident's medical condition.

State statutes are also in place to regulate nursing homes. The Ohio Revised Code, for example, is quite detailed regarding this subject[10]:

[A resident has] *the right to be free from physical or chemical restraints or prolonged isolation except to the minimum extent necessary to protect the resident from injury to himself, others, or to property, and except as authorized in writing by the attending physician for a specified and limited period of time and documented in the resident's medical record. Prior to authorizing the use of a physical or chemical restraint on any resident, the attending physician shall make a personal examination of the resident and an individualized determination of the need to use the restraint on that resident.*

Physical or chemical restraints or isolation may be used in an emergency situation without authorization of the attending physician only to protect the resident from injury to himself or others. Use of the physical or chemical restraints or isolation shall not be continued for more than 12 hours after the onset of the emergency without personal examination and authorization by the attending physician. The attending physician or a staff physician may authorize continued use of physical or chemical restraints for a period not to exceed 30 days, and at the end of this period and any subsequent period may extend the authorization for an additional period of not more than 30 days. The use of

physical or chemical restraints shall not be continued without a personal examination of the resident and the written authorization of the attending physician stating the reasons for continuing the restraint. If physical or chemical restraints are used under this division, the home shall ensure that the restrained resident receives a proper diet. In no event shall physical or chemical restraints or isolation be used for punishment, incentive, or convenience.

Civil Liability and the Standard of Care

When incidents surrounding the use of restraints arise, the injured resident (or his or her family) may file suit and claim damages in civil court. The courts will often examine statutory and regulatory requirements as evidence of the appropriate standard of care. Failure to comply with regulatory guidelines

or the policies adopted by a facility may be prima facie evidence of malpractice or other tort. That is, the practitioner would be presumed to be liable unless disproved by evidence to the contrary. However, not all courts have adopted this approach. Regardless of the stance taken by the judiciary, physical therapists should always be aware of the policies and regulations/statutes they are expected to follow. Compliance with such regulations is the minimally acceptable conduct to expect from health care practitioners. In light of the current Federal and state statutes, the trend is clearly not to use restraints unless alternatives have been identified, discussed, and ruled out.[11]

Informed Consent

Under statutory, regulatory, judicial, and customary informed consent law, long-term-care residents or their surrogate decision makers exercise the right to participate in restraint decisions. Before authorization for the use of physical restraints is valid, health care professionals must disclose the following points to residents or surrogate decision makers:

• Information about the types of restraint recommended, including, but not limited to, the rationale, parameters, and duration for their use, as well as the right of the resident/surrogate to refuse their continued use at any time;
• Material risks of possible harm to the resident associated with restraint use, including, but certainly not limited to, adverse impact on the resident's quality of life;
• Expected benefits of restraint use;
• Reasonable alternatives to the recommended restraint (including those alternatives associated with not utilizing physical restraints, as applicable) and their relative risks and benefits; and
• Solicitation of and satisfactorily answering resident/surrogate questions and respond to comments.

Resident/surrogate informed consent to physical restraint use should be in a signed, written form, even when the law does not mandate that such consent be signed or written, so as to demonstrate the serious nature of this highly intrusive intervention and to avoid misunderstandings and potential claims or litigation. An informed refusal by a resident or surrogate decision maker of necessary physical restraint may operate to limit provider and institutional liability for resident injury under the concept of assumption of the risk (of harm) assuming that the informed refusal is knowing, intelligent, voluntary, and unequivocal.

Need for Restraints?

Is there a need for restraints? In addition to the lack of data supporting the notion that restraints protect the resident from falls, MacPherson et al[12] found that nurses initiated the use of restraints in 73% of the cases in an acute care hospital and that physicians and nurses seldom agreed on the reasons to restrain an individual resident. The authors found an increased use of restraints on the evening shift and suspected that restraints were occasionally used for staff convenience. In addition, a 1992 study found that, despite Federal mandates, nursing staff frequently do not adhere to the Federal guidelines regarding restraint release and repositioning.[13]

Risk Management and Ethical Concerns

Restraint use can be dehumanizing. These devices significantly affect a resident's autonomy—the resident's right to choose his or her own course of medical care. It is that conflict between the resident's autonomy and the principle of beneficence that generates ethical discussion. It has been suggested that nurses (and we could extend the argument to physical therapists) are more likely to pay greater attention to ethical issues that they encounter infrequently such as organ transplants and the right to die, than to ethical problems that involve daily activities such as residents rights and/or abuse of power.

Living in the most litigious society on earth, many may suggest restraint use because they consider it a deterrent to litigation. However, a facility might be found liable for restraining in light of a resident's right to refuse (perhaps more common in the psychiatric setting), alleged injury from

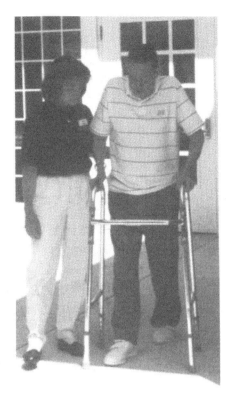

restraint, or allegations of neglect for failure to restrain. This "catch 22" causes consternation among risk management officers who see potential liability in the choice to restrain or not to restrain. Historically, cases claiming injury from restraint far outweigh cases premised on a failure to restrain. Johnson[14] reviewed 247 cases against nursing homes during a 4-year period. There were only 16 claims of failure to supervise and only 8 of failure to restrain—3 of which alleged failure to use bed rails.

Therefore, the fear of liability does not appear to be adequate justification for the use of restraints, particularly in light of data that do not support decreased injury with restraint. More importantly, the fear of liability should never be the determining factor in decisions affecting a resident's care. All health care practitioners need to exercise judgment in applying restraints.

Many facilities have developed restraint reduction committees and have started to create restraint-free environments. There are a variety of risk management strategies that can be used to reduce or eliminate the use of restraints. These include environmental manipulation; behavioral modification; "creative control" for wandering, which may include a lock or closed unit, alarm systems, or nighttime activities; shel-

tered gardens; and changing methods of feeding residents.[14]

Under all laws and regulations, the physician is responsible for the decision to restrain or not to restrain. Although physical therapists may not be the ultimate arbiters regarding the use of restraint, as members of the health care team they can provide valuable insight into the functional status of residents and to environmental alternatives to restraint. Physical therapists, especially those working in long-term-care facilities, must be aware of the laws and regulations governing the use of restraints. *PT*

Jonathan Cooperman, JD, MS, PT, is Director, Rehabilitation and Health Center Inc, Akron, Ohio. He is a member of APTA's Judicial Committee. Ronald Scott, JD, PT, OCS, is Associate Professor, Department of Physical Therapy, School of Allied Health Sciences, University of Texas Health Science Center, San Antonio, Tex. He is past chair of APTA's Judicial Committee and is a member of PT 's Editorial Advisory Group.

References:

1   Kapp MB. Restraining impaired elders in the home environment. *Journal of Case Management.* 1995; 4(2):54-59.
2   Evans LK, Strumpf NE. Tying down the elderly: a review of the literature. *J Am Geriatr Soc.* 1989;37:65-74.
3   Marks W. Physical restraints in the practice of medicine: current concepts. *Arch Inter Med.* 1992;152:2203-2206.
4   Miles SH, Irvine P. Deaths caused by physical restraints. *The Gerontologist.* 1992;32:762-766.
5   Robinson BE, Sucholeiki R, Schocken DD. Sudden death and restricted mechanical restraint: a case report. *JAGS.* 1993;41:424-425.
6   Scott RW. *Promoting Legal Awareness in Physical and Occupational Therapy.* St Louis, Mo; Mosby Year-Book; 1996.
7   Omnibus Budget Reconciliation Act of 1987. Public Law 100-203. Title IV, Subtitle C: Nursing Home Reform Act, codified at 42 USS 1395i-3(c)(1)(A)(ii), 1396r(c)(1)(ii).
8   Omnibus Budget Reconciliation Act of 1987. Public Law 100-203. Signed by President, December 22, 1987. Washington, DC.
9   Code of Federal Regulations 42CFR483.13(a).
10 Ohio Rev Code 3721.13 (A)(13).
11 Braun JA. Legal aspects of physical restraint use in nursing homes. *Health Lawyer.* 1998;11(3): 10-16.
12 MacPherson DS, Lofgren RP, et al. Deciding to restrain medical patients. *JAGS.* 1990;38:516-520.
13 Schnelle JF, Simmons SF, Ory MG. Risk factors that predict staff failure to release nursing home residents from restraints. *The Gerontologist.* 1992;32:767-773.
14 Johnson SH. The fear of liability and the use of restraints in nursing homes. *Law, Medicine, and Health.* 1990;18(3):263-273.

Selected Readings

Furrow BR, Greaney TL, Johnson SH, et al. *Health Law.* 3rd ed. St Paul, Minn: West Group; 1997.

Huckstep A, Wilson JC, Carmody RP. *Corporate Law for the Healthcare Provider: Organization, Operation, Merger, and Bankruptcy.* Washington, DC: National Health Lawyers Association Focus Series Publication; 1993.

Johnson KB, Hatlie MJ, Johnson ID. *The Guide to Medical Professional Liability Insurance.* Chicago, Ill: American Medical Association; 1991.

Prosser WL, Keeton WP. *Prosser Hornbook Torts.* 5th ed. St Paul, Minn: West Group; 1984.

Risk Management for Physical Therapists: A Quick Reference. Alexandria, Va: American Physical Therapy Association; 2001.

Rosovsky F. *Consent to Treatment: A Practical Guide.* New York, NY: Little Brown; 1990.

Rosovsky F. *Liability and Risk Management in Home Health Care.* Gaithersburg, Md: Aspen Publishers Inc; 1998.

Scott RW. *Health Care Malpractice: A Primer on Legal Issues.* Thorofare, NJ: Slack Inc; 1990.

Scott RW. *Legal Aspects of Documenting Patient Care.* Gaithersburg, Md: Aspen Publishers Inc; 1994.

Scott R. *Professional Ethics: A Guide for Rehabilitation Professionals.* St Louis, Mo: Mosby Year-Book Inc; 1998.

Scott RW. *Promoting Legal Awareness in Physical and Occupational Therapy.* St Louis, Mo: Mosby Year-Book Inc; 1997.

Swisher LL, Krueger-Brophy C. *Legal and Ethical Issues in Physical Therapy.* Woburn, Mass: Butterworth-Heinemann Medical; 1998.